Pro SharePoint Migration

Moving from MOSS 2007 to SharePoint Server 2010

Sahil Malik
Srini Sistla

Apress®

Pro SharePoint Migration

Copyright © 2012 by Sahil Malik, Srini Sistla

ISBN-13 (pbk): 978-1-4302-4482-0

ISBN-13 (electronic): 978-1-4302-4483-7

President and Publisher: Paul Manning
Lead Editor: Jonathan Hassell
Developmental Editor: Douglas Pundick
Technical Reviewer: Robert Garrett
Editorial Board: Steve Anglin, Ewan Buckingham, Gary Cornell, Louise Corrigan, Morgan Ertel, Jonathan Gennick, Jonathan Hassell, Robert Hutchinson, Michelle Lowman, James Markham, Matthew Moodie, Jeff Olson, Jeffrey Pepper, Douglas Pundick, Ben Renow-Clarke, Dominic Shakeshaft, Gwenan Spearing, Matt Wade, Tom Welsh
Coordinating Editors: Brent Dubi and Katie Sullivan
Copy Editor: Heather Lang
Compositor: Bytheway Publishing Services
Indexer: SPi Global
Artist: SPi Global
Cover Designer: Anna Ishchenko

Distributed to the book trade worldwide by Springer Science+Business Media New York, 233 Spring Street, 6th Floor, New York, NY 10013. Phone 1-800-SPRINGER, fax (201) 348-4505, e-mail orders-ny@springer-sbm.com, or visit www.springeronline.com.

For information on translations, please e-mail rights@apress.com, or visit www.apress.com.

Apress and friends of ED books may be purchased in bulk for academic, corporate, or promotional use. eBook versions and licenses are also available for most titles. For more information, reference our Special Bulk Sales–eBook Licensing web page at www.apress.com/bulk-sales.

Any source code or other supplementary materials referenced by the author in this text is available to readers at www.apress.com. For detailed information about how to locate your book's source code, go to www.apress.com/source-code.

I would like to dedicate this book to my wife Vijaya and my daughters Anjali and Vaishnavi.
—Srini Sistla

Contents at a Glance

Contents

About the Authors

 **Sahil Malik,** the founder and principal of Winsmarts.com, has been a Microsoft MVP and INETA Speaker for the past 11 years, an author and reviewer of many books and numerous articles in both the .NET and SharePoint spaces, a consultant, and a trainer at conferences internationally. Sahil has trained for the best names in the Microsoft technology space and has architected and delivered SharePoint-based solutions for extremely high-profile clients. Sahil is the author of *Microsoft SharePoint 2010: Building Solutions for SharePoint 2010* and coauthored *Pro SharePoint 2010 Business Intelligence Soltuions*, both published by Apress.

 **Srini Sistla** is an author, Microsoft Certified Technology Specialist, and INETA speaker with over 12 years of experience in designing and implementing IT solutions on a variety of platforms and domains. Srini's core skills have always involved Microsoft technologies, and he has solid experience in building both Windows- and web-based solutions. He has worked with Windows SharePoint Services 3.0, Microsoft Office SharePoint Server 2007, and SharePoint Server 2010, and his expertise in SharePoint includes BI, ECM, the object model, and branding. As a subject matter expert, Srini is often asked to review, improve, and approve a variety of technical designs and approaches. He regularly contributes to several blogs, including his own. He has done a fair amount of speaking at various SharePoint user groups and provides training on SharePoint 2010 and MOSS 2007. Srini hails from Washington D.C. metro area and is currently working as a SharePoint architect and consultant. He coauthored *Pro SharePoint 2010 Business Intelligence Solutions.*

About the Technical Reviewer

 **Robert Garrett** is the author of *Pro SharePoint 2010 Administration* and has extensive experience working with SharePoint 2007 and 2010. Prior to working with SharePoint, Robert developed web applications in ASP.NET and C#. Today, Robert works for Portal Solutions LLC as a lead architect and spends the majority of his time designing new solutions for the SharePoint 2010 platform.

Acknowledgments

This is my second book with Apress, and I would like to thank Apress and Jonathan Hassell for giving me this oppurtunity again. I would like to thank Sahil Malik for organizing the topics and their layout, planning out the entire book, and internal review. I'd also like to thank Robert Garrett for providing deep technical review and very valuable comments that significantly improved the quality of the book. I want to also thank Brent Dubi and Douglas Pundick for managing and scheduling the timelines, content editing, and suchlike. Finally, I am thankful to my family for their support and inspiration.

—Srini Sistla

First of all, I would like to thank my coauthor Srini Sistla. This book would not have been possible without his hard work, sleepless nights, and tireless dedication. Second, I would like to thank Rob Garrett, an author himself; having worked personally on projects with both Srini and Rob, I knew the book was in the right hands. I would then like to thank Jon Hassell; his endless support and attention allow us to focus on what we are good at. Finally, I would like to thank the rest of the Apress team, including Brent and Doug for their discipline, attention to detail, and helping us stick to timelines. Most of all, I would like to thank you, the reader, for your support.

—Sahil Malik

CHAPTER 1

Migration Process

SharePoint 2007 has been an incredibly successful product. Many organizations have reaped the benefits. It is an undeniable conclusion that, sooner or later, you will be faced with the task of upgrading to SharePoint 2010. What are the new capabilities of SharePoint 2010? What are the differences between SharePoint 2007 and SharePoint 2010? What new benefits can you reap, and what unexpected differences will bite you during your eventual upgrade? This book answers all of these questions and more.

SharePoint 2010 is a complete package of powerful capabilities that you surely wouldn't skip as a product by itself. If you are a current user of or have implemented Microsoft Office SharePoint Server (MOSS) 2007, we don't need to explain to you the benefits of SharePoint at all. With SharePoint 2007's capabilities and the enhancements and new features in SharePoint 2010, migrating to the new platform is certainly a good step. This chapter walks you through the different upgrade approaches, as well as offering a high-level comparison of the two versions, including explaining new features, unsupported models, and useful resources that you can benefit from during the overall migration process. In the subsequent chapters, we will walk you through other important aspects, targeting topics that meet needs and some key knowhow for IT analysts, designers, and developers.

Like MOSS 2007, SharePoint 2010 comes in three different flavors: Foundation (free), Standard, and Enterprise. For a feature comparison and licensing overview, see http://sharepoint.microsoft.com/en-us/buy/Pages/Editions-Comparison.aspx. Another edition of SharePoint is the online version known as Office 365. We are *not* going to cover each the edition as well as Office 365 in this book. We'll cover enterprise-edition features, and that way, features of all editions will be covered. To begin with, we will start with the comparison sheet between MOSS 2007 and SharePoint 2010.

Comparing MOSS 2007 and SharePoint 2010

Let's begin with explaining the hardware requirements between the two versions. The biggest change in SharePoint 2010 is in the infrastructure: a 64-bit operating system is now a mandate. Second, SQL Server 2005 Service Pack 3 (SP3) or higher (also running on 64-bits) is required. The rest of the RAM, hard disk, and processor requirements can be scaled. Table 1-1 displays the minimum requirements on the server infrastructure. Note that all servers in the farm where you install SharePoint 2010 need to abide by these requirements, but the server on which SQL Server is installed may have its own additional server requirements.

Table 1-1. Hardware and Operating System Comparison Between SharePoint 2007 and 2010

MOSS 2007	SharePoint 2010
32-bit or 64-bit with Windows Server 2003 SP1 or higher	Requires 64-bit operating system and Windows Server 2008 SP2 or higher or Windows Server 2008 R2
Recommended for dual-core processor (x86/x64) with 2.5GHz	Recommended for dual-core processor (x64) with 3GHz
1GB RAM minimum; 2GB RAM recommended	4GB RAM minimum; 8GB recommended for a multiple-server farm
3GB minimum disk space	80GB minimum disk space
SQL Server 2000 SP4 or higher	SQL Server 2005 SP3 or higher
.NET Framework 3.0	.NET Framework 3.5 SP1

As discussed earlier, SharePoint 2010 has been very popular ever since the beta versions arrived in late 2009, and its popularity grew with the release to manufacturing (RTM) in early 2010 and the SP1 release in during November 2011. Significant features are newly introduced or improved from the previous version, which is MOSS 2007. You have probably seen the feature wheel of SharePoint 2010 in the site http://sharepoint.microsoft.com/en-us/product/capabilities/Pages/default.aspx many times. These feature changes have been broken down in Table 1-2 to show each function and its corresponding features.

Table 1-2. Some New and Improved Capabilities of SharePoint 2010 (All Editions)

Function	Feature	Status
Communities	Blogs	Improved
	Colleague Suggestions	New
	My Content	New
	My Profile	Improved
	Organization Browser	New
	Photos and Presence	New
	Ratings	New

	Recent Activities	New
	Tagging	New
	Wikis	Improved
Composites	Access Services	New
	Browser-Based customizations	New
	BCS (formerly BDC)	Improved
	Sandboxed Solutions	New
	SharePoint Designer	Improved
	Silverlight Web Part	New
Content	Compliance Everywhere	Improved
	Document Sets	New
Insights	Business Intelligence Center	Improved
	Dashboards	New
	Decomposition Tree	New
	Visio Services	New
Search	Contextual Search	Improved
	Metadata-driven Refinement	Improved
	People and Expertise Search	Improved
Sites	Accessibility	Improved
	Cross-Browser Support	Improved
	Multilingual User Interface	Improved
	Out-of-the-box web parts	Improved

	SharePoint Health Analyzer	New
	SharePoint Ribbon	New
	Streamlined Central Administration	Improved
	Unattached Content Database Recovery	New
	Visual Upgrade	New
	Web Parts	Improved
	Windows PowerShell Support	New

As Table 1-2 shows, there have been changes and improvements at every level, from infrastructure right up to the functional aspects. Without a proper understanding of the new version capabilities, planning for migration will be very hard. This chapter provides you with insight into what you need to know and understand to plan and accomplish a successful migration.

There are many steps to ensuring a smooth upgrade process and avoiding failures, including planning that is involved before, during and after the migration. Microsoft provided various mechanisms and tools that help you to have an error-free transition. In the next section, we discuss the available process and ways to upgrade your MOSS 2007 platform to SharePoint 2010.

Overview of Upgrading from MOSS 2007 to SharePoint 2010

Have patience while you upgrade no matter which approach you pick. It is going to take a lot of time, and sometimes, you might end up redoing things if it fails. However, things have changed a lot in this version to make upgrading much better when compared with the upgrade from SharePoint Server (SPS) 2003 to MOSS 2007. Here's an overview of this chapter's coverage of the upgrade process in SharePoint 2010:

- *Hardware requirements*: Upgrading requires meeting specific hardware, operating system, and database needs.

- *Preupgrade checker*: This tool is a "getting ready" application for your infrastructure; it helps you realize what you are missing or need to fix before you start the actual upgrade process.

- *New upgrade methods*: Two new upgrade methods are available to choose, or maybe you'll even use a hybrid of the two.

- *PowerShell cmdlets*: SharePoint administrators have always wanted a scripting language to help them administer the farm. You can use the following command to test an existing content database before attaching it to the SPS 2010 farm:

```
test-spcontentdatabase -name {content db name} -webapplication {webapplicationname}
```

- *Visual upgrade:* This new feature allows you to check how your new web application or site collection looks visually when you finish upgrading. Site and site collection administrators have the option to turn on the new look and feel or delay turning it on for a time, until they can upgrade to the new look and feel. Using visual upgrade is not automatic but can be achieved by manually changing the settings through the UI or by running PowerShell commands. It is also a mechanism by which backward compatibility of visual aspects is achieved.

- *Feature upgrade:* With the help of new members and types, you can upgrade your Windows SharePoint Services (WSS) 3.0/MOSS 2007 features as they are or convert them to the new SPS 2010 type. For more information on feature upgrades, see http://msdn.microsoft.com/library/aa544511(office.14).aspx.

- *Reporting and logging:* Better status reporting and logging mechanisms are provided in this edition.

- *Downtime:* When you do simple math, you can see that the greater the complexity and number of sites, the more time will be needed to upgrade your databases. SharePoint 2010 offers better downtime management during the upgrade process in two ways:

  - *Parallel upgrade:* In MOSS 2007, all the content databases were upgraded in sequence, and this took a lot of time. In SPS 2010, you can decide to upgrade in parallel, or select to upgrade the database manually using a hybrid approach.

  - *Read-only databases for continuous access:* Again, by using a database attach upgrade, you can set MOSS 2007 databases to read-only mode first. This will ensure that the content in the 2007 farm remains accessible in read-only mode, but users cannot perform any write operations on it, thus preventing loss of data during the upgrade process.

Every organization may be unique in its infrastructure. And every SharePoint implementation might or might not have customizations implemented. How would you effectively upgrade your existing farms to new ones? Even before you think you are ready, it is important to verify if your existing MOSS 2007 infrastructure is ready or not? First, ensure that your MOSS 2007 farm is patched with all required hot fixes, most importantly SP2 and the October 2009 cumulative updates. Consider this as one of your key prerequisites. It is particularly important to have SP2, because it comes with a preupgrade checker that you can use to verify how your infrastructure and farm is ready for SharePoint 2010 migration.

■ **Note** We also recommend installing SP3 (optional), but installing SP2 is mandatory.

Hardware Requirements

As discussed earlier, SPS 2010 only runs on a 64-bit platform and requires either the Windows Server 2008 SP2 or Windows Server 2008 R2 operating system. If you have a 32-bit operating system, you must upgrade to 64-bit first. Also, if you have Windows Server 2003, you will have to first upgrade your operating system before you can migrate to SPS 2010. In both cases, an in-place upgrade is not possible, and you will have to use database attach upgrade option (you will learn more about upgrade options in the next section). It is equally important to have either the SQL Server 2005 SP3 or SQL Server 2008 SP1 64-bit version installed.

■ **Note** These infrastructure rules apply to each and every server in the farm.

If none of the infrastructure outlined in the previous paragraph is available, we recommend that you initiate the infrastructure setup changes as a separate project from the migration, to isolate any issues that occur during each type of upgrade.

Preupgrade Check

The preupgrade check command-line tool is to be run on your existing MOSS 2007 environment to find any potential issues as well as review recommendations and best practices. When you run a preupgrade check, you will be provided with information on various features, such as the following:

- *Search content sources and start addresses*: Displays the list of content sources and start addresses for each shared service provider configured in the farm.

- *Search Server Topology*: Details about the office server search topology in the farm and its components, such as shared service providers.

- *Servers in the farm*: Displays details about all the servers that are installed as part of the SharePoint farm.

■ **Note** This list does not include SQL Server. Also, remember to run preupgrade check on each SharePoint Server instance in the farm.

- *Components in the farm*: Displays the current version of the MOSS software running on your farm (e.g., 12.0.0.6421) as well as information such as number of servers, number of web applications, content database (and size), and site collections.

- *Supported upgrade types*: Informs you what types of upgrade approaches are possible on this farm.

- *Site definition information*: Displays all the installed or referenced site definitions. Keep informed that all the out-of-the-box site definitions are upgraded automatically; you need to ensure that custom site definitions are upgraded accordingly (see http://support.microsoft.com/kb/960577).

- *Language pack information*: Displays the current language packs installed. After upgrading, these language packs (other than the global server language) will not work. You will have to install the new versions to ensure that your sites work.

- *Feature Information:* Displays all the installed or referred features. If you have custom features or any missing features, you will have to install each one of them to ensure the site works as expected.

- *Alternate access mapping URLs:* List of alternate access mapping (AAM) URLs in your current environment that you need to consider or configure when upgrading.

- *Lists and Libraries:* List of all lists and libraries.

- *Informational rules to list the WSS Search topology information:* List of all WSS Search topology components that belong to the farm.

- *Hardware:* Informs you whether your existing farm meets the necessary hardware and operating system requirements.

- *Unsupported customizations:* List of unsupported customizations.

- *Databases or site orphans:* List of the content databases and any orphaned sites.

- *Invalid configuration settings including missing web.config file:* List of all configuration settings and related information.

- *Database upgrade requirements check:* List of information about whether or not there is a need for database upgrade requirements.

Note These are informational rules that are part of the preupgrade checker. For a list of all information and errors, see `http://technet.microsoft.com/en-us/library/dd793609.aspx`.

As mentioned earlier, you need to have the MOSS 2007 SP2 and October 2009 cumulative updates; if necessary, you can download and install these from `http://go.microsoft.com/fwlink/?LinkID=169179`. Once you are ready, you can run the preupgrade check using the following SharePoint Team Services Administration (STSADM) command:

```
stsadm –o preupgradecheck
```

The output will look like Figure 1-1, and the results will be saved as an `.htm` report in the `12hive\logs` folder, as shown in Figure 1-2.

You can run the `preupgradecheck` command with additional parameters to detect more routines. For instance, you can define a set of rules in a file and provide the file path as a parameter. Rules can be of different types, including informational, error rules, default, and upgrade checker rules. For more information on rules, see `http://technet.microsoft.com/en-us/library/dd793609(office.12).aspx`. The following line of code shows how to use preupgrade check with the -rulefiles parameter:

```
stsadm –o preupgradecheck –rulefiles <rule file name>
```

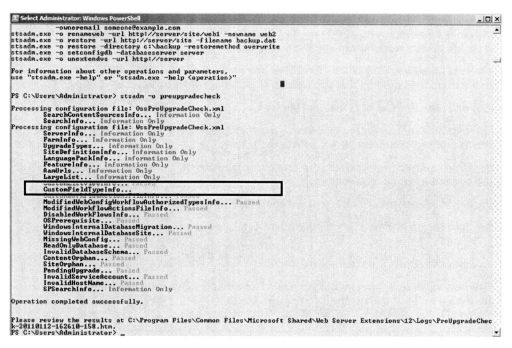

Figure 1-1. STSADM preupgrade check

Figure 1-2. Preupgrade check results

If you find any issues when your preupgrade check is run, it is important to fix them and follow any recommendations offered and subsequently run the check again to confirm that all issues are resolved and you're ready to go for migration. At the same time, ignore errors related to the resources that you are not planning to use anymore or won't migrate. Once the environment is clean, you can plan for the upgrade approach. There are two upgrade approaches that you can follow, as you will learn in the next section.

Supported Upgrade Approaches

Depending on your existing environment, you can pick one of the two upgrade approaches or use a hybrid approach. If you are unsure what to do, at the end of this section, we have provided a decision tree to help you to make the right call. OK, let's dig deep into the two approaches and look at a hybrid model of these two.

■ **Note** There is a Single Click Install—SQL Migration that is not covered in this chapter.

In-Place Upgrade

An in-place upgrade, as the name says, is one in which you run SharePoint 2010 installation software on your existing MOSS 2007 environment. Very few platforms in the market fall into this case because not everyone had the foresight to accommodate the current 64-bit requirement four years back. But if you had (and have) a very good IT professional in your organization who planned ahead well, you are all good to go.

It's pretty much understood that, for an in-place upgrade, your existing environment needs to be 64-bit and meet the operating system requirements as well. If your hardware and infrastructure meet SharePoint 2010 infrastructure requirements, you can use the same hardware and install SharePoint 2010 on it. The advantage of this approach is that all your existing settings and customizations be available after upgrade. However, you will have to make some manual changes to your customizations to get them working. Well, of course, your preupgrade checker will notify you if anything is going to fail during the upgrade. Additionally, all custom solutions should be recompiled with the new SharePoint 14 DLLs and redeployed.

■ **Note** A word about prerequisites—To do an in-place upgrade, you need to ensure that your infrastructure is running MOSS 2007 SP2 x64 on a Windows Server 2008 operating system with the x64 version of SQL Server 2008 R2, or SQL Server 2008 with SP1 and CU 2, or SQL Server 2005 SP3 and CU 3.

Preparing to Upgrade

Before you begin in-place upgrade, it is important to first verify the following:

1. Run the `stsadm -o preupgradecheck` command to learn more details about your infrastructure and make sure it is ready for the upgrade.

2. Create a test environment before trying the upgrade process on actual servers to avoid unknowns and issues.

3. Make sure to certify all the user accounts with the required permissions to run and configure setup.

4. Be prepared for the servers' downtime.

Running SharePoint 2010 Setup and Configuring Your Server

If you have a single server, run the SharePoint Products Configuration wizard on it. However, if you have a server farm, perform installation on each of the servers in the farm, beginning with the server on which Central Administration is running. Make sure that the account you use for installation is a member of db_owner database role. After the installation is complete, you can verify the status of each site from Upgrade Status page in SharePoint Central Administration or by using the `localupgradestatus` operation in `stsadm`.

The following steps need to be performed in sequence after the preupgrade installation is complete:

1. Run SharePoint 2010 Server setup on the server that has Central Administration. In this case, "In-Place upgrade" is automatically selected.

2. Once step 1 is successful, run setup on all the other web front ends, as well as the application servers.

3. Run the SharePoint Products Configuration wizard on the server where Central Administration exists. Once configuration is complete, the configuration database, all the services, and the content databases are upgraded in order.

4. Run the SharePoint Products Configuration wizard on rest of the servers that are part of the farm.

5. Once configuration is successful on all the servers, the upgrade is complete as shown in Figure 1-3.

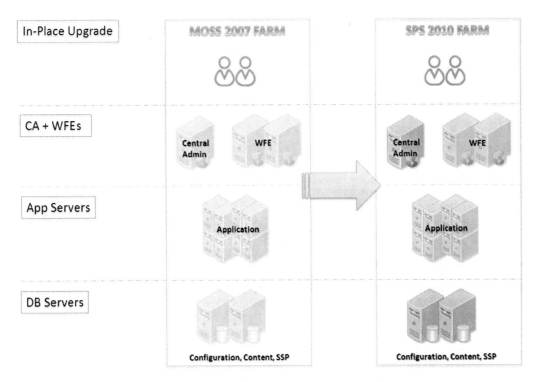

Figure 1-3. In-Place upgrade server status after migration

In-place upgrades generally work well for simple SharePoint installations. When an in-place upgrade is not possible, you can use the database attach upgrade model. Since it is possible to virtualize such environments, it is generally speaking not a bad idea to use the database attach upgrade method.

Database Attach Upgrade

Database attach is similar to the backup-and-restore database operation that you perform with stsadm commands, but in this case, you are migrating from one version to a totally different version. In the database attach upgrade model, one of the best advantages is that your existing environment will not have any downtime. Having said that, let's consider this upgrade approach.

The target database environment is more or less a brand new infrastructure that has been set up in this case, which means that you will have to verify if your new server farm is SharePoint 2010 ready. It can be assumed that database attach upgrade will probably be the most widely adopted model. And it can be performed in four major steps: Preparation, Installation, Upgrade, and Post-Upgrade check.

Preparing to Upgrade

Running the preupgrade check is as important for a database upgrade as for an in-place upgrade. It informs you whether or not your new environment is SharePoint 2010 ready. Since this tool would display issues about your infrastructure along with information, you may need to run it more than once until all the issues are resolved.

Second, prepare a checklist about your existing MOSS 2007 farm that includes any custom solution (.wsp) files that might, in turn, include features, master pages, web parts, timer jobs, event handlers, style sheets, and so on. This comprehensive check-list is very important to prepare as a best practice because this would ensure that you made sure of fixing, verifying any or all related issues, before the migration process. You will also use the same checklist for cross-referencing during the post-upgrade check process.

And finally, ensure that your existing MOSS 2007 environment is functioning healthy. It's time to clean up or delete any unnecessary assets that you wouldn't want to migrate, which might include one or more of the following:

- Orphaned sites

- Unused site collections and subsites

- Unused solutions, features, templates, and web parts

It is also important to take care of the following items for a smooth upgrade process without any problems after or during the upgrade.

- *Large lists*: By default, SharePoint 2010 enforces list throttling. If the lists in your existing sites have views that are large, they may not be migrated correctly. Ensure that views are altered for simple structures. Also, adjust the throttling settings to accommodate your items.

- *Site collections*: The hard limit for the number of site collections in a single content database is 15,000 in MOSS 2007. In SharePoint 2010, the limit is reduced to 5,000. It is important to move additional site collections into different databases to avoid failures during migration.

- *Access control lists*: When you break inheritance and use item-level permissions, they create a larger ACL. Larger ACLs could create performance issues.

- *Document versions*: Multiple document versions or old versions that you do not need can significantly slow the upgrade process. Ensure that you delete the unwanted versions manually or by using object model.

- *Database issues*: Fix any database related issues.

Installing SharePoint 2010 and Configuring Your Server

Install all the required software, which includes the prerequisite software and SharePoint 2010 installation (SPF / SPS) on your new environment. Here are the prerequisites that are installed by the preparation tools:

- Web Server (IIS) role

- Application Server Roles

- Microsoft .NET Framework version 3.5 SP1

- SQL Server 2008 Express with SP1

- Microsoft Sync Framework Runtime v1.0 (x64)

- Microsoft Filter Pack 2.0

- Microsoft Chart Controls for Microsoft .NET Framework 3.5

- Windows PowerShell 2.0

- SQL Server 2008 Native Client

- Microsoft SQL Server 2008 Analysis Services ADOMD.NET

- ADO.NET Data Services Update for .NET Framework 3.5 SP1

- Windows Identity Foundation.

Once the installation is successful, configure your farm; join other servers if necessary as planned and so on. Configure service applications on your new environment. Although, by default, service applications arrive preconfigured, you might need to configure some of the aspects, such as Secure Store Services to very specific needs. Another initiative to be taken during the planning phase is the service applications that are necessary for your farm—identify and retain only those that are required and remove others.

Note Upgrade to SharePoint Foundation 2010 (SPF) is out of scope for this document

---

Also, configure general settings, group permissions, e-mail and SMTP settings, users, groups, logging, and so on. Apply all customizations that you have on your existing platform to the new farm. Create web applications, and configure them as required. Test your environment to make sure everything is up and running as expected before the final upgrade.

Note This book (and chapter) covers only the upgrade and migration process. For more information on installation and configuration, see the TechNet article at `http://technet.microsoft.com/en-us/sharepoint/ee518643`.

Upgrade

While you perform a database attach upgrade, you need to not only consider your new environment but also your existing one. In the database attach upgrade model, your existing environment will go offline and will not be available until the databases are moved to the new environment and upgraded. During this upgrade process, the legacy SharePoint farm is still intact.

Here are the sequence steps that you can use to perform your upgrade:

1. After the new farm architecture is planned with all the Web Front Ends (WFEs), application server, and so on, the server administrator installs the SharePoint 2010 setup, starting from the machine where Central Administration site will

be configured. Subsequently, SPS 2010 is installed on all other machines, and they added to the farm.

2. After the new farm architecture is planned with all the WFEs, application server, and so on, the server administrator installs the SharePoint 2010 setup, starting from the machine where Central Administration site will be configured. Subsequently, SPS 2010 is installed on all other machines, and they added to the farm.

3. Once the setup and configuration are complete, create a new web application and configure all the general settings related to it.

4. Run all customizations that are identified on your existing farm, and make all the necessary changes to the new farm.

5. Run and test the new farm, and make sure web applications and configurations are working fine.

6. Detach all the content and shared service databases from your existing farm. There is no need to move the configuration database to the new farm, because SharePoint 2010 has one already.

7. Use the following command to detach the database from your respective web application. You can use the SQL database backup mechanism as well:

```
stsadm -o deletecontendb -url "<your_sharepoint_siteurl>" -databasename "<database_name>" -
databaseserver "<database_server_name>"
```

8. Take the existing farm to offline mode.

9. Move the databases to the new environment, attach them to the new farm, and upgrade the content.

10. Verify your content database and ensure there are no errors before attaching; you can use the following PowerShell command to do so:

```
Test-SPContentDatabase -Name <your_database_name> -WebApplication <your_web_application_name>
```

11. Once you are ready, you can now attach the database using the following PowerShell command:

```
Mount-SPContentDatabase -Name <database_name> -WebApplication <your_web_application_name>
```

12. Or you can use the following stsadm command:

```
stsadm -o addcontentdb -url <your_web_application_name> -databasename <database_name> -
databaseserver <database_server_name>
```

You can use steps 11 and 12 to upgrade your shared services and My Sites database in the same way. Remember that this process can take many hours, so give yourself plenty of time for this upgrade. It is a better idea to upgrade each one of the databases one at a time and test each before moving to the next database in your list. And while the upgrade happens, it is also important to monitor the progress to ensure there that there are any errors. If errors occur, you need to be ready to roll back your migration process to fix the errors. Once you upgrade all the databases successfully, you need to verify the upgrade and review all the sites. Your new farm could look similar to Figure 1-4.

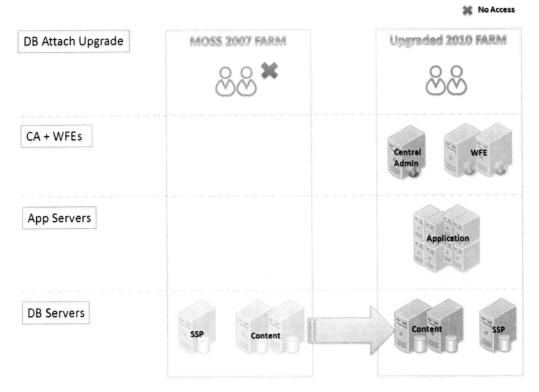

Figure 1-4. Database attach upgrade

Performing the Post-Upgrade Check

Once you finish your high-level review and cursory checks, the availability of the sites on your new platform, it is time to perform a post-upgrade check to ensure the success of the overall upgrade process. These steps can be performed immediately after the upgrade and before the review test:

1. Check administrator permissions for all the service applications.

2. Check profiles that are configured as part of your SSPs in the MOSS 2007 environment. Also, ensure that user photos are updated accurately. If they are not, you may have to manually set the photos for the user profiles. We will discuss more about user profiles in the "Upgrading User Profiles" section of this chapter.

3. Check or configure single sign on and forms-based authentication settings to Secure Store Services.

4. Check all sites that are part of the upgrade process. Ensure that all sites are successfully launched.

5. Run a full search crawl on the newly migrated content.

What if you want to set up your new infrastructure in parallel without taking down your existing MOSS 2007 farm? SharePoint 2010 allows you to perform both the above approaches side by side—you can plan for a hybrid model in this case and take better advantage of both options. In fact, there are two hybrid approaches, which are discussed in the next two sections.

Hybrid Approach 1

In this approach, your MOSS 2007 content and SSP databases should be set to read-only mode. Next, you back them up and restore them onto your new farm, leaving your existing infrastructure in read-only mode. This model is known as the hybrid approach with read-only database. Once the upgrade is completed and tested, your existing infrastructure can be taken down:

1. Server administrators will provision the new farm and set up SharePoint 2010 on all the servers that are part of the farm.

2. Administrators transfer all the customizations to the new farm from existing farm.

3. Existing farm databases are placed in read-only mode by the SQL administrators. SQL administrators then would back up the databases and restore them to the new farm. During this stage, users will not be able to make any modifications on this database. There may be failures if you have any third-party components used, because they would be agnostic about the read-only databases.

4. Server administrators then attach these databases and run the upgrade process.

5. Server administrators confirm whether or not the entire configuration's setup is successful and the new farm is ready to use.

In this model, you have the advantage of having both your environments running side by side, unlike the in-place upgrade, as shown in Figure 1-5. Though the existing farm would be in read-only mode and end users cannot make any modifications, you will have somewhat better control in the new environment, and you can turn off your existing environment after a thorough test of the new environment, as shown in Figure 1-6.

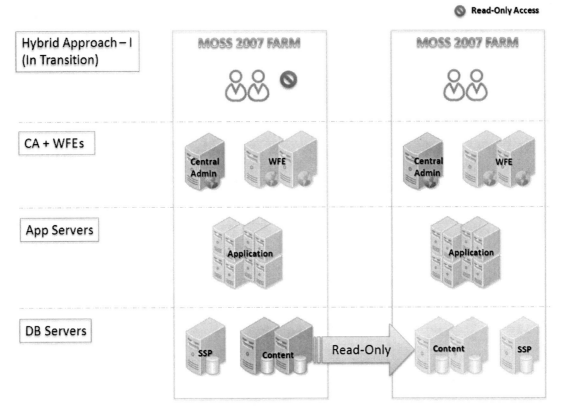

Figure 1-5. Hybrid approach 1 (transition phase)

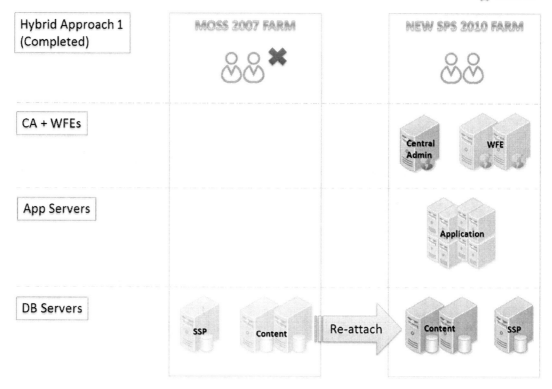

Figure 1-6. Hybrid approach 1 (completed)

Hybrid Approach 2

As an alternate to hybrid approach 1, you can perform an in-place upgrade but with the database detach model, as shown in Figure 1-7. In this model, you will detach your existing infrastructure content databases, which means you are going offline. You can then update your infrastructure and reattach the databases. You can also take this database to a temporarily set-up farm, do a parallel database upgrade, and bring them back to your existing infrastructure, as shown in Figure 1-8. This would speed up the upgrade process. However, until your infrastructure comes back, no one can connect to your infrastructure. Here are the basic steps in hybrid approach 2:

1. The existing farm is taken offline by the server administrator.

2. All content databases are detached from the existing farm.

3. Server administrator runs an in-place upgrade on the existing farm.

4. On success, the server administrator attaches the content databases to the existing farm, and the upgrade is performed on the farm.

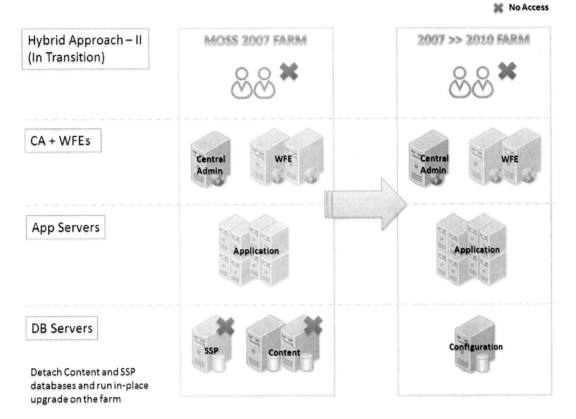

Figure 1-7. Hybrid approach 2 (transition phase)

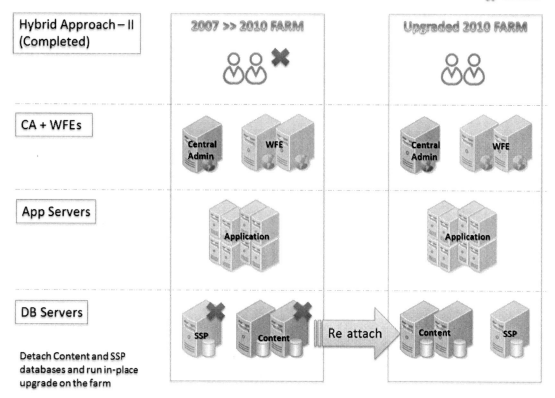

Figure 1-8. Hybrid approach 2 (completed)

Now that you have seen all four models, we will discuss some of the pros and cons of each of these methods, as explained in Table 1-3.

Table 1-3. Comparing the Upgrade Methods

Upgrade Method	Pros	Cons
In-place	• All settings are preserved, but manual steps are required to upgrade customizations if any.	• Significant downtime or offline mode. • Not possible to roll back easily, but you can restore to an earlier snapshot if your environment is virtualized.
Database upgrade	• Parallel upgrade of database possible and results in faster	• Server settings are not migrated.

	upgrade of the overall farm • Multiple farms can further be expanded or combined using the database detach model • If you have taken a backup of the databases before upgrade, roll back is easy in the event of failure.	• All customizations should be manually transferred. • Copying databases over network shall result in consuming time as well as bandwidth.
Hybrid 1 (read-only database)	• Existing farm continues to be available in read-only mode, which results in no downtime for the end user. • Faster upgrade time, because multiple databases can be upgraded in parallel. • Hardware upgrade is possible.	• Server settings are not migrated. • All customizations should be manually transferred. • Copying databases over the network will result in consuming time as well as bandwidth. • Direct access to database servers is required.
Hybrid 2 (in-place upgrade with database detach)	• Farm settings are preserved, but manual steps are required to upgrade any customizations. • Parallel upgrade of database is possible and results in a faster upgrade of the overall farm.	• Copying databases over network result in consuming time as well as bandwidth. • Direct access to database servers is required.

One aspect to consider with any of the upgrade approaches discussed earlier in this chapter is the visuals. The user interface version is completely different in SPS 2010 when compared with MOSS 2007, and there is no such thing as converting your existing visuals or master pages into the new version. Your content has to either adapt to the new visuals or stay with the existing visuals. We will now discuss different options that are available related to the UI. Though we will not discuss what's new in the UI in this chapter, you will learn more about branding aspects in Chapter 3.

▓ **Note** In this and subsequent chapters, you will notice we will be using a version number for UI; UI version 3 is MOSS 2007, and version 4 is SPS 2010.

Visual Upgrade

As discussed earlier, there is no switch you can flip to convert MOSS 2007 branding to SPS 2010 branding during or after an upgrade. Designing new branding to the upgraded site might actually take significant time, depending on the complexity of your UI. This initiative can be a separate process altogether that can be achieved before, during, or after the upgrade process. However, until the new visuals are ready, you probably want to keep your existing visuals as they are and then change to the new look and feel once you are ready. To achieve that new look and feel, the SPS 2010 upgrade process offers you a feature known as Visual Upgrade. In this process, site and site collection owners can preserve the existing look and feel and gradually upgrade to the new interface at a later time. We will revisit Visual Upgrade from a designer's perspective later but will limit our discussion to configuration from an administrative standpoint in this section.

Visual Upgrade is a process in which you are definitely isolating the UI from data. Farm administrators can move ahead with upgrading the content and simply ignore the visual aspects completely. That way, the UI upgrade never gets in the way of migration and can be negotiated at a later stage by simply using the visual upgrade procedures. To have a smooth transition, you can split the process in two ways: first plan and then manage Visual Upgrade.

Note Visual Upgrade for a stand-alone installation with built-in database must use the PSConfig command-line tool for updating and is not supported by the general upgrade process that we are going to discuss now.

In the plan for Visual Upgrade, you can choose to either preserve the existing user interface (version 3), or you can decide to upgrade to the new user interface (version 4). When you choose to preserve the version 3 interface, all data from the existing sites, such as layouts and styles, are preserved. In this state, even the customized content or pages will work as expected, because they are not overridden by new layouts and so on. Once the upgrade process is complete, the UI can be switched to the newer version. When you choose *not* to preserve a version 3 interface and would like to begin using version 4 visuals, you will be overriding control that site and site collection owners have on the Visual Upgrade. This also means that all your customizations will be overridden and default to the new interface. However, you can preserve or reset to the customized pages. Always choose preserve customizations if you are unsure whether or not you have any customizations. If you reset customized pages, SharePoint removes all the customizations, and this step is irrevocable. Next, most importantly, there should be training for the site collections' administrators as well as site owners on how to switch and preview the new visuals and all the new features and layouts in the UI. As a baseline, we recommend having a scheduled timeline between the content and UI upgrades. In fact, there are so many features in SharePoint 2010 that do not work with version 3 UIs that we do not recommend this as an approach to buy time.

Once you have planned the visual upgrade, you can begin managing it. During the in-place upgrade, you will have the option to choose visual upgrade while on the configuration wizard. In the database attach upgrade, you will have to use one of the following commands:

- Using PSConfig:

```
Psconfig.exe -cmd -upgrade [-preserveolduserexperience <true|false>]
```

- Using PowerShell:

```
Mount-SPConentDatabase -Name {ContentDatabase} -DatabaseServer {DatabaseServerName} -
WebApplication {http://yourwebapplication} [-UpdateUserExperience]
```

■ **Note** See http://technet.microsoft.com/en-us/library/ff607581.aspx for more information on how to use the Mount-SPContentDatabase command with PowerShell.

- Using stsadm:

```
Stsadm.exe -o addcontentdb -url {http://yourwebapplication} -databasename
{ContentDatabaseName} -preserveolduserexperience [true|false]
```

To view the status of the current user interface, you can run the following PowerShell command. This is very handy when you wish to impose a deadline on site owners and set a time limit before switching to the new interface, during which time you can monitor the progress.

```
$sitecollection = Get-SPSite http://yourwebapplication;
$sitecollection.GetVisualReport() | Format-Table
```

During the process of using visual upgrade, if site owners would like, for any reason, to revert to the version 3 UI after upgrading to version 4, use the following PowerShell commands. You can run this command either for a single site or for all sites, depending on the need.

For one site in a site collection, use this command:

```
Get-SPSite http://YourSiteInSiteCollection | Get-SPWeb {SiteName} | Foreach
{
        $_.UIVersionConfigurationEnabled=1;
        $_.UIVersion=3;
        $_.Update();
}
```

For all the sites in a site collection, use this command:

```
Get-SPSite http://YourSiteInSiteCollection | Foreach
{
        $_.UIVersionConfigurationEnabled=1;
        $_.UIVersion=3;
        $_.Update();
}
```

If you want to force site owners to apply the new user visual interface to all site collections and sites, use the following command:

```
$webApplication = Get-SPWebApplication http://yourwebapplication
Foreach ($site in $webApplication.sites)
{
        $.VisualUpgradeWebs()
}
```

To upgrade a single site collection, use this one:

```
$site = Get-SPSite http://yoursite
$site.VisualUpgradeWebs()
```

And finally, to upgrade a particular site under a site collection, use this command:

```
$web = Get-SPWeb http://yoursite/site
$web.UIVersion - 4
$web.UIVersionConfigurationEnabled = 0
$web.Update()
```

> ■ **Note** The preceding settings can also be used via the user interface on the site settings page.

Known Issues

The following list contains a few known issues on the Visual Upgrade that you must consider during the upgrade process:

- MySites will inherit the new user interface after upgrade process is performed with the "preserve existing user interface" option.

- You can set properties for an Excel services web part, but the changes are reflected only after inheriting new UI or applying visual upgrade to version 4.

- SharePoint Server 2010 and SharePoint Designer versions and service packs should be the same.

- Project web access sites require the new user interface and will not work with the visual upgrade procedure.

> ■ **Note** There might be some special cases with very specific requirements and goals that you want to achieve during upgrade. Use this URL to understand more about different cases: http://technet.microsoft.com/en-us/library/cc263447.aspx#section2.

Shared Service Provider (SSP) no longer exists in SharePoint 2010, but a new service application architecture has been introduced. After MOSS 2007 SSP databases are upgraded to SPS 2010 (or during uprade), a few steps need to be followed, as we will discuss in the next section.

Upgrading User Profiles and MySites

While using the in-place upgrade, the services and databases are upgraded. However, SharePoint 2010 has its own services with their respective databases, as shown in Figure 1-9.

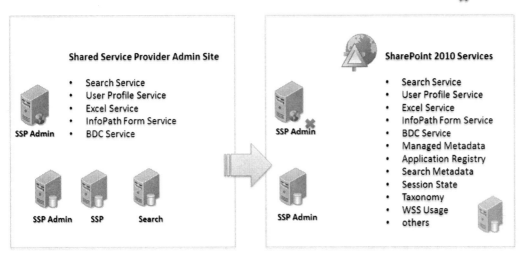

Figure 1-9. In-place upgrade for the services in MOSS 2007

These services are migrated to respective service applications and their proxies with appropriate names. For instance, if the shared service is named SharedService1, it will be renamed SharedService1_<service>. When the Search service is upgraded, it becomes SharedService1_Search in this case. SharePoint 2010 also maintains the associations to the respective web applications and maintains the rights and access to the administrators as well. Similarly, for the service databases, data is copied to the user profile, taxonomy, and other relevant databases. The SSP administrative web application, however, is migrated with only the Business Data Catalog (BDC) profile pages. We will now discuss about how some of these service should be handled during the migration process.

Upgrading User Profiles

In MOSS 2007, profile services that are part of shared services will be migrated to two service applications in SharePoint 2010: User Profile Service and Managed Metadata Service. During an in-place upgrade, these two serives are configured automatically, and the user profile information from MOSS 2007 is upgraded to the new user profile service application accordingly. All the profile properties are preserved as well in this case. Similarly, all the taxonomy-related data is migrated to the Managed Metadata Service application. However, make sure to note the settings configured for timer jobs before upgrading, because they will be set to defaults once upgraded. You will have to reset them as required.

In the database attach upgrade model, since the settings in the configuration database are not migrated, some additional manual configuration steps must be pefrormed. First, verify that the service applications Managed Metadata and User Profile Service Application are started, as shown in Figure 1-10. It is also important to configure the Managed Metadata service before upgrading with the database attach model.

Managed Metadata Service	Managed Metadata Service	Started
Managed Metadata Service	Managed Metadata Service Connection	Started
PerformancePoint Service Application	PerformancePoint Service Application	Started
PerformancePoint Service Application	PerformancePoint Service Application Proxy	Started
PowerPoint Service Application	PowerPoint Service Application	Started
PowerPoint Service Application	PowerPoint Service Application Proxy	Started
Search Administration Web Service for Search Service Application	Search Administration Web Service Application	Started
Search Service Application	Search Service Application	Started
Search Service Application	Search Service Application Proxy	Started
Secure Store Service	Secure Store Service Application	Started
Secure Store Service	Secure Store Service Application Proxy	Started
Security Token Service Application	Security Token Service Application	Started
State Service	State Service	Started
State Service	State Service Proxy	Started
Usage and Health data collection	Usage and Health Data Collection Service Application	Started
Usage and Health data collection	Usage and Health Data Collection Proxy	Started
User Profile Service Application	User Profile Service Application	Started
User Profile Service Application	User Profile Service Application Proxy	Started
Visio Graphics Service	Visio Graphics Service Application	Started
Visio Graphics Service	Visio Graphics Service Application Proxy	Started
Web Analytics Service Application	Web Analytics Service Application	Started

Figure 1-10. Service applications required for User Profile migration

All the relevant service applications, MySites databases, and content databases can be found in the SQL Server (marked) as shown in Figure 1-11. Your Shared Services and My Sites databases are copied from the MOSS environment and attached to the new farm, as shown in Figure 1-11.

```
□ 📇 .\sharepoint (SQL Server 10.0.5500 - SPS\Srini)
  □ 📁 Databases
     ⊞ 📁 System Databases
     ⊞ 📄 Application_Registry_Service_DB_c291b579b9784a1497d2f69f3cf7b1f3
     ⊞ 📄 Rds_Service_DB_7cf2a3620a1642c808b44a4a68150Eba
     ⊞ 📄 Managed Metadata Service_3f0bb1b2ef544457abe6deac697d9332
     ⊞ 📄 PerformancePoint Service Application_58f39a4003bf44159679027dfa424388
     ⊞ 📄 Search_Service_Application_CrawlStoreDB_8aa0b288cde2415eaf3ecd4089326c1f
     ⊞ 📄 Search_Service_Application_DB_774d7392f0964ebd8628aab58cd3bdce
     ⊞ 📄 Search_Service_Application_PropertyStoreDB_83a56ee858314d60bb497b13c286c460
     ⊞ 📄 Secure_Store_Service_DB_23fc450c29ac4dddbcbbd9ab8e52a767
     ⊞ 📄 SharedServicesMoss2007_SocialDB_ad39e3fc7b284fed87a13cb140f21d30
     ⊞ 📄 SharedServicesMoss2007_SyncDB_cf43243c-b3c8-4dd1-95ce-33212ac6171e
     ⊞ 📄 SharePoint_AdminContent_77fee5f3-782a-4cfb-a796-1894fe4849fe
     ⊞ 📄 SharePoint_AdminContent_8d4bad48-2f1c-446f-b68a-bcd955525c37
     ⊞ 📄 SharePoint_Config_baa910a0-2d99-4e56-9e38-9cf0bf3cc81c
     ⊞ 📄 SharePoint_Config_ce0ee430-13fb-4064-8130-ea691b9e6fd2
     ⊞ 📄 StateService_ac5136fd812c4f9aaaf0ddda2da b856d
     ⊞ 📄 User Profile Service Application_ProfileDB_c19b5982c46448de8e9d33f117ac0732
     ⊞ 📄 User Profile Service Application_SocialDB_19b38f7baf444c3894e75bc603950e30
     ⊞ 📄 User Profile Service Application_SyncDB_f8520dfa68d64756bbb410857d60017e
     ⊞ 📄 WebAnalyticsServiceApplication_ReportingDB_64cba7bf0300412a bb18 bdfc4e177c8c
     ⊞ 📄 WebAnalyticsServiceApplication_StagingDB_5f8305b3-ceb0-4298-9779-6fe64653b89c
     ⊞ 📄 WordAutomationServices_5528067d0a204f0492bbcb20610b11bb
     ⊞ 📄 WSS_Content_Default
     ⊞ 📄 WSS_Content_MySites
     ⊞ 📄 WSS_Content_ProMigration
     ⊞ 📄 WSS_Content_SSP
     ⊞ 📄 WSS_Logging
     ⊞ 📄 WSS_Search_SPS
  ⊞ 📁 Security
  ⊞ 📁 Server Objects
  ⊞ 📁 Replication
  ⊞ 📁 Management
```

Figure 1-11. Service application, profile, and MySites databases

Once the databases are attached to the SharePoint server database instance, you will have to create a new service application using this database for which you can run the following PowerShell cmdlet, as shown in Figure 1-12 from the SharePoint 2010 management shell. On success, you shall be returned with the new service application id as shown in the Figure 1-13.

```
New-SPProfileServiceApplication -Name SharedServicesMoss2007 -ApplicationPool
"<ApplicationPool>" -ProfileDBName "<DatabaseName>"
```

■ **Note** In the preceding command, it is important to provide the actual MOSS 2007 database name for the parameter `ProfileDBName`.

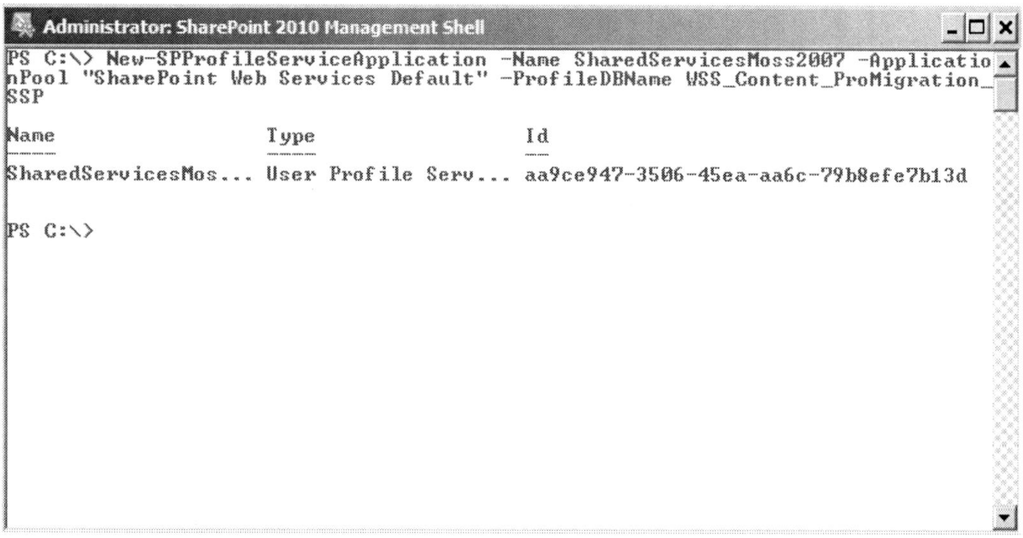

Figure 1-12. Creating a new profile service application

Once the preceding command runs successfully and a new service application is created, you will notice two new databases that have the words "Sync" and "Social." In the preceding example and Figure 1-12, they are User Profile Service Application_SyncDB_{GUID} and User Profile Service Application_SocialDB_{GUID}. You can also check the upgrade status from the Central Administration site, select Upgrade and Migration ► Upgrade and Patch Managemet ► Check upgrade status, as shown in Figure 1-13.

Upgrade sessions

Status	Server	Start	Last Updated	Errors	Warnings
Succeeded	**SPS**	**8/5/2011 11:18:35 PM**	**8/5/2011 11:27:36 PM**	**0**	**4**

Selected upgrade session details

Status	Succeeded
Server	SPS
Start	8/5/2011 11:18:35 PM
Last Updated	8/5/2011 11:27:36 PM
Errors	0
Warnings	4
Starting object	
Current object	
Current action	
Step within the action	0
Total steps in this action	0
Elapsed Time	00:09:01
Percentage completed	100.00%
Process Name	PSCONFIG
Thread Id	4980
Process Id	5468
Command Line	C:\Program Files\Common Files\Microsoft Shared\Web Server Extensions\14\BIN\PSCONFIG.EXE -cmd upgrade -inplace b2b -wait
Log File	C:\Program Files\Common Files\Microsoft Shared\Web Server Extensions\14\LOGS\Upgrade-20110805-231835-438.log
Remedy	Look for possible causes for upgrade issues by searching [ERROR] and [WARNING] strings in the upgrade log file. Refer to "http://go.microsoft.com/fwlink/?LinkId=157732" for more information about how to recover from upgrade failures.

Figure 1-13. Upgrade status screen

Next, you have to create a corresponding proxy for the create service application. To do so, run the following PowerShell cmdlet from the SharePoint 2010 management shell, as shown here:

```
New-SPProfileServiceApplicationProxy –Name SharedServiceMoss2007Proxy –ServiceApplication
{GUID}
```

In this case, the service application GUID is the one previously created (also shown in Figure 1-14).

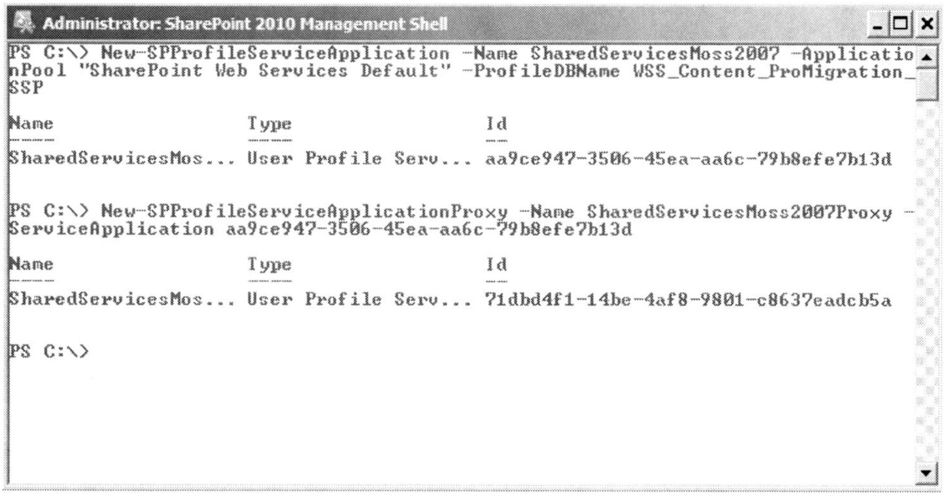

Figure 1-14. Creating a service application proxy

Once the commands run successfully, you'll see the new service application as well as its proxy by visiting the Central Administration Site, and selecting Service Applications ➤ Manage Service Applications, as shown in Figure 1-15.

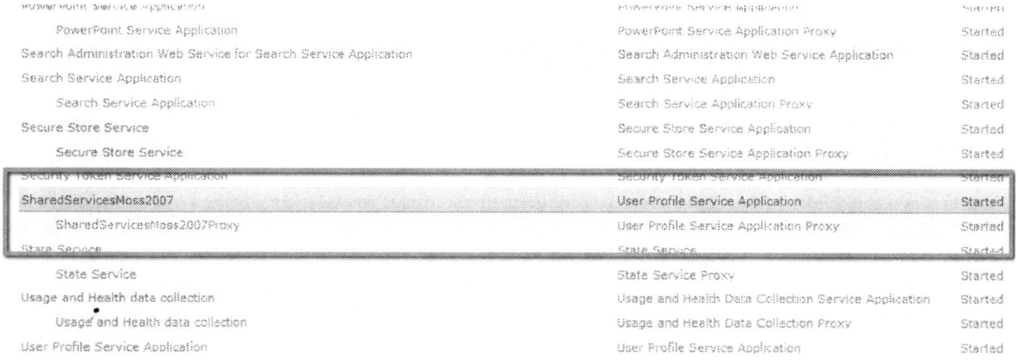

Figure 1-15. Newly created service applications

Since these service applications are created from the legacy databases, it is important to set permissions for them. Click the service application and from the ribbon under operations group, click Administrators, as shown in Figure 1-16.

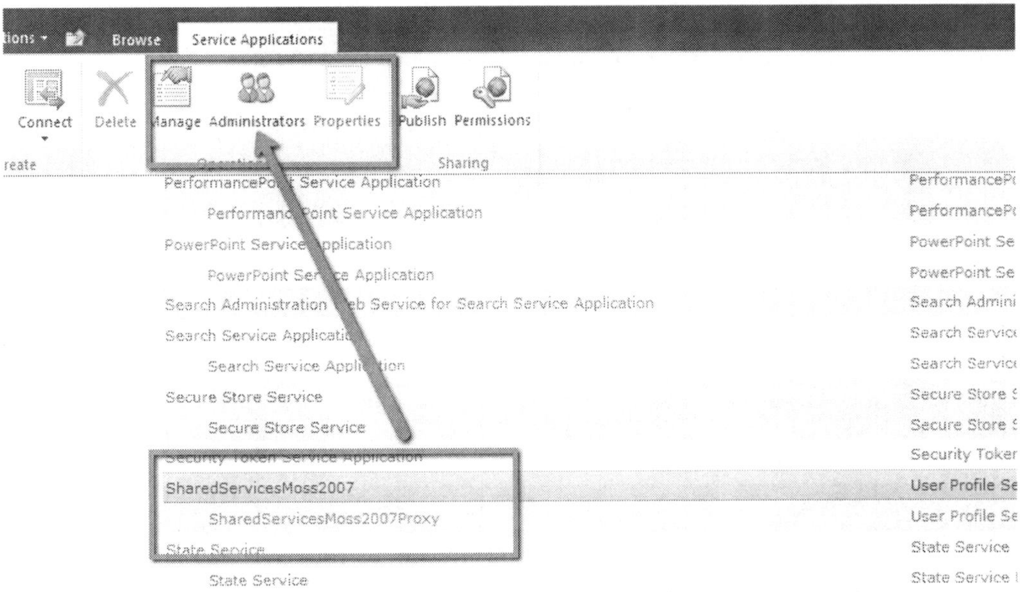

Figure 1-16. Managing service application administrators

In the Administrators for Service Application window, add the users or service accounts that need access and provide needed permissions (see Figure 1-17). Click the OK button when you're finished.

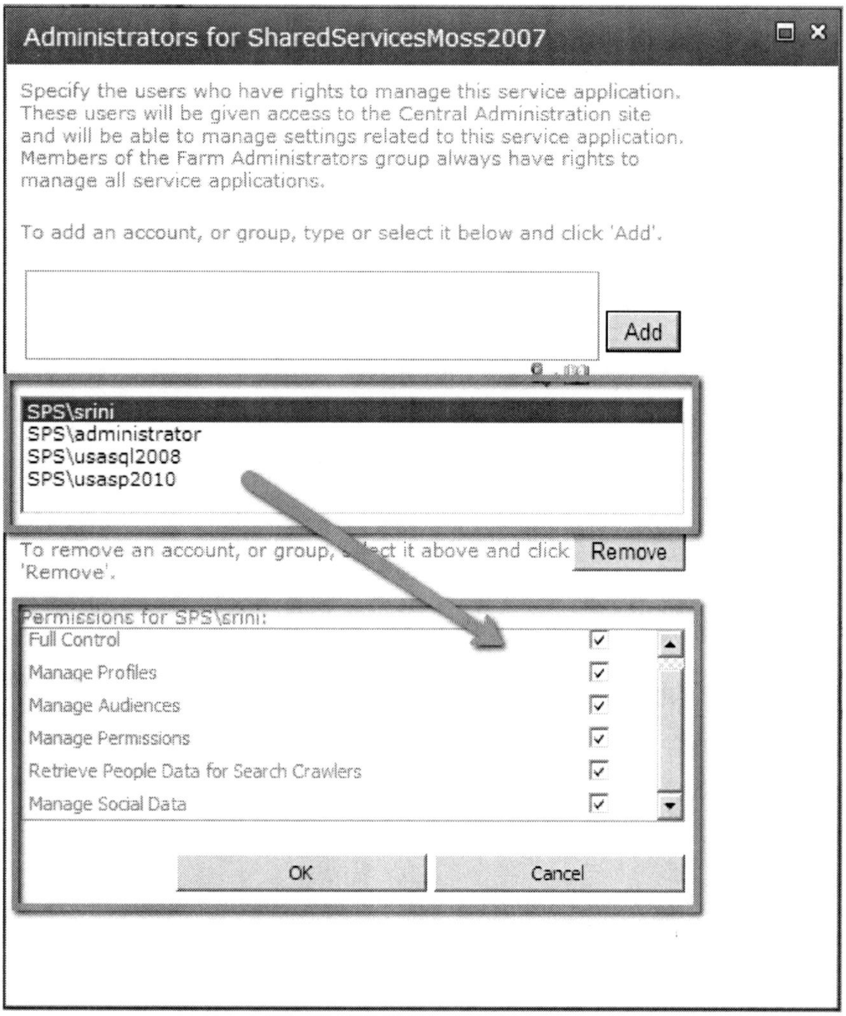

Figure 1-17. Managing permissions for users for a service application

Select the service application, and from the ribbon, click Manage under the operations group. Under People, select Manage User Profiles, as shown in Figure 1-18.

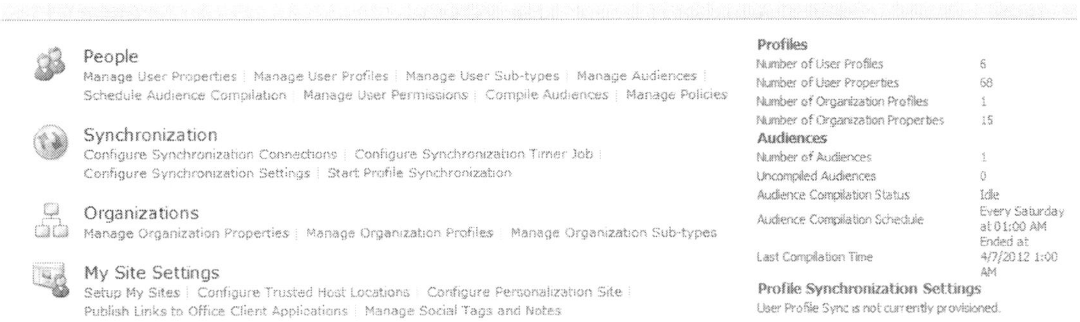

People
Manage User Properties | Manage User Profiles | Manage User Sub-types | Manage Audiences |
Schedule Audience Compilation | Manage User Permissions | Compile Audiences | Manage Policies

Synchronization
Configure Synchronization Connections | Configure Synchronization Timer Job |
Configure Synchronization Settings | Start Profile Synchronization

Organizations
Manage Organization Properties | Manage Organization Profiles | Manage Organization Sub-types

My Site Settings
Setup My Sites | Configure Trusted Host Locations | Configure Personalization Site |
Publish Links to Office Client Applications | Manage Social Tags and Notes

Profiles
Number of User Profiles   6
Number of User Properties   68
Number of Organization Profiles 1
Number of Organization Properties 15
Audiences
Number of Audiences   1
Uncompiled Audiences   0
Audience Compilation Status   Idle
Audience Compilation Schedule   Every Saturday
                                 at 01:00 AM
                                 Ended at
Last Compilation Time   4/7/2012 1:00
                                 AM
Profile Synchronization Settings
User Profile Sync is not currently provisioned.

Figure 1-18. User profile management screen

In the "Find profiles" text box shown in Figure 1-19, you can enter a user name and click the Find button to check the migrated user information.

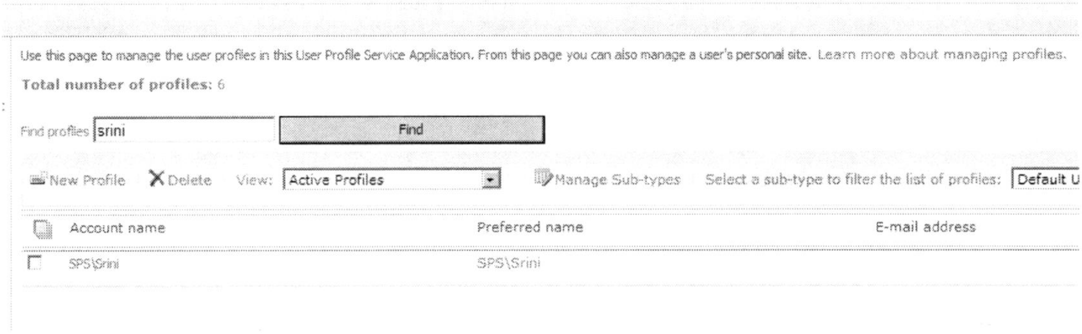

Use this page to manage the user profiles in this User Profile Service Application. From this page you can also manage a user's personal site. Learn more about managing profiles.

Total number of profiles: 6

Find profiles [srini]   [Find   ]

New Profile   X Delete   View: [Active Profiles   ▼]   Manage Sub-types   Select a sub-type to filter the list of profiles: [Default U

Account name	Preferred name	E-mail address
SPS\Srini	SPS\Srini	

Figure 1-19. Finding a user profile

To upgrade the taxonomy data, run the following PowerShell cmdlet from the management shell:

```
Move-SPProfileManagedMetadataProperty
```

MySites

A MySite database can be upgraded while you perform the upgrade on user profile services. MySite databases are usually migrated without issues as part of an in-place upgrade. However, SharePoint 2010 has three different thumbnail variations for the user profile pictures that do not exist in MOSS 2007. When migrated, users' profile pictures aren't automatically converted, hence the same picture is used for all the three thumbnails. To fix that, run the following cmdlet:

```
Update-SPProfilePhotoStore -MySiteHostLocation {your mysite host URL}
```

In the case of the database attach model, first make sure that the MySite content database is in good health. To ensure the same, run the following cmdlet from the management console:

```
Test-SPContentDatabase -Name {MySite Content DB Name} -WebApplication {MySite host URL}
```

If the test fails, you will have to resolve all the issues and subsequently rerun the preceding command until all the issues are resolved. Once the test is successful, you can connect the database to the web application using the following command:

```
Stsadm -o addcontentdb -url {your MySite host URL} -databasename {databasename} -
databaseserver {database server}
```

You can verify the status from the upgrade status page from the Central Administration site. Once the upgrade is successful, you can then visit the MySite Settings page under the User Profile Service Application and configure the MySite URL and other settings. Make sure to perform an IISReset at this point and then launch the MySite instance to view the personal site.

Variations on a Publishing Site

Variations of a publishing site or a page that is introduced in MOSS 2007 is a way to replicate or copy the same content from a source variation site to a target variation site. You can localize or customize the content before publishing to the target site as well. As mentioned earlier, these are applicable only to publishing sites, and if you have enabled variations and have any issues with them, you will have to fix those before the migration. To do so, you have variationsfixuptool, which has been introduced as part of MOSS 2007 SP2 (which is a mandatory preupdate for SPS 2010 migration) that you can run using stsadm commands.

First, to run the command, you will have to log in as the administrator; then, you can control the different versions or variations of a given publishing site. The syntax to run the variationsfixuptool feature with stsadm follows:

```
Stsadm -o variationsfixuptool -url
```

To analyze variations hierarchy and report findings, use the following command:

```
stsadm -o variationsfixuptool -scan -url {http://yourwebapplication/site/}
```

To fix invalid variations, use the following one:

```
stsadm -o variationsfixuptool -fix -url {http://yourwebapplication/site/}
```

And to fix invalid variations recursively, use the following command:

```
stsadm -o variationsfixuptool -fix -url {http://yourwebapplication/site/} -recurse
```

Note For more information on planning variations, see http://technet.microsoft.com/en-us/library/cc262404%28v=office.12%29.aspx, and for more on variationsfixuptool, see http://technet.microsoft.com/en-us/library/dd789658%28office.12%29.aspx.

Unsupported Models

Well, now that you have seen approaches and various steps that you need to perform during upgrade, do not expect that these work like a charm for every version you have. It is also important for you to know what will not be supported as part of the upgrade scenarios.

- You must first upgrade any version before WSS 3.0 SP2 or MOSS 2007 SP2 to at least SP2 with the October 2009 cumulative update.

- If you're upgrading from WSS 2.0, SPS 2003, or an older version, there is a huge gap in the infrastructure itself. Technically, an in-place upgrade is impossible, which leaves you with the database upgrade option. However, you cannot upgrade these databases directly to SharePoint 2010. You need to first upgrade them to WSS 3.0 or MOSS 2007 databases and then upgrade them to SharePoint 2010. As a best practice, it is better to do a test run on a test server before actually performing the upgrade on a production environment.

- If you're planning for side-by-side installation or a gradual upgrade process, you might already understand by now neither of these processes are supported in this edition. But, by now, you know how to achieve a similar model using the suggested upgrade scenarios.

Changes in Key Features

SharePoint 2010 has all new architecture, as well as many new features and upgrades to existing features. Table 1-4 provides you with a list of changes in the key features that you should understand on a high level. This book doesn't provide a deep insight on these, so we recommend you to read many other articles that are mentioned in the appendix of this book on SharePoint administration, architecture, and infrastructure.

Table 1-4. Key Feature Changes

Feature	State	Description
Preupgrade checker	New	<ul><li>STSADM tool that you can run to find any potential issues, analyze status of the farm, and review recommendations and best practices.</li><li>No changes are made to the environment, unlike the prescan tool built for upgrading to 2007 earlier.</li></ul>
Central Administration (CA) web application	Changed	<ul><li>A new interface has been added, along with new functions.</li><li>The ribbon is now part of CA and can be used to access many functions a lot easier.</li><li>You now have the capability to backup and restore from the CA page itself.</li><li>The configuration wizard performs server farm setup step by step.</li><li>Manage service applications (which replaced shared services) using the same CA site instead of using a different web application</li></ul>

		as in MOSS 2007.
Ribbon	New	• A contextual, customizable, and consistent user experience interface is newly introduced in SharePoint 2010. • Previously, the ribbon style was used in Office 2007 products.
Service applications	New	• This is the services architecture that replaced Shared Services in MOSS 2007. • These are very effective to configure, manage, create, and associate with web applications.
Master pages	Changed	• Site owners can now apply branding to their sites. • Site manager pages can be applied to application master pages (files under _layouts folder). • Set custom error pages, login pages, confirmation pages, etc.
Themes	Changed	• Import themes created in PowerPoint 2010. • Themes can be applied to subsites from the interface.
Business connectivity services	New	• This is an updated and newly introduced feature of Business Data Catalog in MOSS 2007. • Perform read/write operations. • Interact with the external systems using a SharePoint list and Office clients.
Claims-based authentication	New	• This new abstract authentication model can connect to many user stores, including ADFS, and works on the principles of identity management.
Throttling and list controls	New	• These new features are targeted for performance and control peak overload.
SharePoint Designer	Changed	• Control settings for whether or not SPD 2010 can be used on a web application by an

(SPD)		administrator.
Developer dashboard	New	• Troubleshoot performance issues, and perform analysis and diagnostics.
Sandboxed solutions	New	• Upload custom solutions by site administrators.

Checklists and References

Plenty of resources are available for your use during migration. Table 1-5 shows checklists that would be handy during either in-place or database attach upgrades. They would help you in all the three stages—preparing for your upgrade, performing it, and post-upgrade.

Table 1-5. Checklists and references

Resource	URL
Checklist for in-place	http://technet.microsoft.com/library/ff608117(office.14).aspx
Checklist for database attach	http://technet.microsoft.com/library/ff607663(office.14).aspx
Worksheets	http://go.microsoft.com/fwlink/p/?LinkId=179928
Feature and template reference	http://technet.microsoft.com/en-us/library/hh801868(office.14).aspx
Web parts reference	www.bluedoglimited.com/SharePointThoughts/Lists/Posts/Post.aspx?ID=333

Summary

In this chapter, we looked at the following (see Figure 1-20):

- Introduction and high-level comparison between MOSS 2007 and SharePoint 2010
- The new features in SharePoint 2010
- Hardware and infrastructure requirements and relative changes
- Various upgrade approaches and hybrid models
- Variations and unsupported models
- Checklists and references

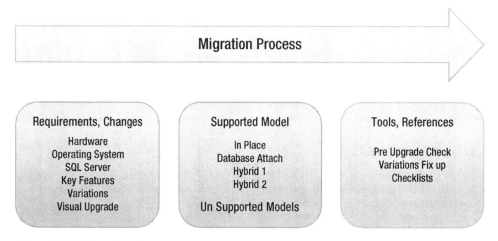

Figure 1-20. The migration process

In the next chapter, you will learn about migration purely from an IT professional's perspective. We will cover migration strategies, migrating old settings to new, how security architecture is impacted in SharePoint 2010, new service applications, taxonomy, and more.

CHAPTER 2

Migration for the IT Administrator

IT administrators play a crucial role during the migration from MOSS 2007 to SharePoint 2010. They perform the majority of the work and there is a need to know almost all the internals of SharePoint 2010, so they can facilitate a smooth transition of existing elements. Many key tasks discussed in Chapter 1 will be planned and performed by IT administrators. Apart from those, administrators also need to ensure that they take care of migrating other settings that we shall discuss in this chapter. Depending on the upgrade approaches we discussed in Chapter 1, strategies will differ, and maintaining continuity and minimizing disruption are of high importance, even critical, from an end user's perspective.

At the same time, from an IT administrator's perspective, it is equally important to

- Plan for and migrate all the existing settings.

- Plan and make changes to prepare ground for new enhancements and design the new environment.

- Make security level changes and required level configurations.

- And finally, monitor the new environment.

While discussing some of the preceding concepts in this chapter, we will also introduce you to changes in SharePoint 2010 from an IT administration standpoint.

Maintaining Continuity

As soon as you mention "migration," these are some of the first questions you will hear:

- What happens to your existing environment during the time of migration to SharePoint 2010?

- Will end users be able to access the sites?

- How many hours of downtime will there typically be?

- Will the old settings be preserved?

Knowing how migration planning is performed is equally important to administrators and end users: Will there be a communication plan? Who will be in charge of performing all the logistics? It's very hard to give the answer to these or any general questions related to migration in a simple statement. Not to be bureaucratic, I would like to deliver an answer such as, "It will depend on which migration approach your organization decided!" If I were to give my subsequent statement, that would be "There is no 100 percent uptime, and there is no 100 percent read-write during the migration period." The following list will help you understand a bit about what that means based on your approach choice (also see Table 1-3, in Chapter 1):

- *In-place upgrade*: There is downtime definitely during the installation and migration.

- *Databases-attach upgrade*: There is a downtime when MOSS databases are attached and upgraded.

- *Hybrid I approach*: There is no downtime; however, you cannot make changes to the content while it is in read-only mode.

- *Hybrid II approach*: There is a downtime, because the farm goes offline.

No matter which mechanism you choose, you face significant downtime or impact to certain operations. If you need some sort of flexibility all in all, you are looking possibly at the Hybrid I approach to best fit your needs. However, this approach may not suit everyone's environment or infrastructure.

Usually, over 90 percent of your assets, settings, and processes will migrate smoothly without any issues. If there are any significant issues, you will be aware of them when you run the preupgrade check. One of the best practices is to fix these issues on a test environment and rerun the preupgrade check to ensure that there are no issues before you begin the actual migration. These steps may be repeated many times before all the errors are resolved. The test environment upgrade can help you

- Fix issues related to customizations around code, settings, hardware, operations, and planning.

- Choose whether or not an upgrade approach works for you, identify user interface issues and make changes, mitigate down time, and so on.

■ **Tip** For building and planning a test environment you can visit `http://technet.microsoft.com/en-us/library/cc262155.aspx`. You can use the URL for troubleshooting issue during initial testing, `http://technet.microsoft.com/en-us/library/cc262967.aspx`.

Even after your test environment is running smoothly, there may be some modifications to perform, which we will discuss later in this chapter and in the next couple of chapters. But, to begin with, we will discuss how workflows get migrated or upgraded to the new platform.

There are different ways one can design workflows in MOSS 2007. You can use the out-of-the-box workflows or workflows designed in SharePoint Designer or design custom workflows in Visual Studio 2008 using Workflow Foundation.

Out-of-the box workflows and SharePoint designer workflows are upgraded automatically, typically without any issues. For custom Visual Studio workflows, you will have to first upgrade the project to Visual Studio 2010 as a new project, and thereby upgrade the workflows' code, and redeploy them to the servers in new environment. On a general note, and especially in the case of database upgrade model, if Workflow Auto Cleanup Timer Job is disabled in the MOSS 2007 environment, make sure to disable the same timer job before migration to SharePoint 2010. If there is a disparity between these two, workflow associations will be lost during the migration. A workflow auto-cleanup timer job runs on a daily schedule (by default) and deletes tasks and instances that are marked as completed for more than x number of days, where x is defined in the workflow association.

■ **Note** By default, all the workflow instances and related tasks are deleted 60 days after the workflows are completed or cancelled.

You can disable an automatic workflow clean up job by selecting Central Administration Site ➤ Monitoring ➤ Timer Jobs ➤ Review job definitions ➤ Worflow Auto Cleanup, as shown in Figure 2-1. You can disable this timer job for each web application.

Variations Create Page Job Definition	SharePoint - 80	Hourly
Variations Create Site Job Definition	SharePoint - 80	Minutes
Variations Propagate Page Job Definition	SharePoint - 80	Hourly
Variations Propagate Site Job Definition	SharePoint - 80	Minutes
Web Analytics Trigger Workflows Timer Job	SharePoint - 80	Daily
Workflow Auto Cleanup	SharePoint - 80	Daily
Workflow Failover	SharePoint - 80	Minutes

Figure 2-1. Workflow Auto Cleanup timer job

On the Edit Timer Job screen shown in Figure 2-2, click Disable to disable this timer job.

Central Administration ▸ Edit Timer Job
Use this page to change or delete a timer job.

Job Title	Workflow Auto Cleanup
Job Description	Deletes tasks and workflow instances which have been marked complete longer than the expiration specified in the workflow association.
Job Properties This section lists the properties for this job.	Web application: SharePoint - 80 Last run time: 2/12/2011 11:51 PM
Recurring Schedule Use this section to modify the schedule specifying when the timer job will run. Daily, weekly, and monthly schedules also include a window of execution. The timer service will pick a random time within this interval to begin executing the job on each applicable server. This feature is appropriate for high-load jobs which run on multiple servers on the farm. Running this type of job on all the servers simultaneously might place an unreasonable load on the farm. To specify an exact starting time, set the beginning and ending times of the interval to the same value.	This timer job is scheduled to run: ○ Minutes Starting every day between ○ Hourly [10 PM ▾] [00 ▾] ● Daily and no later than ○ Weekly [6 AM ▾] [00 ▾] ○ Monthly Warning: The beginning time of the start window is greater than the ending time.

Run Now	Disable	OK	Cancel

Figure 2-2. Disable the workflow auto cleanup timer job

For custom workflows designed in MOSS 2007 using Visual Studio 2008, there are either Sequential or State Machine Workflows (see Figure 2-3).

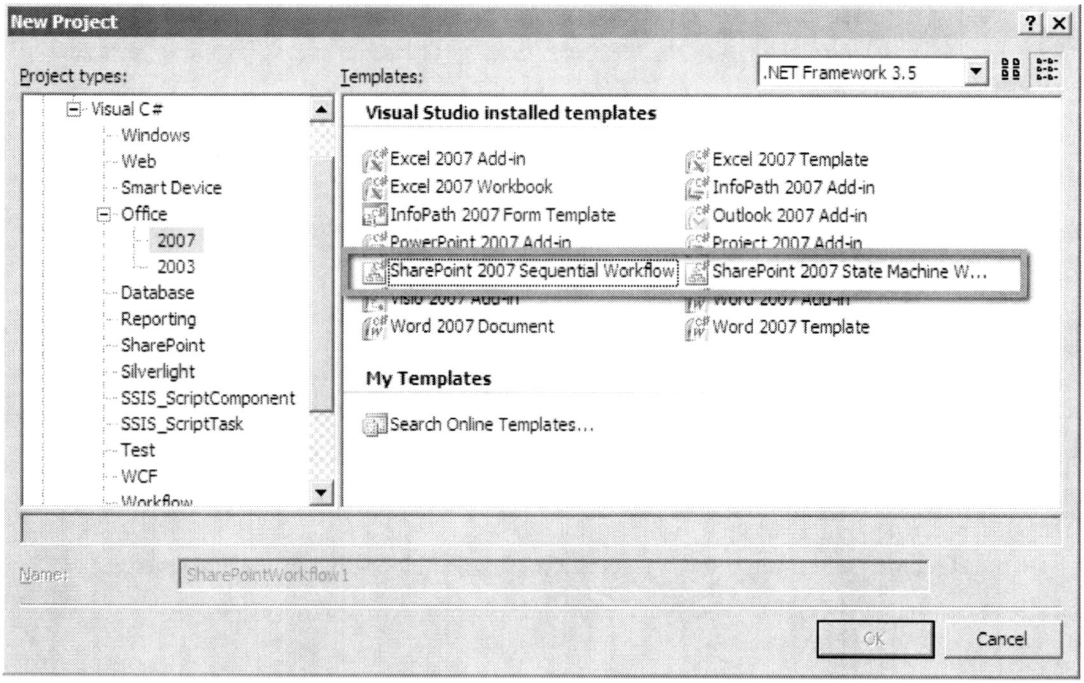

Figure 2-3. Sequential and State Machine Workflows in SharePoint 2007

To migrate these to SharePoint 2010, there are few steps to follow:

1. First, your current project has to be upgraded to a Visual Studio 2010 project. Simply open your existing project in Visual Studio 2010, and follow the upgrade sequence steps.

Tip You cannot migrate MOSS 2007 sequential workflows or state machine workflows directly, because those templates wouldn't work in 2010 as they are. However, the code logic will still be good. So, instead of fixing the existing 2007 code to work for 2010, you copy the code logic into a fresh 2010 project.

2. Create a new SharePoint 2010–based sequential or state machine workflow project. Move your class files (other than the workflow files) to the new project. You can copy the code-behind file but make sure to modify the assembly namespace details etc.

3. Ensure that SharePoint 2007 assemblies are not copied.

4. Copy and refer to any required third-party assemblies.

5. Build and compile the project, and then deploy it to the new environment. Your existing workflows should run fine.

■ **Note** During the preupgrade check, you might receive few warnings on the workflows. Use the following links to smoothly migrate all your workflows:

After upgrading, the WSS.ACTIONS file in the new version and all legacy farm modifications are lost. To handle this scenario, see http://support.microsoft.com/kb/956447.

When database attach and gradual upgrades are performed, custom .ACTIONS file(s) that exist on the legacy farm web frontends have to be manually copied to the new farm to be visible to declarative workflow designers. For more information, see http://support.microsoft.com/kb/956448.

When an upgrade is performed, modified authorized types related to workflows in the web.config file are replaced with the new versions, and all the earlier versions are lost. This will result in the failure of the new authorized types. To handle this scenario, see http://support.microsoft.com/kb/956449.

Minimizing Disruption

For a successful migration, it is very important to have minimal disruption. Because SharePoint 2010 provides you with enough resources, all you need to handle is proper planning and communication. Depending on the complexity of your infrastructure, the number of users that might be affected and the communication plan to reach them will be different. For a small farm, obviously, there might be fewer affected users. However, in a medium to large farm, a proper communication plan must be distributed to all the stakeholders of the farm. To make communication planning and migration strategy easier, you can differentiate your users and stakeholders into three categories.

- Administrators (including local, farm, site collection, and site)
- Developers and designers
- End users of your web application

Once you decide the date, time and estimated duration of the upgrade process, you will have to inform all three of these groups of users about the sequence of the upgrade process and downtime. It is better to give the users as large a window as possible before the upgrade process for better planning, for example, to avoid any other deployment planning on the existing environment or major deliverables during the upgrade dates. It is also important to let the users know what to expect after migration, because they are going to experience a huge visual change from MOSS 2007 to SharePoint 2010. There is also a need to have proper training planned to avoid confusion and surprises while using the new version.

Once all the communications are delivered as per the plan and the upgrade approach model decided, it is then important to ensure that users experience minimal disruption in accessing the existing sites if there is going to be a significant downtime. In MOSS 2007, an upgrade was sequential— you had to upgrade each database one after the other, which takes a lot of time. In SharePoint 2010, you can use the following options to minimize the downtime and achieve a faster upgrade process (again, this model doesn't fit everyone):

- *Set MOSS 2007 databases to read-only mode*: Using the database attach model, you can set your existing MOSS 2007 databases to read-only mode. While the database attach happens, users can still access the MOSS web sites; they just cannot add or update anything. Once the database attaches finish on your new SharePoint 2010 infrastructure, you can switch the users from the MOSS 2007 farm to SharePoint 2010.

- *Parallel upgrade*: Unlike in MOSS 2007, in SharePoint 2010, you perform multiple database upgrades manually using the hybrid approaches. This would reduce the time to upgrade to a large extent. However, the number of databases that you can upgrade in parallel depends on your hardware.

Migration Settings: Old to New

When you upgrade your MOSS 2007 environment to SharePoint Server 2010, there are many aspects that would be affected. First, the most important of them to be aware of are Business Data Catalog (BDC) settings, search features, and user profiles. Second, if you have configured any single sign-on (SSO) settings for external systems, you will have to reconfigure them to the new Secure Store Service (SSS). Before you begin, let's recap: search features, BDC, user profiles, and Excel services settings are stored as part of the Shared Service Provider (SSP) in MOSS 2007. Since SSP does not exist in SharePoint Server 2010, the SSP database, when upgraded, will move settings appropriately to service applications instead. For example, if your shared service's name is SharedServices1 in MOSS 2007, for search services, the application will be named SharedServices1_Search. Let's see how each of these settings can be taken care of during the upgrade process.

Business Data Catalog (BDC)

As discussed earlier, SSP databases are converted to appropriate databases after a migration process. When you perform an in-place upgrade, BDC databases will also be migrated, and new service applications will be initiated to address BDC–related database compatibility and support. In SharePoint 2010, the next-generation BDC is known as Business Connectivity Services (BCS), which comes with its own service application—hence, when you migrate, you get two services. The first one, the Application Registry Service, is for backward compatibility with your existing BDC, and the second, BDC Services, is used for all the out-of-the-box stuff in the BCS architecture, as shown in Figure 2-4.

■ **Note** In a database detach upgrade model, BDC is not automatically upgraded. Also, BDC settings are not part of the content database and are in the SSP database. The steps to upgrade differ from that of a content database upgrade.

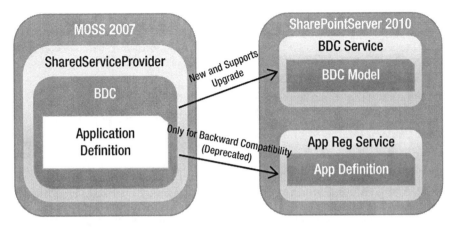

Figure 2-4. BDC and BCS architecture in SharePoint 2010

■ **Tip** BCS is an entirely new world that is rich in enhancements when compared with BDC. To learn more about BCS, see `http://technet.microsoft.com/en-US/sharepoint/ee518675.aspx`. We also recommend that you see Chapter 4 in *Pro SharePoint 2010 Business Intelligence Solutions* (Apress, 2010).

Coming back to the migration, Application Registry Services are only meant for backward compatibility, that is, for supporting your exiting BDC entities; they are already deprecated. So, we highly recommended that you do not extend the services and write extensions over them. Rather, you can now leverage the new BCS architecture and design custom extensions for your needs.

Although BCS is new and has read-write capabilities, it does not reflect the BDC models in MOSS 2007 as-is, but they are more or less similar. If you have custom web parts, logic, and searches relying on the BDC in MOSS 2007, the Application Registry Service will be used in SharePoint. If you are using the out-of-the-box BDC web parts, such as Business Data List, Business Data Association, Business Data Actions, Business Data Details, Business Data Catalog Filter, BCS Services will be used. Upon upgrade, your existing application definition file will be placed in the Application Registry Service and an upgraded version of it is placed under the BCS Service (that contain the new object model) as well as (see Figure 2-4).

All this works well, as mentioned earlier, in the case of an in-place upgrade. In the database attach upgrade scenario, on the custom application definition files solution, you will have to perform some additional tasks. First, export your existing custom application definition files from your MOSS 2007 environment. Using the new BDC service, upgrade your solution so that your application definition files become compatible as BDC models with the new architecture. Once they are ready, upload or import these BDC models into the BCS service.

If you have used SSO for authentication in MOSS 2007, you will now use SSS instead. In the context of upgrade, all the out-of-the-box settings for SSO will be updated to use SSS. However, if you used custom SSO, you will have to manually change your SharePoint Server 2010 environment to configure SSS to your custom solution.

Search

Upgrading from MOSS 2007 to SharePoint 2010 affects search features, functions, and search center sites. For each SSP instance in MOSS 2007, three databases are created in SPS 2010:

- *Search administration database:* Contains all the settings related to the administration of each of the search settings in SSP. There is one and only one search administration database per search service application.

- *Crawl database:* Contains internal information and data about the crawler stored in SSP.

- *Property database:* Contains search related properties that exist in SSP.

Search service in MOSS 2007 is controlled by the OSearch service that actually performs crawling and indexing and facilitates search queries. When migrated, all the settings under the search services shall be moved to a new service application that will now contain the content sources, scopes, crawl rules, and so on. Unlike to the OSearch service, service applications in SPS 2010 are not restricted to a single SSP. Farm administrators can create and configure additional search service applications as farmwide applications.

Just as you have an index server that is used for crawling in the earlier edition, you now have a crawl server that you can use to configure more than one crawl component, and each of these can run in isolation. For a content index, a new index partition will be created in SPS 2010. In an in-place upgrade model you do not need to worry about content, but in a database attach upgrade model, you will have to run the full crawl after your upgrade.

User Profiles

User profiles are among the most important aspects in MOSS 2007, and it is equally important to know about how they are managed during the upgrade process. In SharePoint 2010, two important services will facilitate user profiles: user profile service and managed metadata service. During an in-place upgrade, these two services will take care of your user profiles and taxonomy. The MOSS 2007 SSP database will be upgraded to a new user profile database. After the upgrade is complete, you can run the `Move-SPProfileManagedMetadataProperty` PowerShell cmdlet for the taxonomy to be used by the managed metadata service.

In case of database attach upgrade, you will have to first configure a managed metadata service before you can actually use the upgraded taxonomy and profiles. You then have to attach the SSP database and copy the taxonomy data into taxonomy database for use by your managed metadata service. To do so, you can run the `Move-SPProfileManagedMetadataProperty` PowerShell cmdlet before you actually use the taxonomy.

■ **Note** When you upgrade, timer jobs will be reset to default schedule setting values. To ensure they are run as they were before upgrading, we recommend to take note of them and resetting them after the upgrade.

Finally, properties related to profiles that are stored in the configuration database are not upgraded during the database attach upgrade, although they are preserved during an in-place upgrade. Here are the persisted properties that will not be upgraded using the database attach model:

- MySiteHostURL

- SearchCenterURL

- EnablePersonalFeaturesforMultipleDeployments

- ProfileStoreLanguage

- ProfileStoreLanguagePacksApplied

- ProfileStoreCollationID

- DaysWorthOfEventsToKeep

SSO to SSS

Single sign-on (SSO) has been taken to the next level of enhancements in SharePoint 2010 and is now called Secure Store Services (SSS). SSO in Excel services and BDC are typically used in various scenarios to avoid the double-hop issues. In SharePoint 2010, you will create an unattended service account that would be used in SSS and assigned to a particular service application as Application ID. This service account will take care of impersonating the user to access the backend systems.

■ **Note** Logged-in user credentials are used to impersonate to only some extent and windows will not forward these credentials to a remote resource (requires a second hop). Hence the user's identity is lost even before it reaches the back end. This is known as double hop issue. This requires a mechanism to impersonate logged-in user with the back end which is achieved by using Secure Store Services in SharePoint 2010.

You can configure SSS by following these steps:

1. Launch secure store services configuration by selecting CA ➤ Application Management ➤ Service Applications ➤ Manage Service Applications ➤ Secure Store Services.

2. Before you can configure, you have to create a new key to encrypt the passwords that you store as part of this service. Once you successfully create a new pass phrase for the key, click the New menu on the ribbon, and create new Target Application Settings, as shown in Figure 2-5.

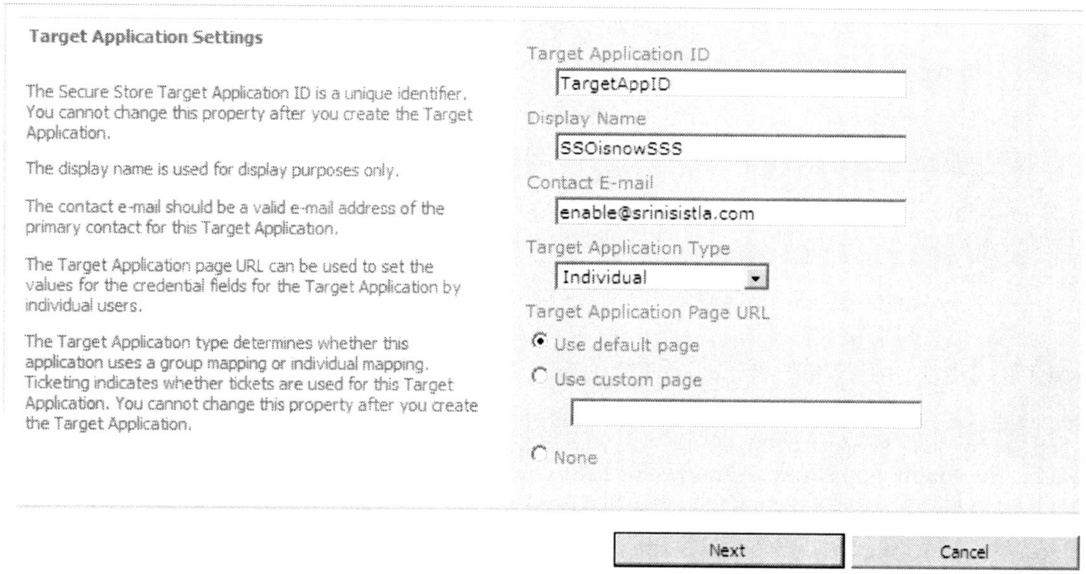

Figure 2-5. Configuring secure store service application ID settings

3. Click Next to furnish the details on the Target Application Settings window, and then provide field names User Name and Password in the following screen.

4. Ensure you choose the accurate Field Type (Windows or a specific account for instance).

5. In the following screen, provide Target Application Administrator(s), and click OK.

6. Once the target application ID is successfully created, SharePoint will return to Manage Target Applications window.

7. Select the previously created Target Application ID, and click the Set menu under the Credentials section to launch the Set Credential window, shown in Figure 2-6.

8. Provide the credential information, and click OK.

9. You application ID is technically ready after successful authentication of the account. You can use this application ID and set it to any service applications application ID.

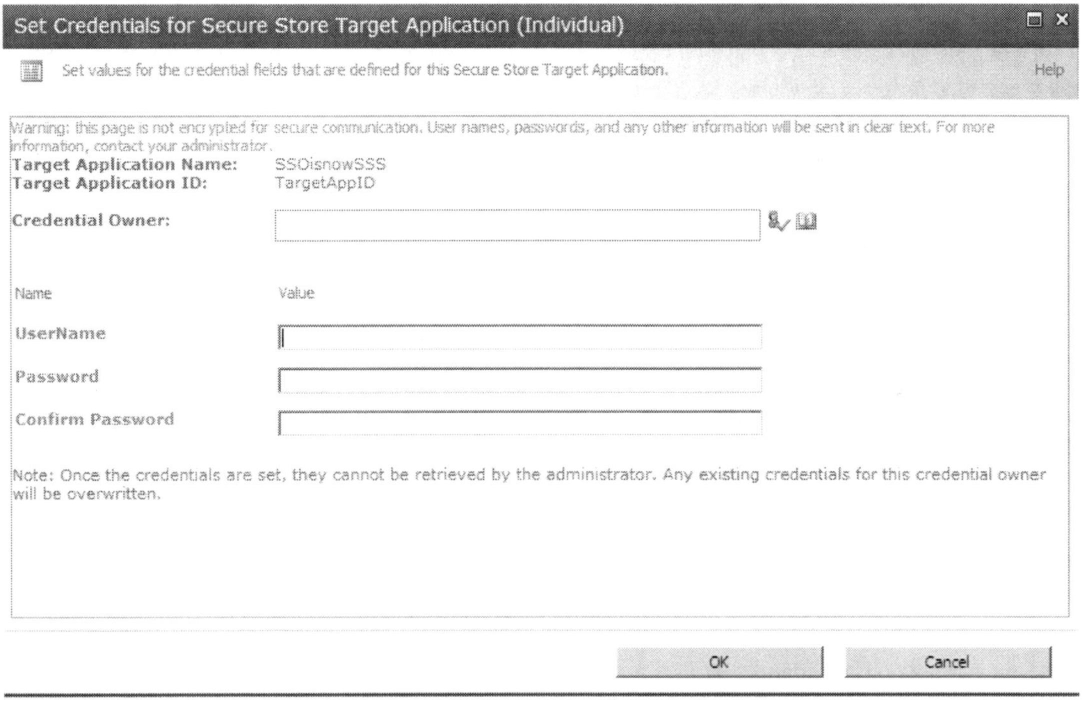

Figure 2-6. *Set credentials for the target application ID*

■ **Tip** For more information on Secure Store Service (SSS), please see Chapter 12 of *Building Solutions with SharePoint 2010* by Sahil Malik (Apress, 2010).

Creating an SSS application ID is very important during the upgrade process, because there is no direct upgrade from SSO to SSS. You will have to configure SSS first and then configure the applications to use this SSS application ID instead of your SSO configuration. However, you can migrate data from the SSO database to SSS database. Once you provision a new SSS application ID using unattended service account, you can upgrade your SSO database using the following PowerShell cmdlet:

```
Upgrade-SPSingleSignOnDatabase -SSOConnectionString <connectionString> -
SecureStoreConnectionString <secureStoreConnectionString> -SecureStorePassphrase <passphrase>
```

where connectionString is the database connection string to your existing SSO database, secureStoreConnectionString is the database connection string to your new SSS database, and passphrase is the security phrase you choose before creating any application ID.

Once the upgrade is successful, disable the SSO service use the following PowerShell cmdlet:

```
Disable-SPSingleSignOn -ServerName <serverName>
```

■ **Tip** For more information on configuring Access Services with Secure Store Services, please Chapter 2 of *Pro SharePoint 2010 Business Intelligence Solutions* by Sahil Malik, Srini Sistla, and Steve Wright (Apress, 2010).

Managing Services

In Chapter 1, we explained how shared services in MOSS 2007 have evolved as service applications in SharePoint 2010. These service applications run as individual services on each server in the farm and are pretty much manageable on a per-server and per-web-application basis, because they are associations to web applications. Managing or, in some cases, configuring the services can be done globally from the central administration itself or by simply starting and stopping the services, as shown in Figure 2-7. Some of the services that you can globally manage are Document Conversion Launcher, Microsoft SharePoint Foundation Workflow Timer, and SharePoint Server Search. Others can be simply started or stopped. To manage these services, access the Services On Server page via Central Administration Site ➤ System Settings ➤ Servers ➤ Manage Services On Server. You can change the server in the Server drop-down, and in the Action column, you can select to Start or Stop the service.

Each of these services has a unique GUID. You can manage the services using PowerShell commands using these GUID's.

Use the following command to start the service:

```
Start-SPServiceInstance –Identity {ServiceGUID}
```

Use the following command to stop the service:

```
Stop-SPServiceInstance –Identity {ServiceGUID}
```

Service	Status	Action
Access Database Service	Started	Stop
Application Registry Service	Started	Stop
Business Data Connectivity Service	Started	Stop
Central Administration	Started	Stop
Claims to Windows Token Service	Started	Stop
Document Conversions Launcher Service	Started	Stop
Document Conversions Load Balancer Service	Started	Stop
Excel Calculation Services	Started	Stop
Lotus Notes Connector	Stopped	Start
Managed Metadata Web Service	Started	Stop
Microsoft SharePoint Foundation Incoming E-Mail	Started	Stop
Microsoft SharePoint Foundation Sandboxed Code Service	Started	Stop
Microsoft SharePoint Foundation Subscription Settings Service	Started	Stop
Microsoft SharePoint Foundation Web Application	Started	Stop
Microsoft SharePoint Foundation Workflow Timer Service	Started	Stop
PerformancePoint Service	Started	Stop
PowerPoint Service	Started	Stop
Search Query and Site Settings Service	Started	Stop
Secure Store Service	Started	Stop
SharePoint Foundation Help Search	Started	Stop
SharePoint Server Search	Started	Stop
User Profile Service	Started	Stop
User Profile Synchronization Service	Stopped	Start
Visio Graphics Service	Started	Stop
Web Analytics Data Processing Service	Started	Stop
Web Analytics Web Service	Started	Stop
Word Automation Services	Started	Stop
Word Viewing Service	Started	Stop

Figure 2-7. Managing services on a server

By now, you must be wondering what happened to the gradual upgrade process. Well, there is no such process in this edition. But you can achieve a near possible solution in this version using alternate access mapping (AAM). You can now depend on its redirect behavior that you had in the gradual upgrade process. Using AAM also significantly minimizes the downtime during the upgrade process. In the next section, you will see how to configure AAM for sites that are in the upgrade process.

Changes to Alternate Access Mapping (AAM)

Alternate access mapping (AAM) provides a mechanism by which you can access a SharePoint web application from different zones with different URLs. For example, if your internal URL of web application is http://myintranetsite and it should be accessed by an external user or from an Internet zone using the URL http://www.spsite.com, AAM would help you achieve this. AAMs are very helpful, particularly in your upgrade process, but just be aware that they should be configured manually.

Before you even try the settings on a test bench, much less a production environment directly, let's discuss how AAM helps and why you should use it in the context of upgrade. When you upgrade your servers in database attach mode, your MOSS 2007 environment is in read-only mode, or it could be offline. If the databases are huge, attaching them to your new SPS 2010 environment might take a significant amount of time, which directly affects your downtime. To avoid excess downtime, you can use AAM and a technique that can manage your requested URLs to be redirected to MOSS 2007 until your SP 2010 environment is ready.

Having said that, it is now evident that you will be depending on your old environment until everything is set right on your new one. The good news is that users will never see any broken links. The not so good news is that you will have to perform a lot of manual changes. But is it worth it? Yes, definitely. Let's see how to configure both environments, MOSS 2007 and SPS 2010, to utilize AAM.

In order to make AAM perform URL redirects, you need to create the list of the source URLs from MOSS 2007 and ensure that these prerequisites are addressed:

- Your destination infrastructure is ready and configured.

- The web application is configured in such a way that the URL matches your MOSS 2007 URL.

- You haven't yet performed the database upgrade method.

- You've deleted the default content database on your SPS 2010 infrastructure.

Then, you will have to perform the following tasks in this order:

1. Ensure that you have configured all managed paths settings on your SPS 2010 server by comparing it with MOSS environment. This step is very important, because URL redirects will fail if the site URL is inaccurate.

2. Configure AAM to redirect URLs using the following stsadm command:

```
stsadm -o addzoneurl -url http://your_new_sp_url/ -urlzone default -zonemappedurl
http://your_new_sp_url/ -redirectionurl http://your_old_sp_url_on_moss/
```

■ **Note** In the preceding command, http://your_old_sp_url_on_moss/ can be derived as an extended web application to your actual moss web application. At this point, all the requests that are coming to http://your_new_sp_url/ shall be mapped to http://your_old_sp_url_on_moss/.

---

3. Upgrade the database using the database detach with read-only model discussed in the previous section.

4. Once you are ready, change the redirection back to the new settings using this stsadm command:

```
stsadm -o addzoneurl -url http://your_new_sp_url/ -urlzone default -zonemappedurl
http://your_new_sp_url/
```

5. At any given instance, you can verify the AAM redirection by enumerating the list with the following stsadm command:

```
stsadm -o enumalternatedomains -url http://your_new_sp_url/
```

If your existing MOSS environment is running in a Windows authentication mode, there is less that you need to worry about. However, if you have any extended web applications or the actual web applications running on forms-based authentication mode, you will need to configure one extra step.

Multiple Authentication Schemes on a Single URL

In MOSS 2007, we used have a single authentication mechanism for each AAM zone, so if you have two different segments, you will end up with two different zones and corresponding authentication mechanisms. For example, you might have extranet with forms-based authentication (FBA), and internally, users access the site authenticated via Windows NT LAN Manager (NTLM) or similar. Also, both zones would have two different URLs, and users would use these URLs differently when they log in from the two different zones. In SharePoint 2010, this model has changed, and now, you can have multiple authentication schemes over a single URL. Let's see how it works.

SharePoint 2010 supports two types of authentications: classic authentication mode, where the authentication scheme is the same as in MOSS 2007, and claims authentication mode, which is new in SharePoint 2010 and authenticates users via claims. This setting value is established when you create a new web application, as shown in Figure 2-8. The multiple authentication over a single URL that we discussed earlier works only in the claims-based, not classic, authentication mode.

Figue 2-8. Authentication modes in SharePoint 2010

SharePoint 2010 allows you to have multiple authentication settings for a given authentication provider in claims based mode. You can configure the claim providers, either FBA or NTLM, and other trusted identity providers and therefore prompt the user for a chosen authentication mode, as shown in Figure 2-9.

■ **Note** The login page you see in Figure 2-9 is the default selection and can be designed or customized to your needs.

We will discuss on how to configure the authentication settings later in this chapter.

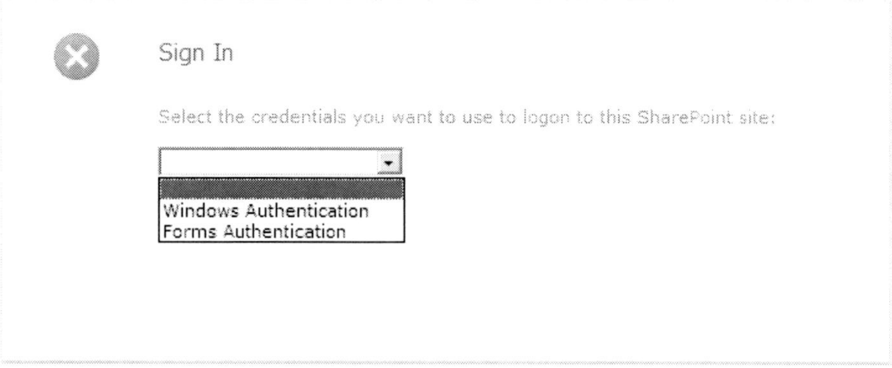

Figure 2-9. *Login page with Multiple Authentication Providers for single web application URL*

You can configure web application authetication settings using either powershell or from the UI in the Central Administrtion Site as shown in the figure 2-10.

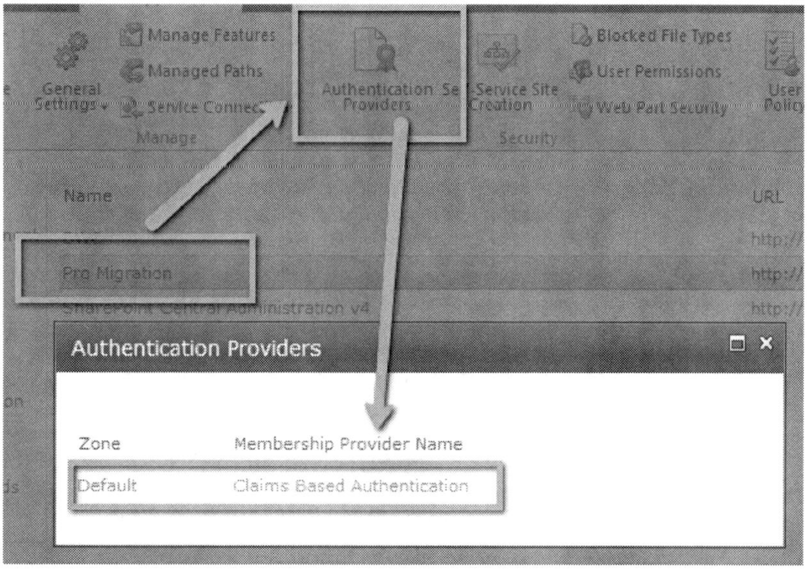

Figure 2-10. *Configuring the authentication provider*

Migrating from FBA to Claims-Based FBA

Once your MOSS 2007 environment is successfully upgraded to SharePoint 2010, web applications that are authenticated against FBA will not work as they are. To enable them to use your existing authentication model (which is FBA), you will have to convert them to claims based FBA (you will learn more about claims based authentication in the next section of this chapter). Once you convert your authentication model, the last step is migrating existing users and their respective permissions to

SharePoint 2010. Converting the authentication model and migrating the users is pretty simple and can be done in two simple PowerShell cmdlets steps. We would recommend you to use PowerShell cmdlets instead of stsadm here, because the latter is deprecated in this version.

Launch Windows PowerShell. Type and run these lines of script:

```
$webApp = Get-SPWebApplication "http://<yourwebapplicationname>"
$webApp.UseClaimsAuthentication =1
$webApp.Update()
$webApp.ProvisionGlobally()
```

The preceding script will set your web application authentication to use claims authentication. Now, to migrate the users and their respective permissions, run these lines:

```
$webApp = Get-SPWebApplication "http://<yourwebapplicationname>"
$webApp.MigrateUsers(True)
```

The preceding command migrates all the existing identities in MOSS 2007 to new token-based identities in SharePoint 2010.

Now, let's see how a web application should be configured for authentication.

Setting Up Authentication for a Web Application

The authentication settings for a web application can be configured during the creation of the application or later by using PowerShell commands. As mentioned earlier, there is new authentication setting for either claims-based or classic mode, as shown in Figure 2-11.

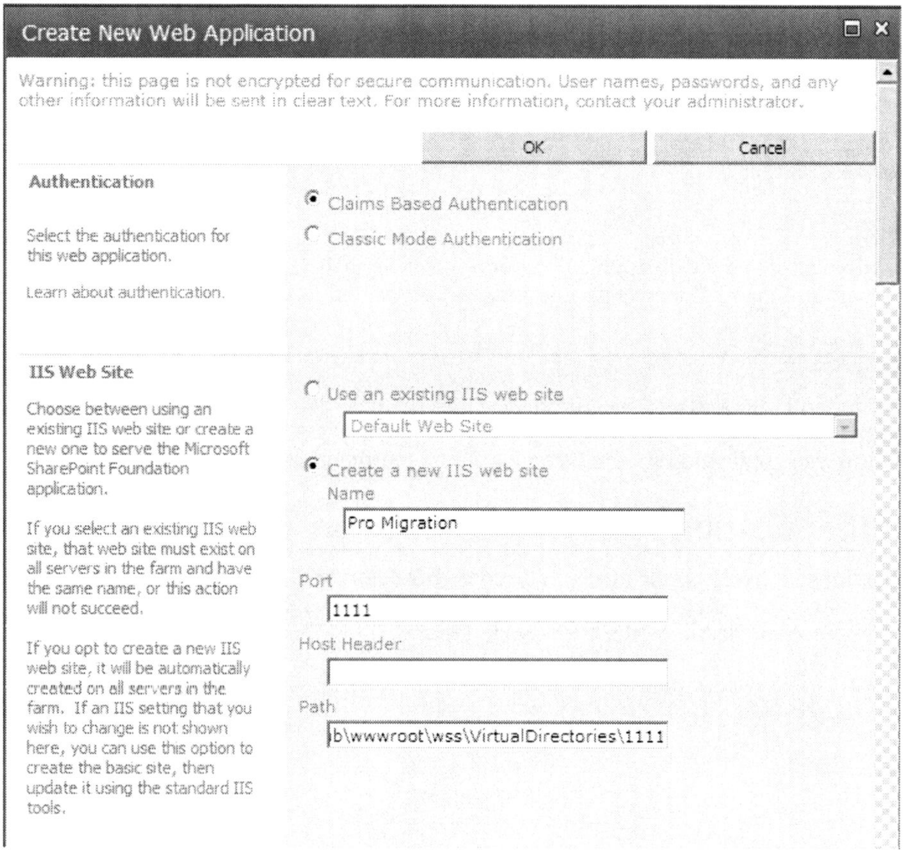

Figure 2-11. *Create a new web application, and select Claims Mode Authentication.*

Here are the steps to create and configure a new web application that is protected with claims-based authentication:

1. Under Application Management ➤ Web Applications ➤ Manage web applications, click the New button on the ribbon under the Contribute group.

2. In the Authentication Settings section, select Claims Based Authetication.

3. Fill in other settings under the IIS Web Site section.

4. Leave the settings under Security Configuration set to the defaults.

5. Under Claims Authentication Types, check the Enable Windows Authentication and Integrated Windows Authentication options, and choose NTLM for the type of authentication. You can choose Kerberos instead, depending on your requirements, as shown in Figure 2-12.

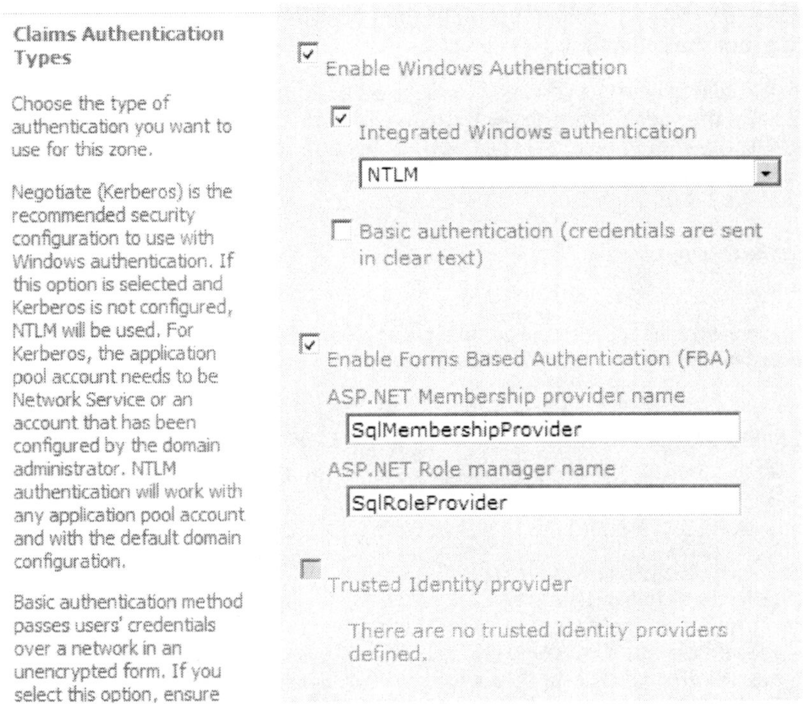

Claims Authentication Types

Choose the type of authentication you want to use for this zone.

Negotiate (Kerberos) is the recommended security configuration to use with Windows authentication. If this option is selected and Kerberos is not configured, NTLM will be used. For Kerberos, the application pool account needs to be Network Service or an account that has been configured by the domain administrator. NTLM authentication will work with any application pool account and with the default domain configuration.

Basic authentication method passes users' credentials over a network in an unencrypted form. If you select this option, ensure

☑ Enable Windows Authentication

☑ Integrated Windows authentication

    NTLM   ▾

☐ Basic authentication (credentials are sent in clear text)

☑ Enable Forms Based Authentication (FBA)

ASP.NET Membership provider name

    SqlMembershipProvider

ASP.NET Role manager name

    SqlRoleProvider

☐ Trusted Identity provider

    There are no trusted identity providers defined.

Figure 2-12. Setting Claims Authentication Types

6. To enable the trusted identity provider, you will have to first configure available providers using PowerShell. Otherwise, you have the option to set the Enable Forms Based Authentication option. Enter the ASP.NET membership provider and ASP.NET role manager names, as shown in the Figure 2-12.

7. Next, set the Sign In Page URL to default, as shown in Figure 2-13, or if you have designed a custom sign in page, choose that option.

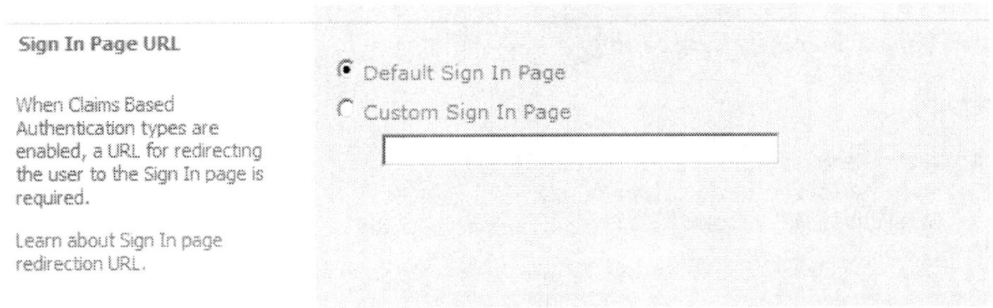

Sign In Page URL

When Claims Based Authentication types are enabled, a URL for redirecting the user to the Sign In page is required.

Learn about Sign In page redirection URL.

⦿ Default Sign In Page

◯ Custom Sign In Page

    [   ]

Figure 2-13. Selecting the default or custom sign in page

8. Once the settings are completed and the web applications is provisioned, you will have to create a root site collection.

9. Further, there are web.config settings you need to make on both the central administration site and the specific web application on which claims are configured. These settings should be made via a web application scoped feature, and you should avoid manual changes. Settings that are to be made are as shown in Listings 2-1 through 2-3.

Listing 2-1. Setting the Connection Strings

```
<connectionStrings>
        <add name="MembershipConnectionString" connectionString="Data Source=datasource;Initial
Catalog=aspnetdb;User;Password=pass;" providerName="System.Data.SqlClient" />
</connectionStrings>
```

Listing 2-2. Membership and Role Manager Settings

```
<membership>
        <providers>
                <clear/>
                        <add name="SqlMembershipProvider"
type="System.Web.Security.SqlMembershipProvider"
connectionStringName="MembershipConnectionString" enablePasswordReset="true"
requiresQuestionAndAnswer="false" requiresUniqueEmail="false" maxInvalidPasswordAttempts="5"
passwordAttemptWindow="10" passwordFormat="Hashed" minRequiredPasswordLength="7"
enablePasswordRetrieval="false" applicationName="/" />
        </providers>
</membership>
<roleManager>
        <providers>
                <clear/>
                <add name="SqlRoleProvider" connectionStringName="MembershipConnectionString"
type="System.Web.Security.SqlRoleProvider, System.Web, Version=2.0.0.0, Culture=neutral,
PublicKeyToken=b03f5f7f11d50a3a"/>
        </providers>
</roleManager>
```

Listing 2-3. Setting the People Picker Wild Card Settings

```
<PeoplePickerWildcards>
        <clear />
        <add key="AspNetSqlMembershipProvider" value="%" />
        <add key="SqlMembershipProvider" value="%" />
        <add key="SqlRoleProvider" value="%" />
</PeoplePickerWildcards>
```

Understanding the Basics of Claims-Based Authentication

In general, when you try to access web applications with different authentication models and user data stores (AD, SQL, Oracle, etc.), you will end up extending your web applications to different zones, such as intranet, Internet, custom, or extranet. However, working with multiple web applications that require the SSO model with single authentication, though not impossible, is not easy in MOSS 2007. Although third-party vendors provide the SSO model, Microsoft did not have its own until recently. However, now you have better solution from Microsoft that will address the identity management and authentication abstraction. Being able to use multiple authentication mechanisms in SharePoint 2010 with claims-based authentication is a very nice benefit in the larger picture.

Claims-based authentication (CBA) (formerly known as the Geneva Framework) was introduced more than two years ago with a very simple idea and solution—isolate authentication from your application. CBA came about to support identity management and authentication abstraction. Since applications need some kind of authentication token, CBA will provide the necessary token on a basis of trust. In addition, that token is actually the identity, which is very important for any application to allow access to users on respective web applications. Of course, authorization comes later and can purely depend on the application rules. First, what does an identity consists of?

Consider an application's identity as analogous to your own. Your identity contains your essential information like you address or where you belong. Your Social Security Number can be considered as one attribute of your identity: your current information, history, and so on can be accessed just by using your SSN. In SharePoint, carrying your identity wherever you go is important, because that helps you get access or at least request access to a system. Although each person can have multiple flavors of identity, the actual physical identity (what defines the user) is singular. Regardless of which identity flavor is chosen, the relying party can identify the user when described and matched with several claims of the user. Technically, user identity can stay in any system as long as that system can be reached to retrieve the identity information. To be more precise, Active Directory, SQL Server, Oracle, and People Soft can be some of the data sources, or identity providers, where you might have your credential information. And each web application might need to authenticate users from one of these authentication providers.

CBA provides you with a mechanism of using multiple identity providers with one web application (or more) by using either Active Directory Federation Services (ADFS) 2.0 or a custom system using the set of assemblies provided by the Windows Identity Framework (WIF) or any other federated Secure Token Service (STS)–based service. Let's see how it works. But before we get there, there are other important entities of the entire CBA model. Mainly you need to understand the buzz words Claims, Security Token Service (STS). A *claim* is necessary user information. Each of the tokens contains claims, and these tokens are generated by the STS. Each web application server will be installed with the WIF packs that will communicate with ADFS, or a similar custom service. When the end user request access, a token is generated by ADFS (let's say you are using it for this example) with the help of corresponding identity provider and STS. As long as the token with such a claim is generated by your ADFS, your end user is considered trusted. In Figure 2-14, for Web Application 1, when a token is generated, the user will be able to authenticate using that token as long as Web Application 1 is added as a trusted member to your ADFS. Now, here is the interesting part: If Web Application 2 is also one of your ADFS trusted parties, a user need not reauthenticate on Web Application 2 since that user has already been identified as trusted through Web Application 1.

This facilitates the often-required SSO model. In the preceding example, Web Application 1 can be your SharePoint 2010 farm, which arrives with built-in STS. If you are considering using STS on a MOSS 2007 environment, you will have to install the necessary service packs or packages for ADFS 2.0, WIF, and so on. As long as your web applications are built on the .NET Framework, you are CBA ready.

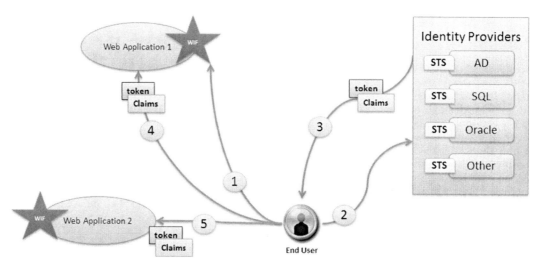

Figure 2-14. *Claims-based authentication model*

STSADM vs. PowerShell

SharePoint Team Services Administration (STSADM, as you know it popularly) has been our best friend for performing administrative tasks using a command line utility. It is a very powerful tool that can execute many operations when passed with right parameters. For instance,

```
stsadm -o addsolution -filename <somesolutionpackage.wsp>
```

would add the `.wsp` package to the solution gallery.

The preceding command is very simple, and there are many such. However, the only thing missing from STSADM that every one of us wanted was the ability to execute a series of such scripts with return parameters. Although creating a batch file with sequential `stsadm` statements will solve the issue partially, to execute the batch files or `stsadm` statements, you need to be logged in as a local administrator.

So what happened to STSADM in SharePoint 2010? The good news is that it still exists! But the not-so-good news is that it will be deprecated in the next version. There have been some changes to STSADM in this version. Although commands such as `associatewebapp`, `editssp`, `mysite`, and `restoressp` no longer exist, commands like `add-adsdefaultapplication`, `monitordb`, and `remove-adsdefaultapplication` have been added. Beyond wondering why there have been new additions, what's most important is considering what's new in SharePoint 2010 to take over for STSADM—PowerShell.

SharePoint 2010 Management Shell loads up a Windows PowerShell console application, which does all that STSADM can and even more. It surpasses STSADM in many ways. PowerShell is built on the Microsoft .NET Framework, which can accept and return objects. It is possible to access the file system, registry, and so on using PowerShell. You weren't able to access the object model using STSADM, but now, you can do so using PowerShell. Administrators can write small scripts called *cmdlets* (pronounced as "commandlets") that can access the API and interact with and manipulate SharePoint objects. Consider the following code:

```
$site = New-Object Microsoft.SharePoint.SPSite("http://yoursharepointsite/")
$site.RootWeb.Lists | Select Title
```

■ **Note** You can test the preceding code by launching SharePoint 2010 Management Shell.

The preceding code connects and retrieves your SharePoint site object; it gets the list information and prints the title of each list to the console. Thus, PowerShell makes administration tasks much easier than the earlier version. For a full comparison of commands in STSADM and PowerShell, see the books appendix.

Monitoring Your SharePoint 2010 Environment

There are significant improvements in many areas around monitoring the environment in SharePoint 2010. For example, MOSS 2007 offers no one easy way to monitor the health of your environment, debug an issue, or assess the overall performance overall. To obtain some of these results, administrators and developers used to seek help from many third-party tools or end up writing a lot of trace logs in their code. This kind of monitoring on the platform took a significant paradigm shift in SharePoint 2010. All the monitoring features are available from the Monitoring link on the Central Administration screen, as shown in Figure 2-15.

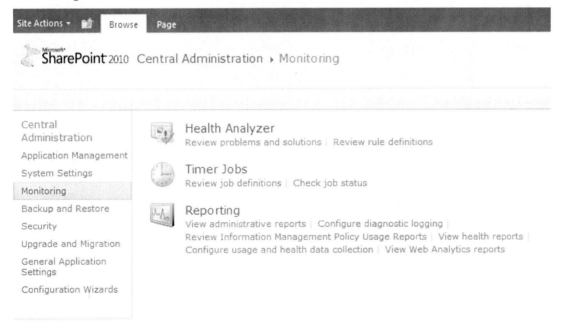

Figure 2-15. SharePoint 2010's new Monitoring screen

Similar to MOSS 2007, the first place to start looking for more details about errors in SharePoint 2010 is in the log files. SharePoint trace log files are under the location {SharePoint root folder}\logs. Now, we will begin explaining the log files themselves.

Correlation IDs

What would you say is one of your biggest pain points in MOSS 2007? I would say finding information about an error. Before you could pinpoint exactly where the error is and what caused it, you would end up searching multiple areas on the SharePoint environment. The first place, of course, is the log files, where you'd search for recent errors and so on. And I would say that *one* of the best things SharePoint 2010 offers is the ability to find information about errors using correlation IDs. It's not just the errors—there are huge improvements in all aspects of overall monitoring of the environment itself.

Correlation IDs are among the best things that could ever happen. What are correlation IDs? Did you happen to see an error message, like the one shown in Figure 2-16, in a SharePoint environment?

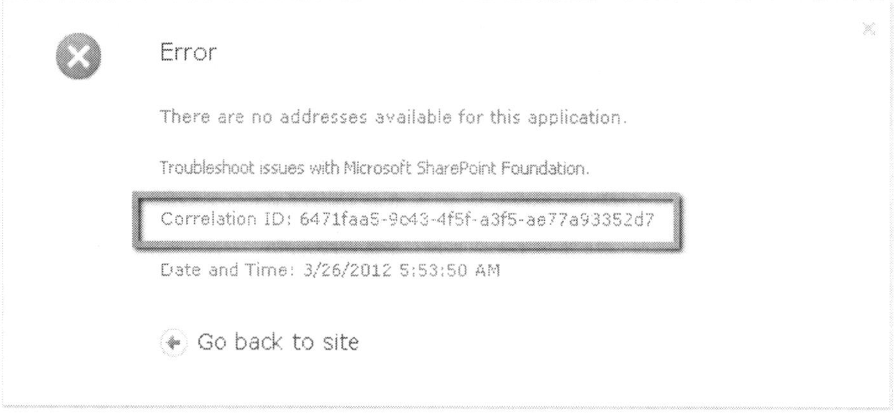

Figure 2-16. *Correlation ID error message*

Errors in SharePoint 2010 are associated with correlation IDs. These, as you must have noticed, are Global Unique Identifier's (GUID) generated whenever an error occurs, and more details about this correlation ID are basically saved to the default log files' folder. Tracking an error with a correlation ID now becomes very simple and easy. In the earlier version, to fiind an issue in the log files, you used to open the latest file and search on a particular bit of text. As the search text parses through the entire document, your search text might appear in multiple locations. In that case, you end up with a secondary search criteria, such as time factor. In SharePoint 2010, all you need to do is simply search for the correlation ID in the log file, and since it is unique to an error instance, you will be directed to the exact error log location. And the log files' location is the same as in the previous version, except for the version number "14" instead of "12," as shown in Figure 2-17.

By default, a new trace log file is created every 30 minutes. To change the log interval, you can run a simple PowerShell command:

```
Set-SPDiagnosticConfig –LogCutInterval 60
```

The preceding command will set the trace log files to be generated every 60 minutes (or every hour).

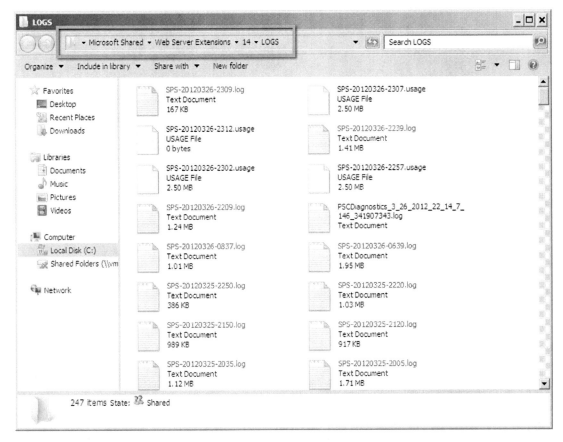

Figure 2-17. Default log files location

With the new Unified Logging Service (ULS) viewer, you can read and understand the logs very easily as well. The default log location from which the files are loaded is the default \root folder for the logs itself. Some of the very good features include error filtering, warnings, the Toggle Correlation Tree button, and notification levels. The ULS Viewer window is shown in Figure 2-18.

■ **Tip** You can download ULS Viewer at `http://archive.msdn.microsoft.com/ULSViewer`.

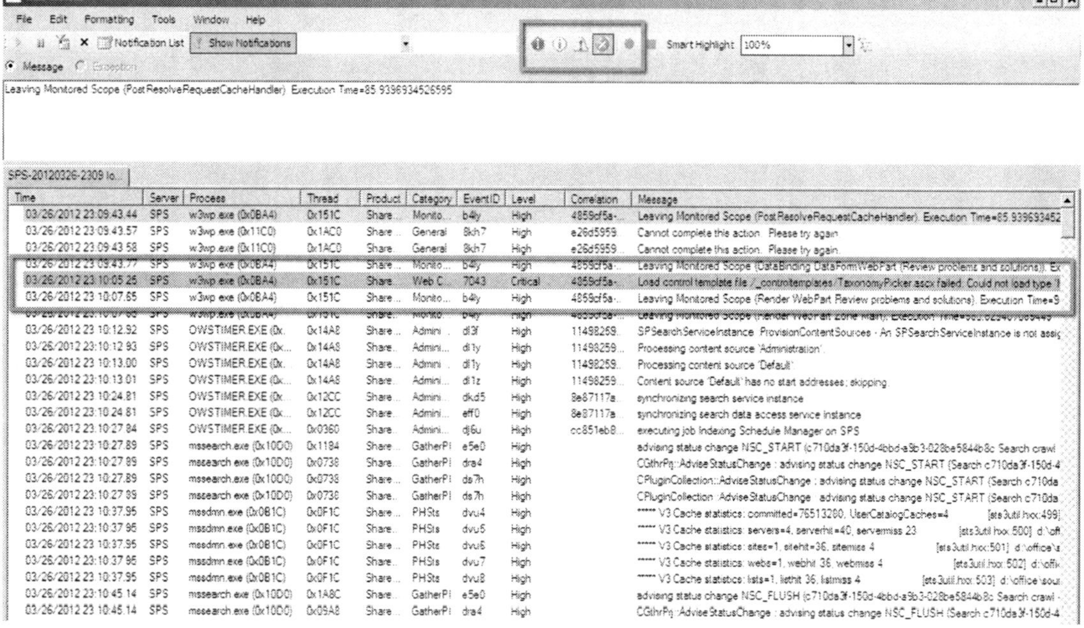

Figure 2-18. ULS Viewer

Another very important enchancement that you cannot fail to miss is the Health Analyzer message on the Central Administration home page.

Using the Health Analyzer

SharePoint 2010 now monitors your environment based on certain rules that are built over best practices. These rules are checked and verified periodically by timer jobs, and in the event that a rule is not met, information about the failed rule is alerted to the administrator, as shown in Figure 3-19. From the Central Administration, you can get to the health analyzer page via Monitoring ➤ Health Analyzer ➤ Review Problems and Solutions. All these rules against which the jobs run are defined under Monitoring ➤ Health Analyzer ➤ Review rule definitions. This will allow you to make modifications to an existing rule and so on.

Figure 2-19. Health Analyzer warning

Each of these rules are categorized under groups logically—Security, Performance, Configuration and Availability—as shown in Figure 2-20. You can verify each of the errors by simply clicking the item.

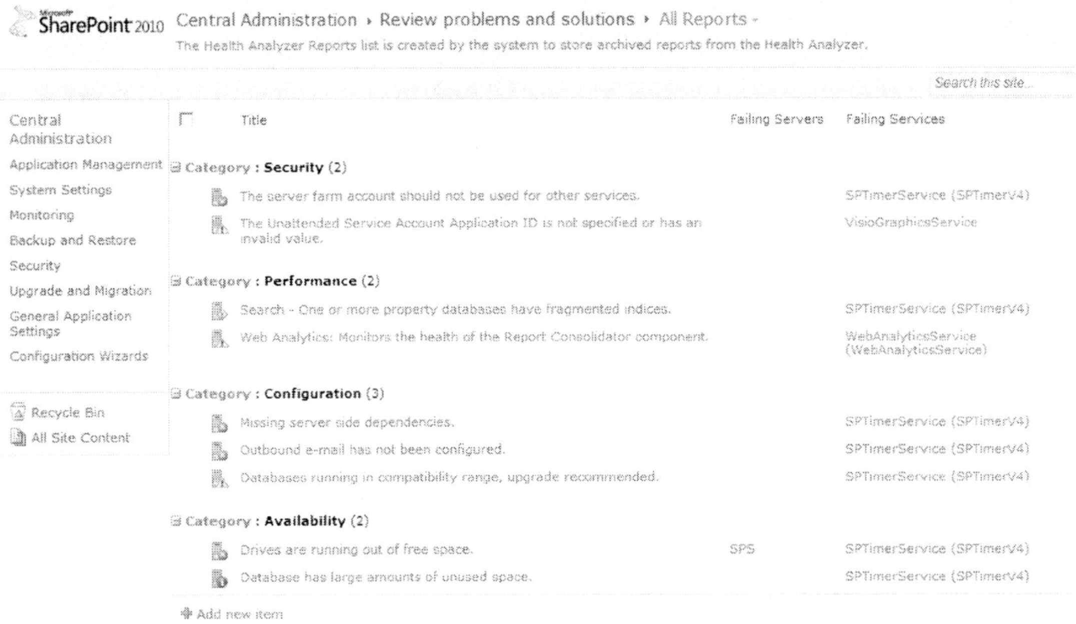

Figure 2-20. Health Analyzer report

Detailed information on the issue is then provided to the administrator, with an explanation as well as a remedy, so administrators can fix the issue and then use the Reanalyze Now option, shown in Figure

2-21. Another very interesting feature (not in the image) is the Repair Automatically function, which attempts to fix the issue for you.

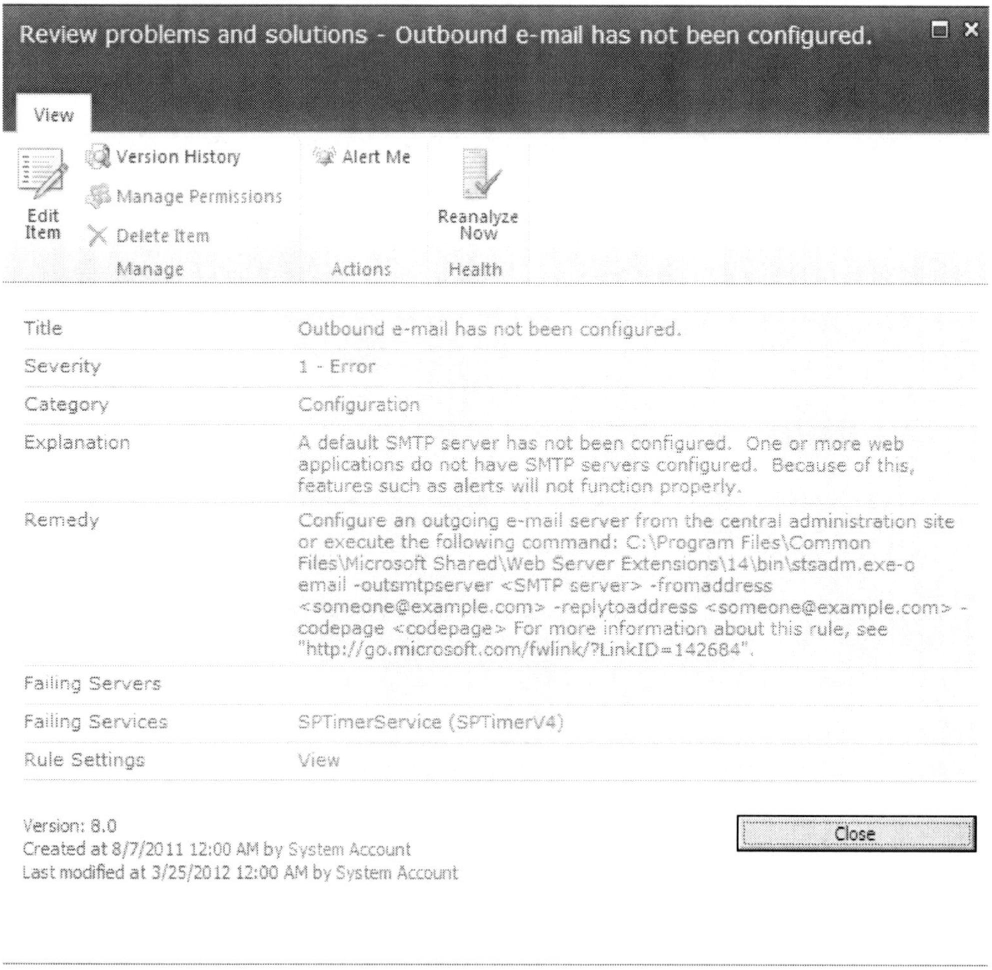

Figure 2-21. Health Analyzer reported issue

MOSS 2007 had two major limitations with respective to logging. First, there is no option to monitor a particular event, and second, there is no resetting or going back to original settings once the monitoring task is complete. This is addressed in SharePoint 2010 under the usage and health data collection screens.

Usage and Health Data Collection

Figure 2-22 displays the settings for individual services that can be monitored and checked for the severity of the events. You can individually select these events and configure them for more detailed diagnotics. Once the settings are selected and the required diagnotics logging is performed, you can reset to the default settings a shown in Figure 2-22.

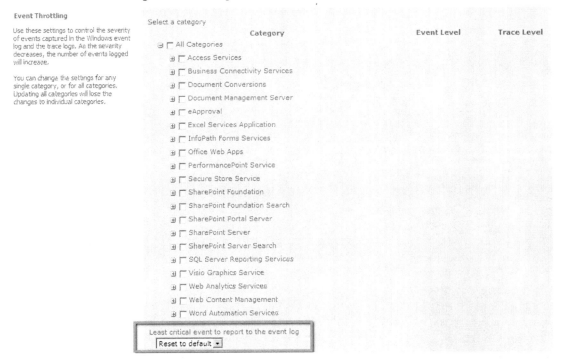

Figure 2-22. Usage and health event throttling settings

At the same time, in the same window, you can also set the Event Log Flood Protection option. This mechanism identifies repeated events and suppresses those events until they become normal. You can set other Trace Log settings as well in the same window, as shown in Figure 2-23. You can access the usage and health data collection configuration from Central Administration ➤ Monitoring ➤ Reporting ➤ Configuring Diagnostic Logging.

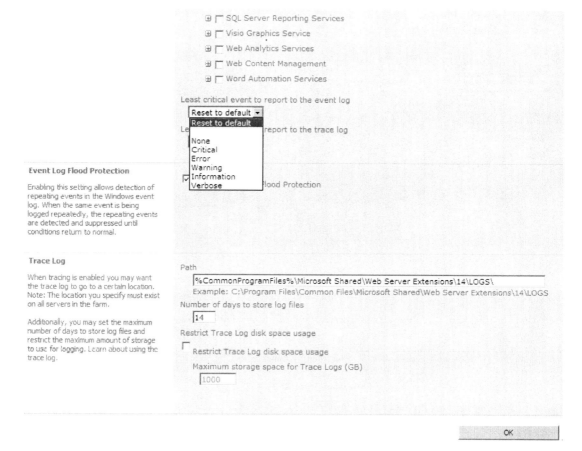

Figure 2-23. Usage and health diagnostic logging settings

Configuring the Logging Database

All the information about logging, events and so on that we have been discussing actually goes to the logging database. If you see the screen shown in Figure 2-24, you have the option to enable logging. You can log 11 different types of events (note that these are selected by default). The usage data collection settings can also be configured with the location as well as the maximum log file size. Toward the end of the screen are the settings to configure the database server, under which logging databases reside.

"Configure logging database" is available under Central Administration ➤ Monitoring ➤ Reporting ➤ Configure usage and health data collection.

Central Administration ▸ Configure web analytics and health data collection

Web Analytics tracking will log events whenever the selected events occur on your SharePoint system. Use the Web Analytics Reports once the collected data has been processed to better understand how your system is being used.

I Like It   Tags & Notes

Warning: this page is not encrypted for secure communication. User names, passwords, and any other information will be sent in clear text. For more information, contact your administrator.

Usage Data Collection

Usage data collection will log events whenever various events occur in your SharePoint deployment. Usage Logging enables analysis and reporting, but also uses system resources and can impact performance and disk usage.

☑ Enable usage data collection

Event Selection

Logging enables analysis and reporting, but also uses system resources and can impact performance and disk usage. Only log those events for which you want regular reports.

For sporadic reports or investigations, consider turning on logging for specific events and then disabling logging for these events after the report or investigation is complete.

Events to log:

☑ Sandboxed Requests
☑ Content Import Usage
☑ Workflow
☑ Content Export Usage
☑ Page Requests
☑ Feature Use
☑ Search Query Usage
☑ Site Inventory Usage
☑ Sandboxed Requests Monitored Data
☑ Timer Jobs
☑ Rating Usage

Usage Data Collection Settings

Usage logs must be saved in a location that exists on all servers in the farm. Adjust the maximum size to ensure that sufficient disk space is available.

Log file location:
`C:\Program Files\Common Files\Microsoft Shared\Web Server Extensions\14\LOGS\`

Maximum log file size:
`5` GB

Figure 2-24. Web anaytics and health data collection and logging database configuration

Adminsitrators are not always notified of errors via correlation IDs and log entries. Sometimes, a page-level web part error or performance needs to be tracked and monitored as well. To do that, the Developer Dashboard has been introduced in SharePoint 2010.

Developer Dashboard

After viewing the Developer Dashboard, don't jump to the conclusion that it is meant to replace your fiddler tools or IE developer toolbar. Also, it's not just for developers. The Developer Dashboard provides a lot of information about what is happening on the page at the time it's rendering. Examples are request event details, execution timing, events, database query processing duration, and other service calls that are very important to know in order to analyze the overall page performance, diagnose issues, and so on.

The Developer Dashboard is not turned on by default. It has to be enabled using either PowerShell commands by the administrators (to be performed on the server) or by writing a code snippet using the SharePoint Object Model. To enable the Developer Dashboard using PowerShell cmdlets, use the script shown in Figure 2-25.

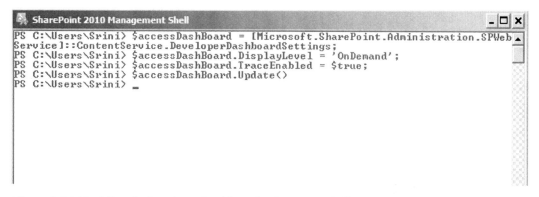

Figure 2-25. Enabling the Developer Dashboard using PowerShell

There are three display levels: OnDemand, On, and Off. When you set the mode to OnDemand, you will have the Developer Dashboard as a toggle window that can be controlled via a small icon in the top-right corner on the ribbon, as shown in Figure 2-26. When set to On, the Developer Dashboard is always available on the bottom of the window, as shown in the Figure 2-27. And when set to Off, which is the default mode, the window is hidden.

Figure 2-26. The Developer Dashboard link on the web application

---

■ **Tip** If you would like to control the Developer Dashboard using the SharePoint Object Model, use the following URL: www.srinisistla.com/blog/Lists/Posts/Post.aspx?ID=73.

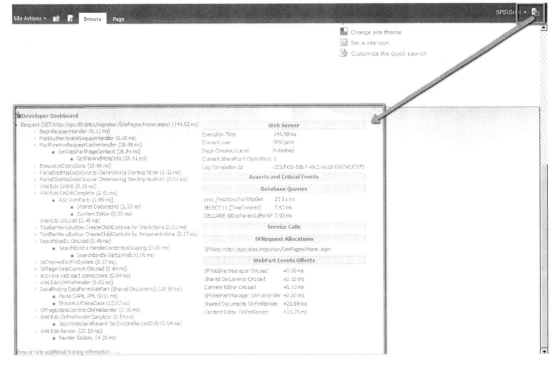

Figure 2-27. Developer Dashboard report

Monitoring Workflows

As a site owner you can monitor the workflows that are running at the site collection level, similar to the way many things can be monitored. You can access workflows from Site Actions ➤ Site Settings ➤ Site Administration ➤ Workflows, as shown in Figure 2-28.

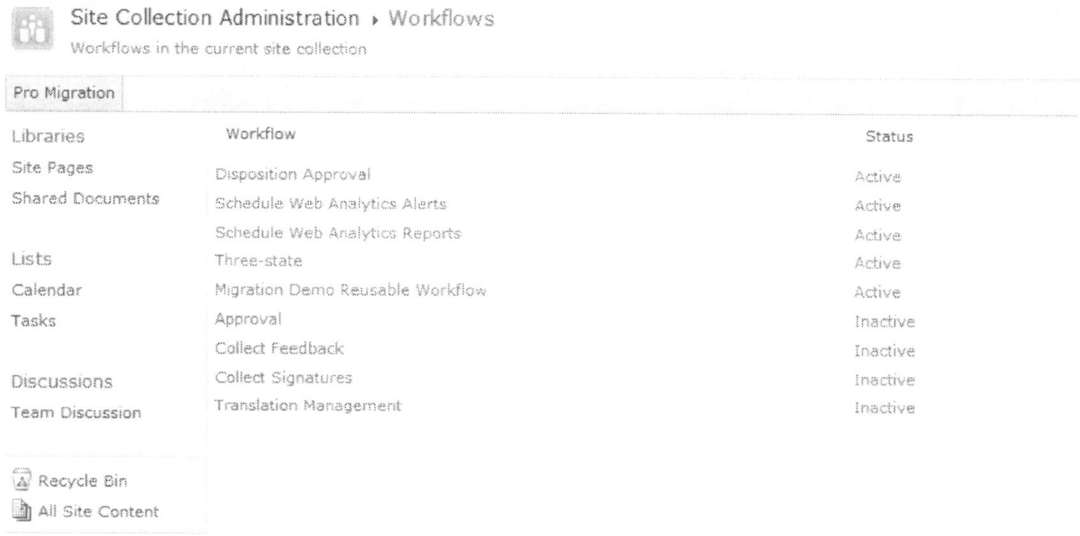

Figure 2-28. *Site Collection Administration Workflows*

Then too, users with Edit Item permissions can view an individual item workflow status, as shown in Figure 2-29.

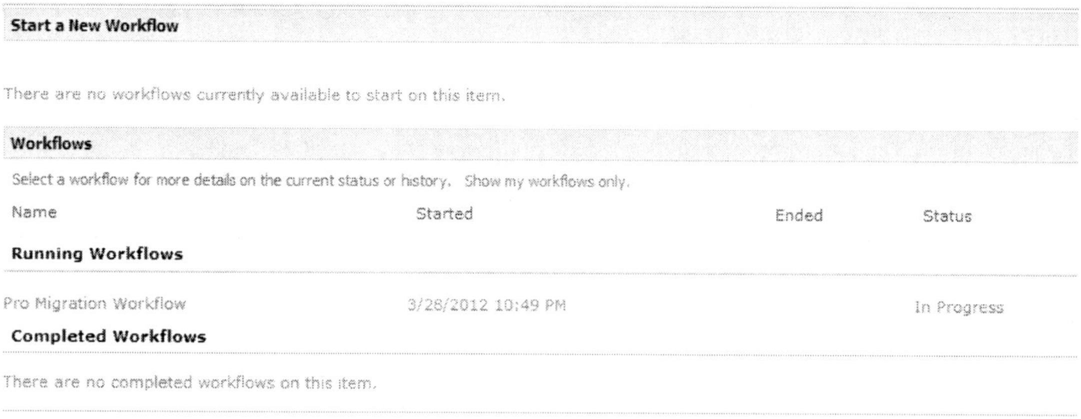

Figure 2-29. *Item-level workflows*

■ **Tip** On a different note, we highly recommend using the Administration Tool Kit for general purposes, not in specific to the migration effort. See `http://technet.microsoft.com/en-us/library/cc508851.aspx`.

Summary

In this chapter, we looked at the following:

- Maintaining continuity and migration strategy to minimize disruption
- Migrating old settings to new, including BDC, search, user profiles, SSO to SSS, and changes to AAM
- Migrating security settings from forms-based to claims-based authentication
- Introductions to monitoring features in SharePoint 2010, including Correlation IDs, Health analyzers, and the Developer Dashboard

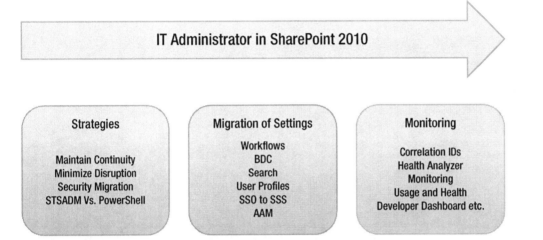

Figure 2-30. IT administrator roadmap in SharePoint 2010

In the next chapter, you will learn about branding and design aspects in SharePoint 2010. We will discuss themes, master pages, and the visual upgrade model as well as CSS and jQuery-based changes. Then, we will discuss some of the changes and enhancements in the Enterprise Content Management (ECM) area and before moving on to ribbon customizations.

CHAPTER 3

Branding and Design Changes

There is no special need to mention the new user interface (UI) in SharePoint 2010—*the UI is an entirely new incarnation.* Comparing the old and new would be very difficult, so it is easier to say, "Do not compare; everything has changed, so start adapting to the new look and feel."

Comparatively, there were very few UI changes from version 2 to version 3. However, version 4 is a new world and leaves you to learn a lot of new "better" things, of course. Believe us, you will soon realize that the changes are for your own good and ease. Let's now dive right into the new UI, but first, look at Figures 3-1 and 3-2 to see how different these versions are with respect to the UIs.

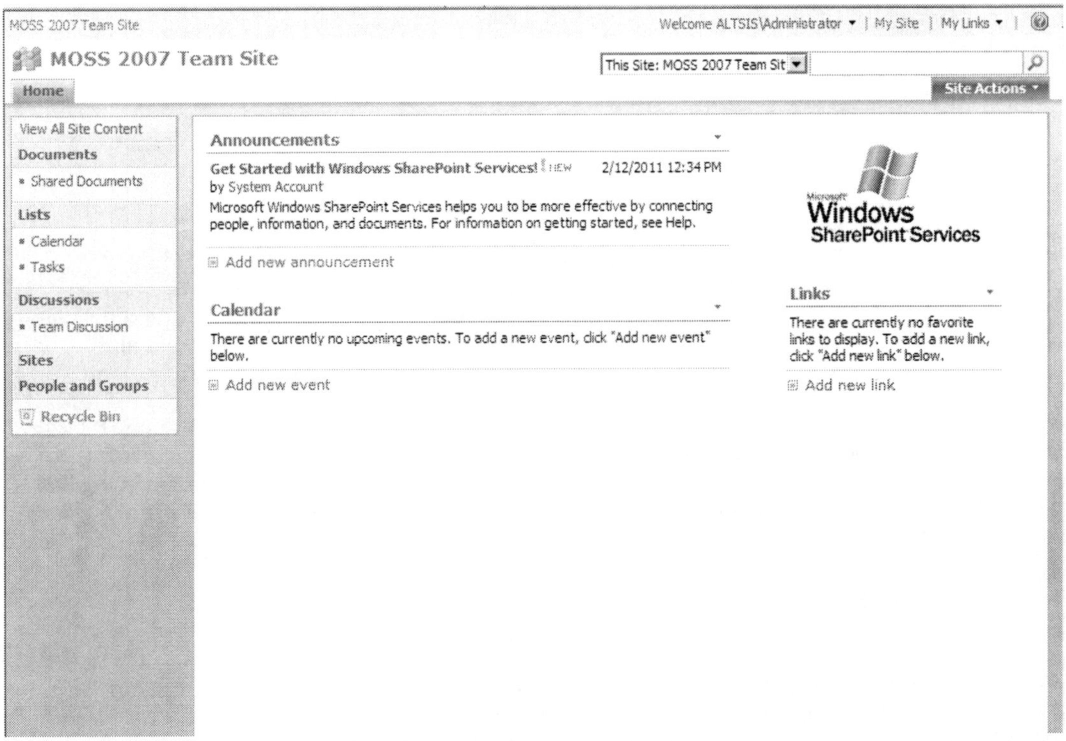

Figure 3-1. Team Site's look and feel in MOSS 2007

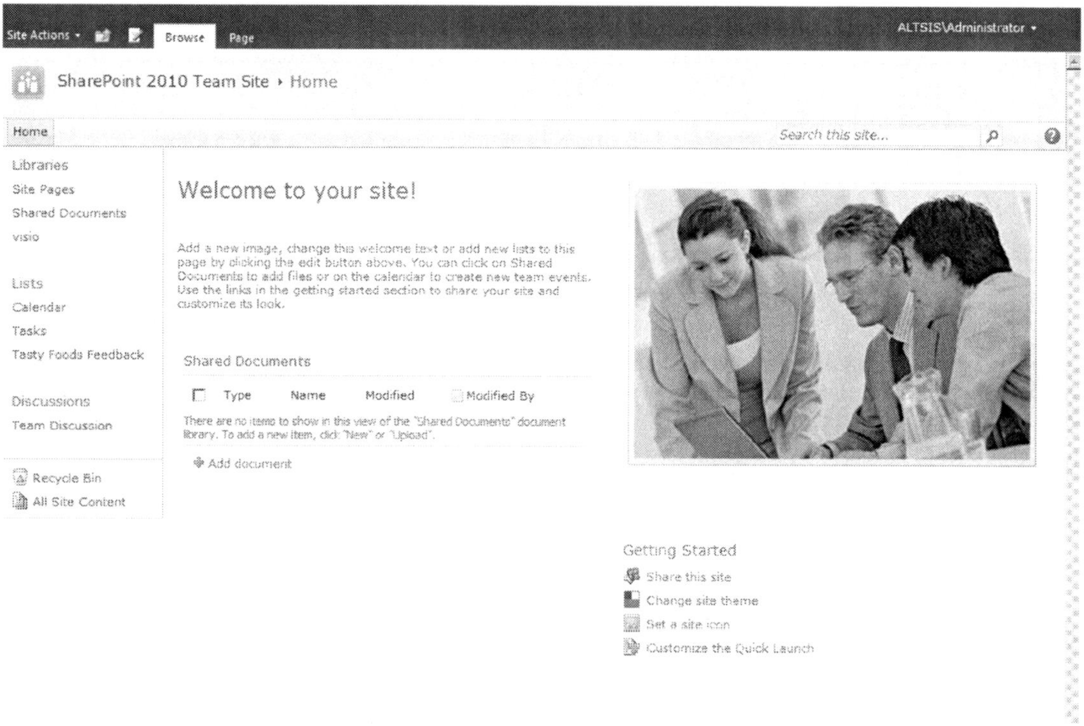

Figure 3-2. SharePoint 2010 Team Site's look and feel

There have been changes in SharePoint 2010 in every aspect with respect to branding: themes, master pages, and CSS files and so on. Writing one single chapter to cover all aspects of branding would be impossible, because the topic by itself could fill a book. There are many topics, internals, and advanced concepts, and we don't want to write another book—particularly since many are already out there. Instead, we will try to cover concepts such what branding means to you during your migration from MOSS 2007 to 2010, what the new features are, and changes and improvements in some of the key areas. To begin with, we would like to make a statement: *You cannot directly migrate your existing 2007 master pages or branding artifacts to 2010*. We guess that makes your life easier—the reason being that there is one less thing to worry about during migration. So let's start with some of the newly introduced and enhanced features in SharePoint 2010 related to branding and visuals.

Changes to Themes

Themes are a way to change the visual aspects of the site without changing the master pages. Themes mainly target background colors, text, links etc. and in some cases fonts as well. They are completely different to that of your site branding files and don't require any knowledge about CSS files or master pages to build one. And probably they are the easiest ones to create, may be for someone like a business user. By default there will be no theme set for your site, but you can change it from Site Actions ➤ Site Settings ➤ Look and Feel ➤ Site Theme.

Themes that are created in MOSS 2007 are not automatically upgraded or compatible with SharePoint 2010. If you still want to use the old themes from the 2007 version, the only way is to use the visual upgrade approach (see Chapter 1). But, honestly, this solution is only temporary until the new UI shall be applied.. Even the location of the themes has changed. In MOSS 2007, they used to be under 12hive\Template\Themes; in SharePoint 2010, they are now globally available under 14hive\Template\Global\Lists\Themes. Also, the files now have the extension .thmx. A .thmx file is a compressed zip file that contains few XML files and the metadata about the theme.

However, as per the best practices, we recommended using the new version and themes. You can choose the themes from one of the available out of the box themes or customize the preinstalled theme before you can apply it.

■ **Note** To perform these changes or apply a theme, you need site owner or higher permissions at the site level.

With SharePoint 2010, you now have the capability or ability to create new themes using Microsoft Office PowerPoint 2010 and publish them. We will now discuss on how to create one theme, publish the same to SharePoint and apply it.

Creating Themes Using PowerPoint 2010

You can create custom themes using PowerPoint 2010 by choosing colors and fonts for various elements of the page. The key to the themes in SharePoint 2010 is that Office and SharePoint 2010 now share the same theme types. Here below are the steps to set up your custom theme:

1. Launch PowerPoint 2010, and create a blank presentation.

2. Under the Design tab, select Themes Group ä Colors drop-down menu, select Create New Theme Colors link.

3. Under the Create New Theme Colors window, change the Theme Colors for the available HTML elements, as shown in Figure 3-3.

---

[2] IIS – Internet Information Services

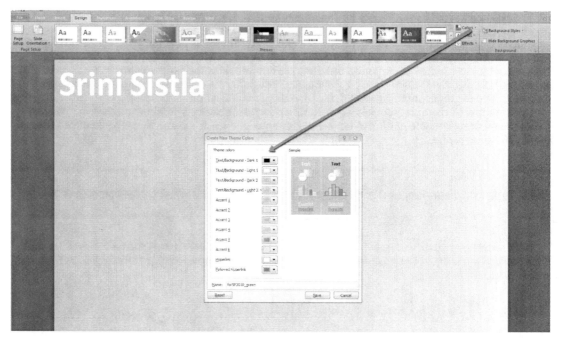

Figure 3-3. Creating themes in PowerPoint 2010

4. Provide a name to the new set of theme colors chosen, and click Save button.

5. From the backstage window, under file menu, choose Save As button. Select Save as type as Office Theme (*.thmx), and provide a file name as for SP2010_green (or as per your choice), and click Save button.

6. There are two ways to use the saved theme file. In the first approach, you can upload the themes file to your site collection under the themes gallery (Site Actions ä Site Settings ä Galleries ä Themes) that can be applied to site collection or site under the site collection.

■ **Note** This approach of manually uploading the file would restrict the themes very much to your site collection or its sub sites.

---

7. In the second approach, upload a theme so that it can be used globally, you will have to save the .thmx file physically to the C:\Program Files\Common Files\Microsoft Shared\Web Server Extensions\14\TEMPLATE\GLOBAL\Lists\themes location. Once you have chosen one of the above methods, do an IIS2 reset and simply browse to the location Site Actions ä Site Settings ä Look and Feel, and select the Site Theme link.

8. You can then choose the new theme, as shown in the Figure 3-4. When you apply the theme to a blog subsite, it looks as shown in the Figure 3-5.

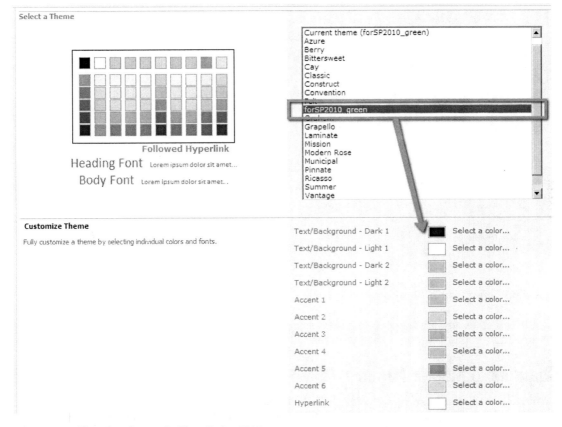

Figure 3-4. Choosing themes in SharePoint 2010

***Figure 3-5.** SharePoint 2010 blog site applied with new theme*

While themes are very easy and simple to create when compared to any other visual aspects in SharePoint 2010, one of the huge changes actually arrived in the form of master pages.

Changes to Master Pages

We have mentioned master pages previously in this book. Yet again, there has been a phenomenal upgrade to the master pages in SharePoint 2010. It would be a bold attempt to compare the editions; it would be wiser to just start with the new SharePoint 2010 edition. Do not get scared away by changes or how much you need to redo your master pages; rather, consider that the new changes bring lots of benefits. Although you can continue using your MOSS 2007 master pages using the visual upgrade model, sometime in the future you will have to move to the SharePoint 2010 master pages. The good news is that the new master pages are built over ASP.NET master page technology and the same framework as MOSS master pages, so you are not learning any new technology here.

To begin with, as we mentioned earlier, there is no migration of master pages; technically, everything will start from zero. After migration, you can use Visual Upgrade until your 2010 master pages are built, and for that, your site will inherit your current version 3 master pages. During this phase, your site under SharePoint 2010 looks the same as your MOSS 2007 site. The downside is you do not get the famous ribbon and other new UI functionalities.

The most important master page within SharePoint 2010 is the `v4.master`, which is the default master page for 2010 and is used for the team site. It consists of the ribbon and all the new visual changes. You also have the `minimal.master` page that is used on search and Office web application pages. And the last important page is `simple.master`, which is used on the error, login, logout, request access, and access denied pages as well as other similar application pages that reside in the `layouts` folder.

Similar to MOSS 2007, SharePoint 2010 contains the other master pages mentioned in Table 3-1. You will notice that some of these master pages serve specific to version 4 and some to version 3.

Table 3-1. Master pages compared in SharePoint 2010 and MOSS 2007

Version 4 SharePoint Master Pages	Version 3 MOSS Master Pages
Applicationv4.master	Application.master
V4.master	Default.master
Dialog.master	
Layouts.master	Layoutsv3.master
Minimal.master	
Pickerdialog.master	
RteDialog.master	
Simplev4.master	Simple.master
	Sspadmin.master

■ **Tip** When you begin creating a new master page, a good place to start is the "Starter Master Pages" article by Randy Drisgill (http://startermasterpages.codeplex.com).

One of the important changes in the master page attribute is DynamicMasterPageFile (which replaces MasterPageFile). This new attribute causes application pages to refer to the site master page instead of the default application master page. The advantage of using this is that you do not need to create a special custom master page for your layout pages; you can use the site's master page instead. Note that, by default, the attribute is set to true. You can turn off the automatic referencing at any time. To do so, simply select Central Administration ➤ Application Management ➤ Web Application ➤ "Manage web applications," and select the web application you want to configure. From the ribbon under the Web Applications tab, select Manage ➤ General Settings. Scroll down to reach the Master Page Setting for Application_Layouts Pages section, and select No, as shown below in Figure 3-6, to disable referring of the site master page.

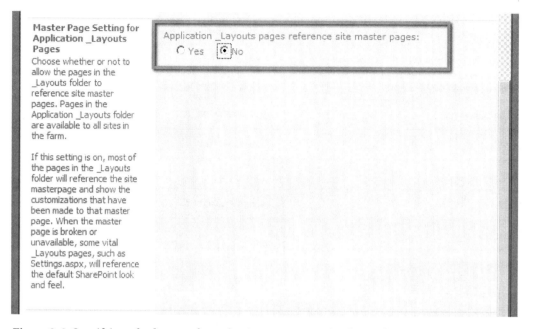

Figure 3-6. *Specifying whether to refer to the site master page for the application master page*

As part of the new master page, many actions that you used in MOSS 2007 are now included on the ribbon, for example, the site actions menu and login and logout controls. Because of the new ribbon design, the content placeholders' location has shifted as well. Hence, you need understand the design of the new structure before beginning your migration to version 4. Understanding placeholders and the placement of web part zones is essential; more information, you can see Appendix B. Finally, scripting and styling resources to support the new master pages have also been updated.

Note You will learn how to deploy master pages, apply them to the site using a feature, and create a feature stapler model in SharePoint 2010 in the section 'Migrating MOSS 2007 Branding Artifacts'

CSS Changes

Like other resources, Cascading Style Sheets (CSS) has also been updated in this version, and there are a lot of new UI enhancements such as the ribbon and pop-up dialogs. Similar to what you have in MOSS 2007 (a `core.css` file of about 5000 lines), you now have the `corev4.css` file at `14hive\layouts\1033\styles\themable\`, which is one of the most important CSS files. However, unlike in MOSS 2007, where you have all the CSS data in one file, now, the data has been logically split into multiple CSS files as shown in Listing 3-1 (view the page source on a team site page). The interesting part is that these files are loaded dynamically. For instance, if you are not using search functionality in the master page, `search.css` will not be loaded.

Listing 3-1. New CSS Links in Version 4 Master Pages

```
<link rel="stylesheet" type="text/css"
href="/_layouts/1033/styles/Themable/search.css?rev=UocOfsLIo87aYwT%2FGX5UPw%3D%3D"/>
<link rel="stylesheet" type="text/css"
href="/_layouts/1033/styles/Themable/wiki.css?rev=9pXM9jgtUVYAHk21JOAbIw%3D%3D"/>
<link rel="stylesheet" type="text/css"
href="/_layouts/1033/styles/Themable/corev4.css?rev=iIikGkMuXBs8CWzKDAyjsQ%3D%3D"/>
```

Though you can customize the CSS files, best practices recommend creating your own custom CSS files and using then to override the CSS classes. There is no specific rule with respect to the location of a custom CSS file; you can upload it to a style or document library. However, it is a good practice that such (or any other) files should be created as part of the branding project in Visual Studio; then, deploy them to the layouts folder. This allows you to reuse the branding and its assets across multiple site collections. You can edit the corev4.css using SharePoint Designer as well.

As a developer, you might have the situation where your custom CSS needs to be rendered after the core CSS file or maybe after another style file, so that it can override some of the classes that belong to the core or other CSS file. There is a new, simple way of loading custom CSS in SharePoint 2010. Consider the following line of code, which adds a link to the corev4.css file.

```
<SharePoint:CssLink runat="server" Version="4"/>
```

To add your custom.css file after the corev4.css file, you can add the following line, using CssRegistration server control:

```
<SharePoint:CssRegistration name="custom.css"  After="corev4.css" runat="server"/>
```

▪ **Note** There are many other new SharePoint server controls added in this edition; you can learn about them in Appendix E.

What about jQuery? Is it part of SharePoint 2010, and does it come out of the box? The answer is "not exactly." To use jQuery, you have to make some customizations to your site, which we will discuss in next section.

Customizing with jQuery

jQuery is an open source standard library built on JavaScript to create powerful applications. The query mechanism is simple yet very powerful, and it parses though HTML DOM elements. In SharePoint, jQuery can be used to retrieve SharePoint objects via web services. This is similar to the Client Object Model, except that the Client Object Model uses specific assemblies instead of web services. To use jQuery with SharePoint 2010, you will have to use the jQuery script reference in your site. You can download jQuery related script files at http://docs.jquery.com/Downloading_jQuery or use the libraries directly from the Content Delivery Network (CDN) URL http://ajax.microsoft.com/ajax/jquery/jquery-1.4.2.min.js.

▪ **Note** Loading library from CDN incurs a performance overhead while your site waits to download the AJAX library over the Internet for various page requests.

There are two versions of the jQuery script file: jQuery-{verion}.js has script functions that you can read and that can be used in a development environment. jQuery-{version}.min.js is a compressed version of the same file, which is highly recommended for use in production environments.

You can load the above mentioned jQuery library in many ways. You can upload the library's .js file to a document library and add the reference on your master page. If you need it on a specific page, you can use the `script` tag wit a content editor web part, as follows:

```
<script src="custom_location/jquery-1.4.2.js" type="text/javascript"></script>
```

An alternate method is to use the `ScriptLink` control, as follows:

```
<SharePoint:ScriptLink ID="scriptLink" runat="server" Defer="false" Localizable="false"
Name="{scriptlayoutlocation}/jquery-1.4.2.js">
</SharePoint:ScriptLink>
```

However, to load the script, you will have to copy the jQuery library file to the location `14hive\Template\Layouts\` or in a specific folder under `layouts` folder. We recommend using feature deployment to do so. Using feature deployment also ensures that the all required dependencies are loaded first.

▪ **Note** In either case, make sure that you have only one instance of the jQuery script link on your page at any given time. You cannot have the reference on the master page as well as on a content page

---

Listing 3-2 provides an example of using jQuery to retrieve list items (in this example, retrieving titles from the Shared Documents library) using a Simple Object Access Protocol (SOAP) envelope. To use the example code, follow these steps:

1. First, make sure that the required jQuery script is deployed to appropriate location, in our case, `_layouts/Pro Migration VS2010`.

2. Under your Visual Studio project, add the `Layouts` mapped folder. Create a project specific subfolder, and add the jQuery file as shown in Figure 3-7.

3. Once the solution is deployed, the jQuery file will be added to the `{sharePointroot}` folder, which you can add as a reference as shown in Listing 3-2.

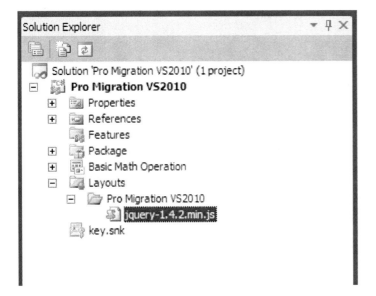

Figure 3-7. Adding a jQuery file to the Layouts mapped folder

4. Edit a page on your SharePoint Site, and add content editor web part.

5. To the content editor web part, add the code in Listing 3-2. Make sure to modify the links in the script to match of your web application or site collection.

6. Once the document is in ready state, the script will invoke the GetSharedDocuments() method.

7. GetSharedDocuments() queries the SharePoint list web service list.asmx with the specific list name and related columns.

8. Once the request is complete, it returns to the callback function GetListItemsComplete() along with the results.

9. The results can be iterated and then appended to the SharedDocuments div element.

Listing 3-2. Retreiving List Items Using jQuery

```
<script src="http://{yourwebapplication}/_layouts/Pro Migration VS2010/jquery-1.4.2.min.js"
type="text/javascript"></script>

<script type="text/javascript">
        $(document).ready(function()
        {
          GetSharedDocuments();
        });
</script>
```

```
<script type="text/javascript">
function GetSharedDocuments() {
var soapEnv =
        "<soap:Envelope
              xmlns:soap='http://schemas.xmlsoap.org/soap/envelope/'> \
                        <soap:Body> \
                          <GetListItems
xmlns='http://schemas.microsoft.com/sharepoint/soap/'> \
                                <listName>Shared Documents</listName> \
                                <viewFields> \
                                        <ViewFields> \
                                                <FieldRef Name='Title' /> \
                                        </ViewFields> \
                                </viewFields> \
                          </GetListItems> \
                        </soap:Body> \
              </soap:Envelope>";
jQuery.ajax({
        url: "/_vti_bin/lists.asmx",
        type: "POST",
        dataType: "xml",
        data: soapEnv,
        complete: GetListItemsComplete,
        contentType: "text/xml; charset=\"utf-8\""
        });
}
function GetListItemsComplete(xData, status) {
        jQuery(xData.responseXML).find("z\\:row").each(function ()
        {
                $("<li>" + $(this).attr("ows_Title") + "</li>").appendTo("#SharedDocuments");
        });
}
</script>

<ul id="SharedDocuments"></ul>
```

Changes to Publishing Templates

There have been some significant changes to the publishing infrastructure in SharePoint 2010. A couple of important ones to note are a missing site template and one new publishing site template. The Collaboration Portal template (see Figure 3-8) has been decommissioned, and Enterprise Wiki has been added as new template under the Publishing group (see Figure 3-9).

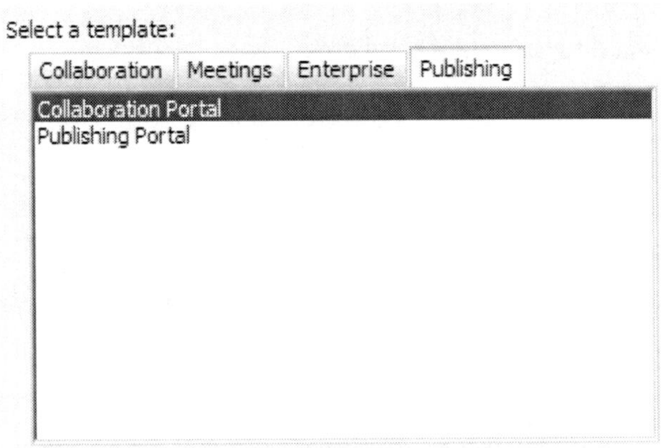

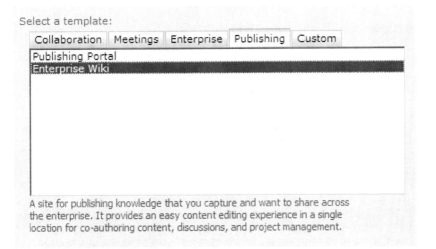

Figure 3-8. Publising templates in MOSS 2007

Figure 3-9. Publishing templates in SharePoint 2010

In SharePoint 2010, Team Site Collaboration Templates provide very flexible way to create and edit the content on a page. These templates feature wiki-style pages with a ribbon providing necessary editor controls, and they address

- *Editing:* Subsets of users are permitted to make changes on the page, as granted by the administrators with full control.

- *Versioning:* Previous versions can be viewed and rolled back if needed.

The Enterprise Wiki template has all the publishing features, such as ratings, managed metadata, customizable options, page layouts, and branding. Enterprise Wiki pages are used when there is a need for many-to-many communication, tagging with enterprise keywords, and, of course, exchanging collaborative information. Changes that are performed on a site and saved can be viewed by others instantly without publishing those pages and going through the approval process.

■ **Tip** Use the following link to plan Enterprise Wiki template-based sites: `http://technet.microsoft.com/en-us/library/ee721055.aspx`.

Because of the power of this template, Enterprise Wiki sites might attract a huge audience and therefore end up with huge amounts of data. These sites are meant to store and share large-scale data; however, this very fact makes the site perform slower when compared to the team sites. Then too, pages under this site template cannot be converted or migrated to pages on a team site (you would have to write some custom code logic to do so). Though using an Enterprise Wiki template site offers significant advantages, you need to plan for these template sites even before you think of using them.

■ **Note** Enterprise Wiki sites have fewer available page layouts than publishing sites.

Changes to Web Content Management Web Parts

There are many good changes and enhancements to some of the out-of-the-box web parts that are very popular and commonly used in MOSS 2007. You need to be aware of the changes for these web parts so that you can plan for them, for a lot of good reasons that you will see in this section.

Content Query Web Part

One of the most widely used web parts in MOSS 2007 is the Content Query web part (CQWP). For power users and developers in MOSS 2007, this web part needs no introduction at all. If you are a beginner and you hear the phrase "aggregate or rollup information," the first thing you should look at using is the CQWP. The simplicity of this web part and its tool part is that they provide you an easy configuration wizard with which you can retrieve data from a list or document library from any site or site collection or from all sites. If you are a power user, knowing XSLT would be added advantage, because you can use it modify the related `itemstyles.xslt` file to add additional columns to the display.

In SharePoint 2010, you no longer need to modify out-of-the-box files or write complex XSLT (it's good to learn though) to parse the list information. CQWP has been well upgraded; it brings more features and it is easier to configure. Figure 3-10 shows the CQWP and the tool part when edited.

Figure 3-10. Content Query Web Part

Furthermore, with managed metadata in SharePoint 2010, now CQWP can be configured to use managed term fields, and you can query based on context. For instance, in MOSS 2007, if you design a CQWP to retrieve data from a list based on a page layout filter, the CQWP settings will not change for any instance of the page layout when it is used. If you build a context based on the metadata provided, you will have different results even though same page layout is used in multiple instances.

You have two filters that you can use at each page level to accomplish the preceding scenario, PageFieldValue and PageQueryString. When values are passed to these tokens, your CQWP dynamically generates the necessary the output. As mentioned earlier, to add more than one field to CQWP in MOSS 2007, you have to use XSLT. However, in SharePoint Server 2010, you have the functionality to use it by configuring the tool part appropriately without even touching XSLT. Finally, the good news is that there is a huge performance improvement in this edition of CQWP. You can access CQWP from the web part gallery under Categories ➤ Conent Rollup ➤ Web Parts ➤ Content Query, as shown in Figure 3-11.

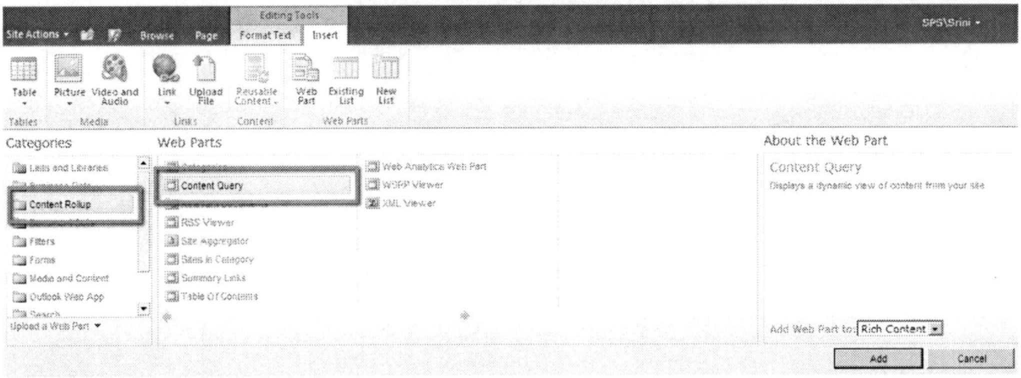

Figure 3-11. Content Query Web Part

■ **Note** If you are using a team site, you will have to activate the site collection feature SharePoint Server Publishing Infrastructure and site feature SharePoint Server Publishing, similar to what you must do in MOSS 2007 to obtain CQWP.

Content Editor Web Part

Another very popular web part in MOSS 2007 is the Content Editor web part (CEWP); there is probably not one person who has not used it. Adding custom HTML on a page, hiding a quick launch menu, applying custom styling, and executing a JavaScript function are some of the tasks for which CEWP comes in very handy. And it absolutely does not require any kind of deployment and can be used quickly. Changes made to a page using CEWP stay on the page itself and live on the page forever unless deleted. Migrating a page with a CEWP from MOSS 2007 to SharePoint 2010 will have impact on the migrated page or the control itself.

■ **Tip** Some very useful tips and information on the CEWP can be found at `http://blah.winsmarts.com/2009-11-The_new_content_editor_WebPart_in_SharePoint_2010.aspx`.

Similar to CQWP, CEWP also went through a big change in SharePoint 2010. First of all, you have the ribbon, by which you can change the source of the web part. It's much cleaner and better than what you used to have. As shown in Figure 3-12, simply click the HTML menu under Markup section, and add any HTML Source, including script.

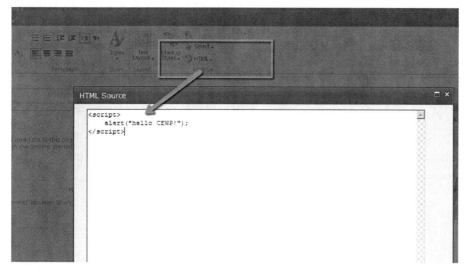

Figure 3-12. CEWP editor

Even better, you can now convert the HTML markup to XHTML and make your markup pretty clean; you don't have to worry about unclean HTML. You can also have your HTML source or script in a text (.txt) file stored in a document library and can refer to this CEWP, which would render the contents as a HTML file. Another outstanding feature of the new CEWP is that links under the markup will be converted to relative paths based on your alternate access mapping settings on your web application's farm.

You can access CEWP from the web part gallery under Categories ➤ Media and Content ➤ Web Parts ➤ Conent Editor, as shown in Figure 3-13.

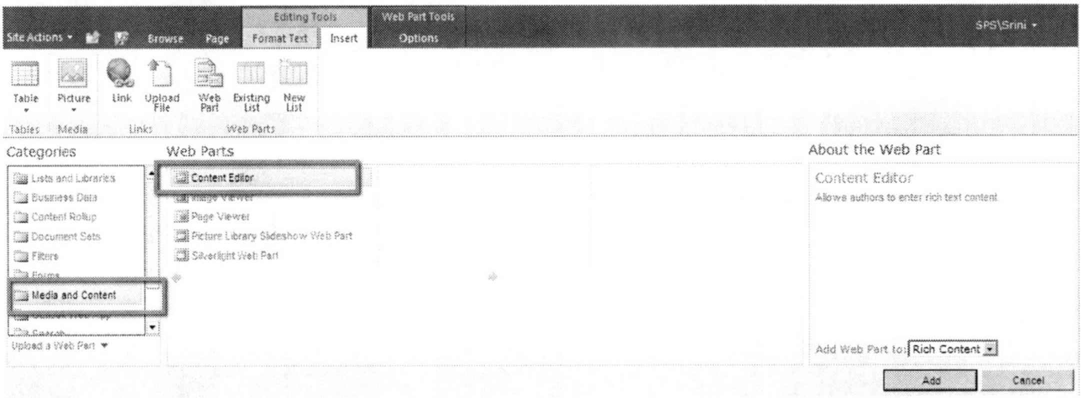

Figure 3-13. *Content Editor Web Part*

XML Viewer Web Part

If you need to add XML content on your page and apply style sheet to transform the data using XSLT, you can use the XML Viewer web part. You can refer to both structured and unstructured XML data or even XML–based documents. An XML Viewer web part can be added or referenced from the web part gallery under Categories ➤ Content Rollup ➤ Web Parts ➤XML Viewer, as shown in Figure 3-14.

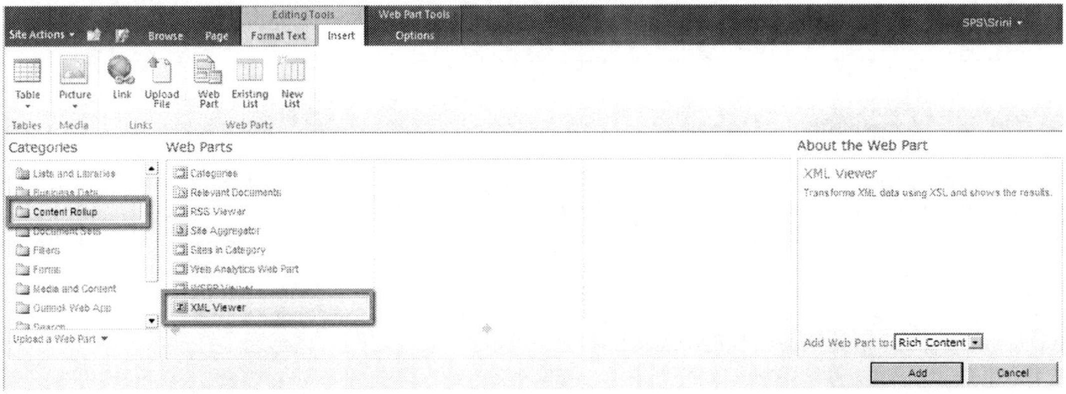

Figure 3-14. *XML Viewer Web Part*

The XML Viewer web part enables you to add XML directly or refer to an existing XML file link (as shown in Figure 3-14). You can either add the corresponding XSLT using the editor or refer to an existing XSLT file link (see Figure 3-15).

Figure 3-15. Adding content to the XML Viewer web part

■ **Note** Do not add any HTML content to the XML Viewer web part; if you need to do so, use a Page Viewer or Form web part.

XSLT List View Web Part

Who has not used the famous Data View or List View web parts in MOSS 2007? They are very easy to configure (of course with SharePoint Designer 2007) and quick to design, which made them very popular for use with lists. Many would not share our excitement about the Data View or List View web parts in MOSS 2007, because these web parts bring extensive Collaborative Application Markup Language (CAML) and do not render HTML so well. But they are very good for a quick development to display data on a SharePoint page. They are powerful, yet they can look ugly sometimes. While they still exist in SharePoint 2010, the good news is that there has is an all-new component, the XSLT List View web part, that solves many concerns around cleaner HTML and has many other advantages. So, you can either live with your existing Data View or List View web parts, or consider moving on to the XSLT List View web part.

XSLT List View web part (let's call it "XLVWP") is the default web part to display list data in SharePoint 2010. The first thing that will attract you is the ribbon UI with sections or menus for each individual functionality, as shown in Figure 3-16. It allows you to perform customizations, including defining custom styles and conditional formatting for the data. Second, you can now use XSLT instead of CAML; this is one of developers' wish list items for SharePoint 2010. Unlike in MOSS 2007, this edition supports in-line editing capabilities and rich end user friendliness via the ribbon UI. Finally, you can also connect to enterprise-level data using Business Connectivity Services (BCS) (using external lists), retrieve data from another web application, and merge data from different lists to display it as one list.

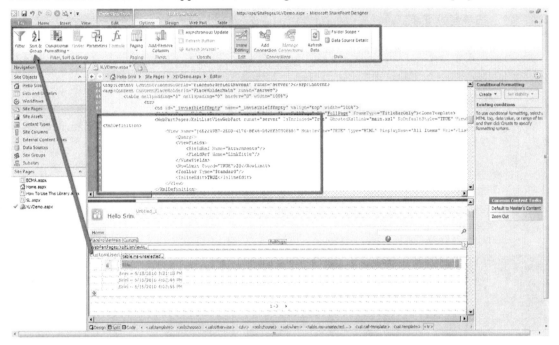

Figure 3-16. XSLT List View web part

■ **Note** The XSLT web part is only available via SharePoint Designer 2010.

Complying with WCAG and ARIA

There is so much to talk about the material in this section, but we prefer to put it simply. First, if you are not sure of what Web Content Accessibility Guidelines (WCAG) and Accessible Rich Internet Applications (ARIA) standards are, we recommend you read more about them at www.w3.org/TR/WCAG20 and www.w3.org/TR/wai-aria, respectively. Simply put, these standards outline guidelines for two main reasons:

- How simply and easily your web application can be accessed by users with a wide range of abilities

- Providing semantic information about the contents of your web application.

SharePoint 2010 came up with a good upgrade to be compliant with and reach the expectations of the WCAG and ARIA standards. Meeting these standards was one of the key reasons for the huge UI facelift and ribbon features in what you see now. There have also been improvements in many core areas, including these:

- *Accessibility guidelines*: SharePoint 2010 guarantees interoperability of the web sites over a wide range of operating systems and multibrowser support across many platforms and handheld devices such as iPad, iPhone, and Blackberry. Supported browsers include Internet Explorer, Safari, Firefox, and Chrome.

- *Dialogs everywhere*: One of the biggest changes, apart from the ribbon, that you will notice in this edition is the use of modal windows or dialogs. This feature keeps you in context to the current page and avoids unnecessary page refreshes. Every action on a dialog is asynchronous, so a page reload is not required to reflect the changes.

- *The ribbon itself*: Again, in the context, this is a familiar interface similar to your Office applications, which is integrated with accessibility mode (shown in Figure 3-17).

- *Keyboard friendliness*: Keyboard lovers will be astonished to see the new user friendliness and quick access. For instance, to access the Browse tab, use the shortcut keys Ctrl+[.

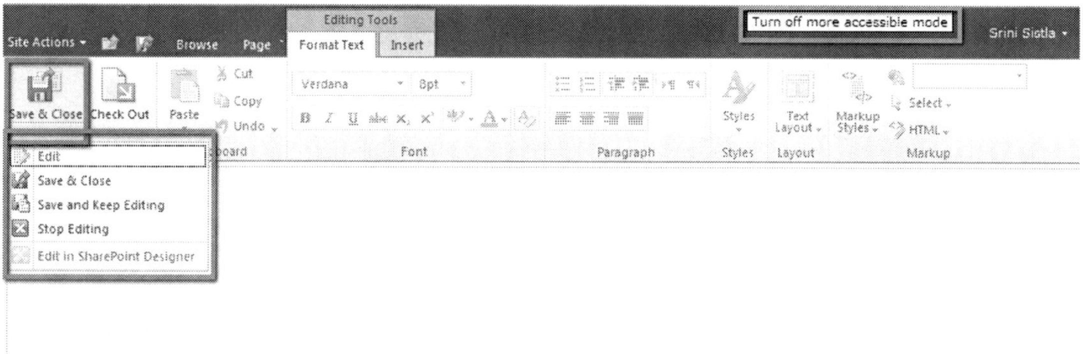

Figure 3-17. Accessible mode

- *Tab key*: Simply use the Tab key to move across the ribbon to any menu, as shown in the Figure 3-17.

- *Tooltips*: Tooltips everywhere describe command behavior in detail.

In addition to the accessibility features, there has been tremendous improvement with respect to the rendered HTML.

■ **Note** For a detailed quick check and reference on these standards and accessibility features, see www.aiim.org/community/blogs/expert/SharePoint-2010-Web-Standards-Accessibility-and-Usability-Quick-Reference-Guide.

Creating Cleaner HTML

We have to admit that the rendered HTML is not clean enough in MOSS 2007. It has nothing to do with the product itself, but the nature of HTML, CSS, JavaScript, tables and so on make the code sometimes look a bit untidy and difficult to manage. There have been a lot of improvements in SharePoint 2010. For that matter, you can simply right-click the rendered page to view the source and notice how clean the output is. SharePoint 2010 uses divs rather than tables, and using technology, such as Ajax, mess less code and much cleaner rendering.

The server controls are much improved now too. For instance, SharePoint 2010 contains a new property for ASP.NET menu navigation called UseSimpleRendering. SharePoint:AspMenu is primarily used to dynamically create the navigation elements. In MOSS 2007, that control renders output as HTML. In SharePoint 2010, when the property is set to true, it renders cleaner HTML with divs, as shown in Listing 3-3.

Listing 3-3. Rendering with the Simple Rendering Option Set to true

```
<DIV id=zz15_TopNavigationMenuV4 class=ms-topNavContainer>
  <DIV class="menu horizontal menu-horizontal">
    <UL class="root static">
      <LI class="static selected">
        <A accessKey=1 class="static selected menu-item" title="Home Page"
href="/Pages/default.aspx">
          <SPAN class=additional-background>
            <SPAN class=menu-item-text>Home</SPAN>
            <SPAN class=ms-hidden>Currently selected</SPAN>
          </SPAN>
        </A>
      </LI>
```

When set to false, it renders HTML as shown in Listing 3-4 andgives you an opportunity to ensure a cleaner HTML when you write code.

Listing 3-4. Rendering with the Simple Rendering Option Set to false

```
<TABLE id=zz1_TopNavigationMenuV4 class="ms-topNavContainer zz1_TopNavigationMenuV4_2"
border=0 cellSpacing=0 cellPadding=0>
<TBODY>
  <TR>
    <TD id=zz1_TopNavigationMenuV4n0 onmouseover=Menu_HoverStatic(this) title="Home Page"
onkeyup=Menu_Key(this) onmouseout=Menu_Unhover(this)>
      <TABLE class="ms-topnav zz1_TopNavigationMenuV4_4 ms-topnavselected
zz1_TopNavigationMenuV4_9" border=0 cellSpacing=0 cellPadding=0 width="100%"
hoverClass="zz1_TopNavigationMenuV4_13 ms-topNavHover">
```

```
        <TBODY>
          <TR>
            <TD style="WHITE-SPACE: nowrap">
              <A accessKey=1 style="BORDER-BOTTOM-STYLE: none; BORDER-RIGHT-STYLE: none;
BORDER-TOP-STYLE: none; FONT-SIZE: 1em; BORDER-LEFT-STYLE: none"
class="zz1_TopNavigationMenuV4_1 ms-topnav zz1_TopNavigationMenuV4_3 ms-topnavselected
zz1_TopNavigationMenuV4_8" href="/Pages/default.aspx"
hoverHyperLinkClass="zz1_TopNavigationMenuV4_12 ms-topNavHover">Home</A>
            </TD>
          </TR>
        </TBODY>
      </TABLE>
    </TD>
```

Customizing the Ribbon

One of the most significant changes, which we have been discussing in this chapter, is the addition of ribbon interface originally introduced in Office 2007. While the ribbon interface has been implemented over other thick clients, such as Paint, it brings a great advantage to the web pages. If the end user is coming with Office 2007 experience, adapting to the new user experience is easy. Simply put, the ribbon provides ease of access, fewer steps to perform a task, and context sensitive operations.

Introducing New Styles

The ribbon provides contextual editing capabilities to the current page. Operations that you can perform using the ribbon are laid out logically as groups. Each group has menus, which are the actual operations that user may perform. You then have tabs for various page-related operations. Items under these groups, menus, and tabs (shown in Figure 3-18) are object dependant, which means that they are subject to change when different objects on the page are referred or selected. Ribbon and ribbon elements appear contextually when you click the relevant tabs on the ribbon or any edit elements on the page. We will discuss them now in detailed.

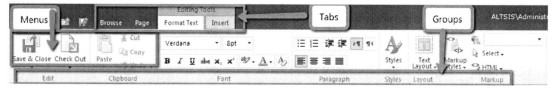

Figure 3-18. Ribbon 101

Format Text Tab

Table 3-2 outlines the functions available by selecting Editing Tools ➤ Format Text tab.

Table 3-2. *Format Text Tab Functions*

Group	Description
Edit	As soon as the page changes to edit mode, you can begin typing in the editable area on the page because pages in SharePoint 2010 are wiki-like. You can exclusively edit the page by checking it out (automatic in publishing pages). Later, check in the page, and then save and close it.
Clipboard	A simple cut/copy/paste operation from any other source to the page can be performed. You can also undo or redo the changes, if required, through menus under this group.
Font	This is a no-brainer group. You might have seen it more than a thousand times while using SharePoint Designer 2007 or Office Word and PowerPoint to make your artifacts fancy. This feature is now available for your web pages too.
Paragraph	Again, this is a familiar functionality that you must have used with Office applications, such as Word, to align or indent text, create bulleted or numbered lists, or lay out bidirectional text.
Styles	These are styles that you can apply to HTML text on the page. A few out-of-the-box styles are available, and you can build your own custom styles and add to the styles group.
Layout	Text and page layouts are available under team and publishing sites, respectively; these are preconfigured content and page layouts that can be used on your page.
Markup	This group has functions for page-level branding. You can apply specific styles to the text that is embedded on the page by selecting the required and specific text. You can also apply a specific language attribute to the selected text. Another very helpful functionality is related to the HTML markup on your page. You have two options, first, edit HTML source to modify your HTML specific layouts. And secondly, make your HTML mark up as XHTML compliant.

Insert Tab

Table 3-3 outlines the functions available by selecting Editing Tools ➤ Insert tab.

Table 3-3. *Insert Tab Functions*

Group	Description
Tables	Insert an HTML table with your required number of rows and columns.
Media	Add pictures, video, or audio to the page from your local drive (using the From Computer option) or from a specific web URL (using the From Address option). The media can belong to a SharePoint or non-SharePoint site.

Group	Description
Links	Add a link to the specific page by URL or something that is available on your SharePoint site already. Another wonderful feature here is the ability to upload files to a SharePoint site to a specific library directly without going to the library first. We're sure you will wonder how many clicks will be saved with this new functionality when compared with that in MOSS 2007.
Web	Add a web part or an existing list, or even create a new list and add to your existing page directly. Because there are no web part zones in this version, you can simply add and move your web parts anywhere on the page.

Page Tab

Table 3-4 outlines the functions available by selecting the Page tab.

Table 3-4. Page Tab Functions

Group	Description
Edit	Refer to the Edit group in Table 3-3.
Manage	You can rename a page, except the default home page and review the page history related to any modification over the current page. You can set the page-level permissions and delete the page if needed. (This feature not available for publishing sites.)
Share & Track	Launch e-mail with a link to the page, if required, and send a message to any individual.
Page Actions	You can make the current page the default home page and find a list of all pages linked to the current page.
Page Library	You can configure library settings and permissions for the current page and view all the pages under the library that the current page belongs to.
Publishing Site Specific Page Settings	*Edit Properties:* View and edit page metadata properties and content type of the page. *Alert Me:* Set alerts (immediate, daily, or weekly) for any changes that happen on the current page. *Preview:* Preview the current page after editing and before it will be published and viewed by the end user. *Page Layout:* Can create page-level templates, which are controlled by developers and designers.

	Draft Check: Highlight changes made on the current page until they're published or the draft check button on the ribbon is deselected.

Publish Tab

Table 3-5 outlines the functions available by selecting the Publish tab.

Table 3-5. Publish Tab Functions

Group	Description
Publishing	This feature is only available for publishing sites or when publishing is enabled; it can be used to publish checked out pages.

Browse Tab

Clicking the Browse tab actually hides the ribbon and displays how the actual page looks after editing is complete. You can click any other tab to begin editing once again.

While the ribbon provides many new features, as you have seen, you can also tailor the branding of the ribbon to match your site branding.

Ribbon control is an integral part of the version 4 master page in SharePoint 2010. Unless you are using the out-of-the-box master pages (that is, whenever you have a custom, branded master page), it is equally important to brand the ribbon. We will now discuss how to make changes to the ribbon styles and the related CSS files in the next section.

Branding the Ribbon

The easiest way to find the ribbon control on a master page is to simply search for the text "ribbon". Easy, isn't it? You will reach to the specific div tag with the ID s4-ribbonrow and contents under this division comprise and relate to the ribbon control. However, if you would like to know what the ribbon control is, it is tagged with <SharePoint:SPRibbon>, which is found under the same s4-ribbonrow div. Overall, the ribbon is encapsulated and its styles are controlled with many CSS files. We will discuss a few of them here, but for a designer or developer, the fastest way to learn how to modify a ribbon style on the fly is to play around using either Firefox Firebug or the Internet Explorer Developer tool bar. OK, let's get to some internals now.

Primarily, SharePoint 2010 CSS files are all defined under the corev4.css file located in {SharePointRoot}/_layouts/1033/Styles/Themable/. This file controls not just the ribbon but the entire look and feel of your web application.

■ **Note** In `v4.master`, you can find the `corev4.css` reference, as follows:

```
<SharePoint:CssLink runat="server" Version="4"/>
```

It's virtually impossible to override all the classes in this file, hence you can only change those that are relevant to your design. What does that mean? The `corev4.css` file and your custom CSS file will coexist in your master page.and to override the corev4.css classes, you will have to make sure of couple of things.

First, you will have to register your custom CSS file using `CssRegistration` on the master page and make sure to set the `After` attribute to `corev4.css`. This will ensure that your custom CSS file is loaded after the `corev4.css` file, as shown in Listing 3-5.

Listing 3-5. Loading a Custom Style Class in the Master Page

```
<SharePoint:CssRegistration name="customstyle.css" After="corev4.css"
runat="server"/>
```

Second, in your custom CSS file, wherever you are overriding core classes, make sure to use the `!important` override model for those classes. Now, as discussed earlier, ribbon control is under the div tag `s4-ribbonrow`, as shown in Listing 3-6.

Listing 3-6. Listing Ribbon Control Elements

```
<div id="s4-ribbonrow" class="s4-pr s4-ribbonrowhidetitle">
        <div id="s4-ribboncont">
                <SharePoint:SPRibbon
                    runat="server"
                    PlaceholderElementId="RibbonContainer"
                    CssFile="">
                    <SharePoint:SPRibbonPeripheralContent
                        runat="server"
                        Location="TabRowLeft"
                        CssClass="ms-siteactionscontainer s4-notdlg">


        <!-- Site Actions Content Goes Here -->


                    </SharePoint:SPRibbonPeripheralContent>
                    <SharePoint:SPRibbonPeripheralContent
                        runat="server"
                        Location="TabRowRight"
                        ID="RibbonTabRowRight"
                        CssClass="s4-trc-container s4-notdlg">


        <!- Global Navigation Goes Here -->
```

```
                </SharePoint:SPRibbonPeripheralContent>
            </SharePoint:SPRibbon>
    </div>

    <div id="notificationArea" class="s4-noti">
        <!- All Notifications Go Here -->
    </div>

    <asp:ContentPlaceHolder ID="SPNavigation" runat="server">
                <SharePoint:DelegateControl runat="server"
ControlId="PublishingConsole" Id="PublishingConsoleDelegate">
            </SharePoint:DelegateControl>
    </asp:ContentPlaceHolder>
    <div id="WebPartAdderUpdatePanelContainer">
            <asp:UpdatePanel
                    ID="WebPartAdderUpdatePanel"
                    UpdateMode="Conditional"
                    ChildrenAsTriggers="false"
                    runat="server">
                <ContentTemplate>
                        <WebPartPages:WebPartAdder ID="WebPartAdder" runat="server"/>
                </ContentTemplate>
                <Triggers>
                        <asp:PostBackTrigger ControlID="WebPartAdder" />
                </Triggers>
            </asp:UpdatePanel>
    </div>
</div>
```

Table 3-6 shows the CSS elements around the ribbon; a detailed list is provided in Appendix C as well.

Table 3-6. Ribbon CSS Elements

CSS Class	Description
s4-ribbonrow	Top div of the ribbon
s4-ribboncont	Used to globally control the ribbon, such as its background
ms-cui-groupSeparator	Controls the ribbon separators
ms-cui-ribbonTopBars	Controls the area around ribbon top tabs
ms-cui-tt-s ms-cui-tt-a	Controls the styles for the ribbon selected tabs (Browse, Page, etc.)
ms-cui-tabBody	Controls the style for the selected tab body

`ms-cui-cg-db`
`ms-cui-cg-t`
`ms-cui-cg-gr`
`ms-cui-cg-s`
`ms-cui-cg-t`
	Controls the text on the tab headers

`ms-cui-cg-db` `ms-cui-tt-a:hover`	Controls the text on the tabs and the anchor links

`ms-cui-cg-db`
`ms-cui-cg-i`
`ms-cui-cg-db`
`ms-cui-cg-s`
`ms-cui-cg-i`
`ms-cui-cg-gr`
`ms-cui-cg-s`
`ms-cui-tt-a:hover`
`ms-cui-cg-gr`
`ms-cui-cg-s`
`ms-cui-tt-s`
`ms-cui-tt-a:hover`
	Controls the borders of the tab groups (Library Tools, etc) and subgroups (Documents, Library, etc.)

`ms-cui-cg-db`
`ms-cui-cg-s`
`ms-cui-ct-ul`
	Controls the spaces between the menu items under a group

`ms-cui-cg-db`
`ms-cui-cg-s`
`ms-cui-cg-t`
	Controls the background elements when a subitem is selected

`ms-cui-cg-db`
`ms-cui-ct-first`
`ms-cui-tt-a`
`ms-cui-cg-db`
`ms-cui-ct-last`
`ms-cui-tt-a`
	Controls the borders of the tabs

`ms-cui-cg-db`
`ms-cui-cg-s`
`ms-cui-tt-a`
	Controls the submenu item background, text, etc.

`ms-cui-cg-db`
`ms-cui-cg-s`
`ms-cui-tt-a:hover`
`ms-cui-cg-gr`
`ms-cui-tt-a:hover`
	Controls hover settings of submenu items

`ms-cui-cg-gr` `ms-cui-cg-s`	Controls styles for ribbon menu buttons

ms-cui-tt-s ms-cui-tt-a	

As mentioned earlier, not every CSS class needs to be overridden, you can verify your requirements, and based on them you can override, customize, or add custom CSS classes to define your new ribbon branding CSS file. This is all good and easy. Now, what do these changes mean to your existing master page migration and your already branded artifacts?

Migrating MOSS 2007 Branding Artifacts

Throughout this book, and especially in this chapter, we have been mentioning that there is no migration of your existing MOSS 2007 master pages; instead, you have to rewrite and design them from scratch again. You have already seen the changes related to visuals, master pages, CSS, and the ribbon. Now, we will discuss how your existing artifacts can be migrated, leaving the design part for new custom development. Your existing master page artifacts might be some of the following (all with respect to your branding of course):

- Custom CSS

- Custom JavaScript, jQuery, and Ajax files

- Images, banners, logo files, and so on

- Web controls that are part of the master page

- SharePoint features that take care of applying the master pages or staple them when a site collection or site is provisioned

There might be other assets, but the preceding ones are the primary areas that branding artifacts usually fall under. When you build your project structure in Visual Studio 2010, mappings to features and the layout folder are now built in, so you don't need to create a structure (see the Visual Studio section in Chapter 4 for more information). In this chapter, we will cover some high-level aspects of migrating branding artifacts. All of the listed artifacts could be re-created in the same structure you have been using so far. Usually, these files are deployed to the layouts folder with specific project folder unless there is a special need to add them under site document or asset libraries. This means that all custom assets would be deployed under _layouts, as in the following examples:

- _layouts/{brandingspecificfolder}/styles/: Where styles are deployed

- _layouts/{brandingspecificfolder}/images/: Where images and logos are deployed

- _layouts/{brandingspecificfolder}/scripts/: Where custom scripts (jQuery or JavaScript) are deployed

And master pages, of course, will be part of the SharePoint 2010 resource files that will be added to the feature elements file. All other web controls will be either added to the control templates folder or will composite controls that are deployed to either the global assembly cache (GAC) or bin.

Though you can design your master pages by editing the out-of-the-box v4.master file using SharePoint Designer, we wouldn't recommend doing so. It's a best practice to write your custom master page and deploy it as a feature, rather than editing the master pages, directly unless or otherwise required or suggested by your architects.

You may have already noticed some of the visual changes. A couple more interesting things you need to keep in mind while designing master pages are explained here. First, the dialogs that appear as part of some of the actions you perform might contain a number of visual aspects that you don't want to display on the branding, especially when it comes to the dialogs. For example, top navigation is one control that would look very odd and clumsy on a dialog box. To avoid displaying any of the elements in the master page, you can simple add the following CSS tag to restrict the specific control or tag under the dialogs. For example, to hide a custom control on a dialog, you would do as follows:

```
<div class="s4-notdlg">
  // Your Custom Control Tag Goes Here
</div>
```

You can use the same tag with other elements, as shown here:

```
<div id="s4-leftpanel" class="s4-notdlg">
  // Quick Launch
</div>
```

The preceding example is very specific to the quick launch feature that you would notice under the default v4.master page.

Next, in case of fixed-width design, you need to add a specific class s4-workspace. Locate it in the master page, and add the s4-nosetwidth CSS class, as follows. If you do not set it on an out-of-the-box master page, the page would use 100 percent width.

```
<div ID="s4-workspace" class="s4-nosetwidth">
```

The location of the master pages in SharePoint 2010 hasn't changed. All the out-of-the-box, as well as custom, master pages are deployed to the _catalogs/masterpage library. Once you finish designing your master page based on the starter master pages (or other mechanism you wish to choose) and following the CSS script changes that are mentioned earlier, you can begin designing your features that deploy these master pages to the _catalogs/masterpage location. You can refer to the final project structure, as shown in Figure 3-19.

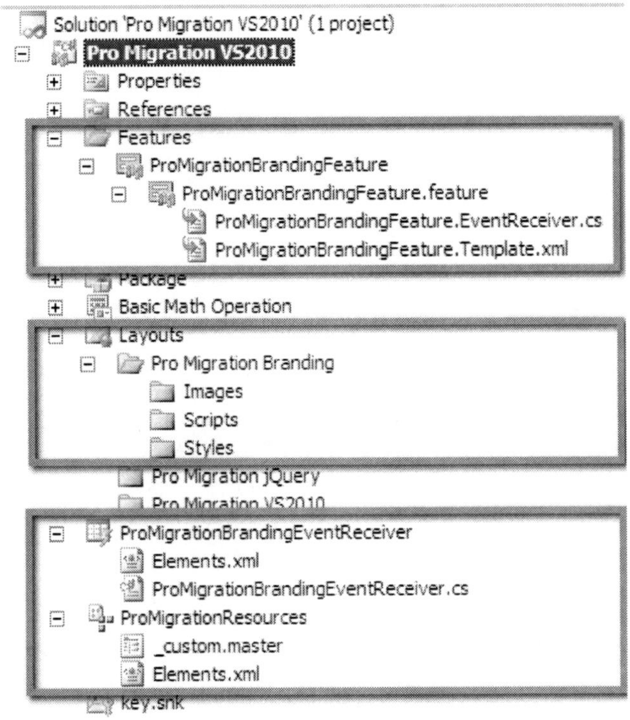

Figure 3-19. Build master page structure in Visual Studio 2010

You will have the following items in the project specific to the branding aspects:

- Layouts mapped folder, with specific folders for images, scripts, styles

- Resource folder (ProMigrationResources in this case) for your master page and its elements file

- Feature and feature receiver code to add the master page on activation or retract and apply the v4.master file when a feature is deactivated

- Specific web events receiver that would work as a feature stapler to attach the master page

You will have to map your existing files as shown in Figure 3-19. Let's now observe the contents under each of these assets. The elements file will look like Figure 3-20. Module and File elements are not new, but notice the Property Name UIVersion that is set to a value of 4. This specifies that the deployed master page is version 4, that is, a SharePoint 2010 master page.

```xml
<?xml version="1.0" encoding="utf-8"?>
<Elements xmlns="http://schemas.microsoft.com/sharepoint/">
  <Module Name="ProMigrationResources" Url="_catalogs/masterpage" Path="ProBrandingResources">
    <File Url="_custom.master" Type="GhostableInLibrary" IgnoreIfAlreadyExists="TRUE">
      <Property Name="UIVersion" Value="4"></Property>
      <Property Name="ContentTypeId" Value="0x010105"></Property>
    </File>
  </Module>
</Elements>
```

Figure 3-20. Code for the elements file

Under the event receiver, again the code logic is not special. Feature activation and deactivation events have not changed, as shown in Figures 3-21 and 3-22. You can use the `CustomMasterUrl` property to define the master page for a publishing site.

```csharp
public override void FeatureActivated(SPFeatureReceiverProperties properties)
{
    SPWeb currentWeb = properties.Feature.Parent as SPWeb;
    if (currentWeb != null)
    {
        string webAppRelativePath = currentWeb.ServerRelativeUrl;
        if (!webAppRelativePath.EndsWith("/"))
        {
            webAppRelativePath += "/";
        }

        SPFile file = currentWeb.GetFile("/_catalogs/masterpage/_custom.master");
        if (file.Exists)
        {
            if (file.CustomizedPageStatus == SPCustomizedPageStatus.Customized)
            {
                file.RevertContentStream();
            }
        }

        Uri masterUri = new Uri(currentWeb.Url + "/_catalogs/masterpage/_custom.master");

        currentWeb.MasterUrl = masterUri.AbsolutePath;
        // Very Important for Publishing Site and not required for other templates
        currentWeb.CustomMasterUrl = masterUri.AbsolutePath;
        currentWeb.UIVersion = 4;
        currentWeb.Update();
    }
}
```

Figure 3-21. Master page feature activation code

```
public override void FeatureDeactivating(SPFeatureReceiverProperties properties)
{
    SPWeb currentWeb = properties.Feature.Parent as SPWeb;
    if (currentWeb != null)
    {
        string webAppRelativePath = currentWeb.ServerRelativeUrl;
        if(!webAppRelativePath.EndsWith("/"))
        {
            webAppRelativePath += "/";
        }

        Uri masterUri = new Uri(currentWeb.Url + "/_catalogs/masterpage/v4.master");

        currentWeb.MasterUrl = masterUri.AbsolutePath;
        // Very Important for Publishing Site and not required for other templates
        currentWeb.CustomMasterUrl = masterUri.AbsolutePath;
        currentWeb.UIVersion = 4;
        currentWeb.Update();
    }
}
```

Figure 3-22. Master Page feature deactivation code

The feature stapling aspects in SharePoint 2010 have also changed. Though the feature stapling concept still exists, it's kind of obsolete, and the recommended approach is to use web event receivers. To add one such event, on a Visual Studio project, add a new event receiver. Under the customization wizard (shown in Figure 3-23), select Web Events; select the "A site was provisioned" event handler, and click Finish.

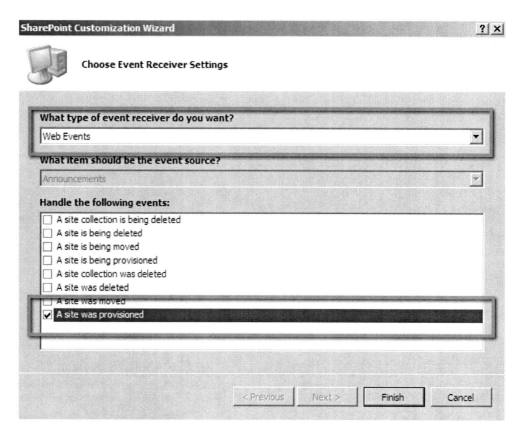

Figure 3-23. Creating web events

Once the corresponding event receiver class is created, under the WebProvisioned event, add the code shown in Figure 3-24. This event will fire whenever a new site is provisioned and apply the master page that has been choosen in the code logic.

```
/// <summary>
/// Web Events
/// </summary>
public class ProMigrationBrandingEventReceiver : SPWebEventReceiver
{
    /// <summary>
    /// A site was provisioned
    /// </summary>
    public override void WebProvisioned(SPWebEventProperties properties)
    {
        base.WebProvisioned(properties);

        SPWeb currentWeb = properties.Web;
        if (currentWeb != null)
        {
            string webAppRelativePath = currentWeb.ServerRelativeUrl;
            if (!webAppRelativePath.EndsWith("/"))
            {
                webAppRelativePath += "/";
            }

            SPFile file = currentWeb.GetFile("/_catalogs/masterpage/_custom.master");
            if (file.Exists)
            {
                if (file.CustomizedPageStatus == SPCustomizedPageStatus.Customized)
                {
                    file.RevertContentStream();
                }
            }

            Uri masterUri = new Uri(currentWeb.Url + "/_catalogs/masterpage/_custom.master");

            currentWeb.MasterUrl = masterUri.AbsolutePath;
            // Very Important for Publishing Site and not required for other templates
            currentWeb.CustomMasterUrl = masterUri.AbsolutePath;
            currentWeb.UIVersion = 4;
            currentWeb.Update();
        }
    }
}
```

Figure 3-24. Web provisioned event handler

■ **Tip** For more information specific to creating master pages, see http://msdn.microsoft.com/en-us/library/gg430141.aspx.

Summary

In this chapter, we have looked at the following (see Figure 3-25):

- Overall visual changes in themes, master pages, CSS, and jQuery customizations

- The evaluation and rendering of publishing templates

- Changes to the WCM web parts, particularly around the Content Query, Content Editor, XML Viewer, and XSLT List View web parts

- SharePoint 2010 compliance with WCAG and ARIA

- Ribbon customizations and branding your ribbon

- Migrating your existing branding artifacts

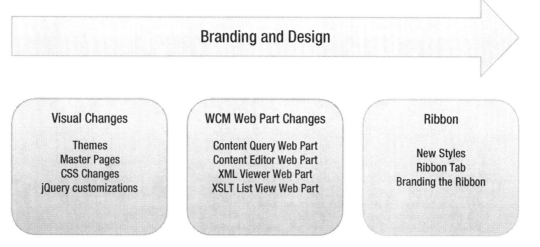

Figure 3-25. Developer Roadmap in SharePoint 2010

In the next chapter, you will learn some very good enhancements in SharePoint 2010 for savvy business developers and .NET developers. We will discuss SharePoint 2010 Designer changes and new enterprise content management (ECM) features from a business developer standpoint, as well as Visual Studio 2010, ribbon, and API changes from a .NET developer standpoint.

CHAPTER 4

Migration for the Developer

Developers working with MOSS 2007 as well as WSS 3.0 know some of the shortcomings of these products, as well as Visual Studio 2008 and associated tools, such as SharePoint Designer 2007. Usually, these were complimented by various third-party tools, such as STSDEV, WSPBUILDER, BDC Metaman, and VseWSS. In the current edition of SharePoint and its tools, these shortcomings have been very well addressed with enhancements in Visual Studio and SharePoint Designer 2010.

The greatest benefits in this version are features to help in building applications faster and easier without depending on third-party tools. At the same time, SharePoint designer 2010 has been enhanced to help both developers and power users a lot. In this chapter, you will learn about some of the features these enhancements for advanced users.

Savvy Business User Developers

In MOSS 2007, a savvy business user developer, or power user (the terms "power user" and "business user developer" are used interchangeably in this chapter) must rely heavily on developers for customizations and advanced changes on the platform. That, obviously, creates stress on both sides of the team and will usually lead to delays, dependencies, and suchlike, as you know already. In SPS 2010, this interdependency has changed somewhat, if not dramatically, in each area. In this section, you will learn how to add value to your organization as a business user developer with very little or no dependency on developers.

SharePoint Designer 2010

One of the best things that happened in the arena of tools in SharePoint 2010 is SharePoint Designer 2010 (SPD 2010). You can call it as a complete revamp over its previous edition 2007 in regards to the user interface and many enhancements. It has evolved as a powerful mechanism, wherein one can design and develop no-code solutions and rapidly meet business needs. Many areas have been improved by which you can now build many common scenarios that you would usually develop using code. Then too, SPD 2010 also helps .NET and SharePoint developers to a greater extent. You might have heard a lot of new terms either in this book or others, including "BCS," "Secured Store Services," "external lists," "external content types," and "Visio workflow design capabilities." You will also soon realize that some of these terms are familiar to you from the earlier version; however, previously, they required custom code development or the use of third-party tools.

SharePoint Designer 2010 natively supports many no-code features rather than requiring you to developing custom solutions, at least for some basic needs. For instance, to communicate with an external data source in the earlier edition, you had to write either custom code-based logic or design large XML files for Business Data Catalog (BDC). The same now can be designed using SPD 2010 without writing a single line of code or touching any XML files. Also, not only will you be able to connect to data sources but you will be able to design and enable operations, such as create, read, update, and delete (CRUD), over the data sources you connect to.

In MOSS 2007 master pages, site pages written in HTML were basically designed with tables, and once they were opened, edited, and saved in SharePoint Designer 2007, the HTML, though undisturbed, became very *unclear*. To save the files and repurpose them, you had to first clean them up. SharePoint 2010 pages are mostly div-based HTML. And guess what? Even when you open them in SPD 2010 and edit them, you will still have a clean version of the files.

Finally, without limiting the capabilities of SPD 2010, you can hand over the customization by exporting them to developers so that further development and changes can be achieved using Visual Studio 2010. This is another big leap in handshaking between two different roles and teams. For example, a business user developer can design the workflows in Visio, bring them to SPD 2010, and then export them to developers for further changes. There are many such instances where interoperability with Visual Studio is possible that was lacking in the earlier version.

Figure 4-1 shows how SharePoint Designer 2010 looks, and in the next section, we will delve deeper into how some of these aspects work in real time.

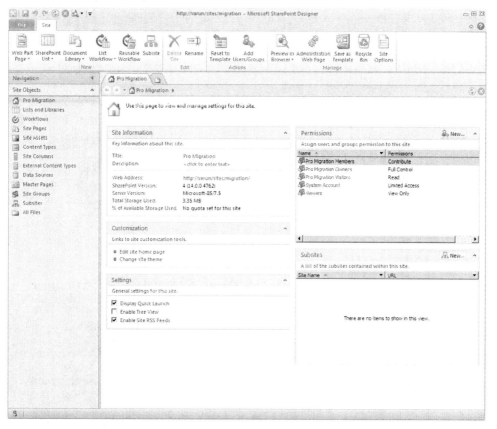

Figure 4-1. *SharePoint Designer 2010*

If you are concerned about the power of SharePoint Designer 2010, you can control the customizations at the web application level in Central Administration, as shown in Figure 4-2.

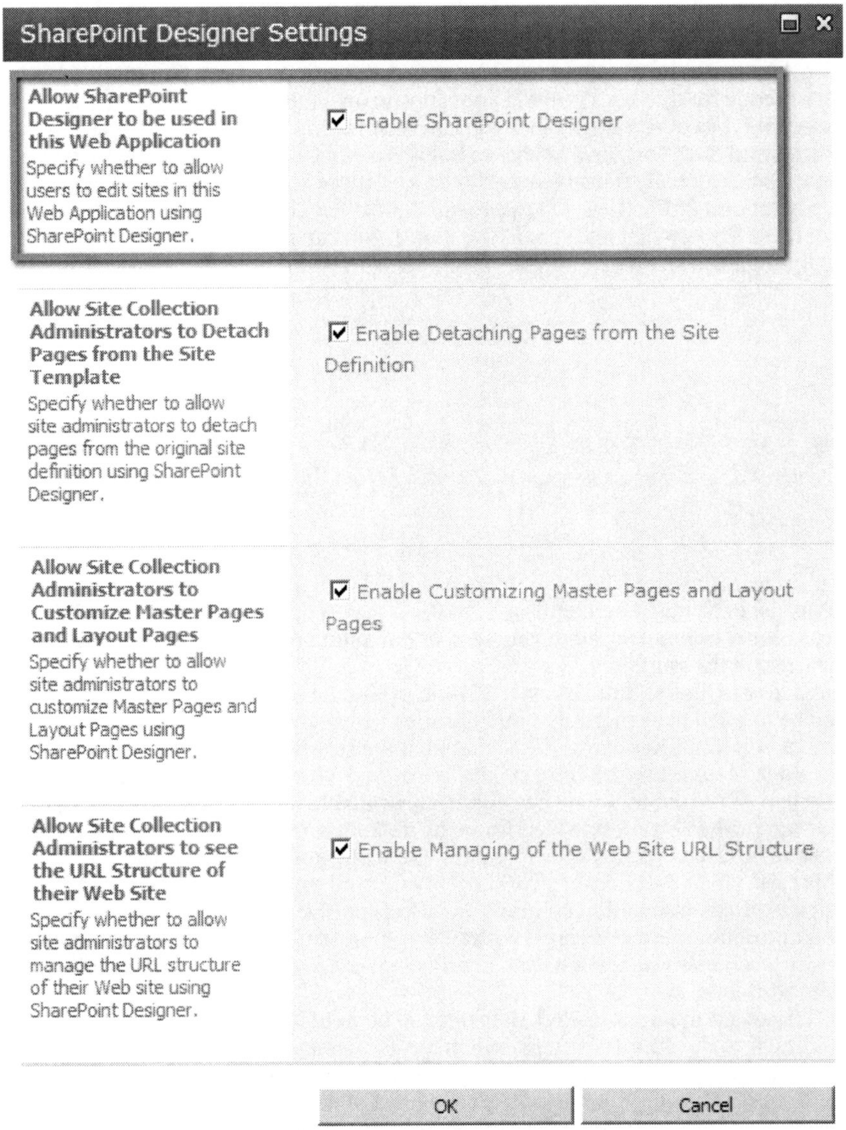

SharePoint Designer Settings

Allow SharePoint Designer to be used in this Web Application Specify whether to allow users to edit sites in this Web Application using SharePoint Designer.	☑ Enable SharePoint Designer
Allow Site Collection Administrators to Detach Pages from the Site Template Specify whether to allow site administrators to detach pages from the original site definition using SharePoint Designer.	☑ Enable Detaching Pages from the Site Definition
Allow Site Collection Administrators to Customize Master Pages and Layout Pages Specify whether to allow site administrators to customize Master Pages and Layout Pages using SharePoint Designer.	☑ Enable Customizing Master Pages and Layout Pages
Allow Site Collection Administrators to see the URL Structure of their Web Site Specify whether to allow site administrators to manage the URL structure of their Web site using SharePoint Designer.	☑ Enable Managing of the Web Site URL Structure

OK   Cancel

Figure 4-2. Enabling SharePoint Designer settings for a web application in Central Administration

SharePoint Designer Workflows

We can define a *workflow* as a simple process that is followed while performing any specific task. *A workflow is like a flowchart.* There can be many different levels of steps that you can assign to tasks or jobs, but when it comes to SharePoint, certain out-of–the-box workflows can be attached to various

SharePoint types, such as lists, libraries, content types, and list items. You can define, design, and automate these workflows. Workflows can be simple or complex, depending on the business requirements. Advanced workflows can be designed using Visual Studio and Windows Workflow Foundation, which are out of scope for this book; we will concentrate on what SPD 2010 can facilitate.

To begin, there are different types of workflows that you can select using SPD 2010, such as List Workflow, Reusable Workflow, and Site Workflow, as shown in Figure 4-3. Out-of-the-box workflows that are available are categorized as globally reusable workflows, and these are the ones available in MOSS 2007 but rebuilt for SharePoint 2010. These are Approval, Collect Feedback, Collect Signature, and Publishing Approval. Using these (by copying and modifying them), you can build your own custom workflows, rather than beginning from scratch.

Figure 4-3. Different types of workflows

You might have used a *list workflow* in MOSS 2007; it is associated with a list or library and has access to the items within the list or library. Each of these workflows is very specific to one list or library and cannot be shared across others or repurposed. If you need to have similar functionality on another list or library, you have to re-create the workflow.

The *reusable workflow* is new in SharePoint Designer 2010. Workflows of this type are created at the site collection level and can be applied to as many lists and libraries within the context of the site collection (and sites within) as you like. They can also be created at the subsite level, but in that case, they are limited to that site alone. Reusable workflows can be associated with a particular content type, with those columns that are part of the content type automatically available under the workflow when reused for other sites. However, primarily reusable workflows, by default, provide columns that are very common across all the lists and libraries. To add additional new columns, you can choose to have association columns. In this case, when the reusable workflow is exported from one site and uploaded and activated on a different site, these association columns are also exported.

Site workflows, as the name defines, are associated with sites rather than lists, document libraries, or their items. Since they are site level, many operations and actions that are available for a list workflow are not be available for a site workflow.

When any of these workflows are to be associated, they need to be built first with the help of certain building blocks. These are similar to the flowchart steps, which are associated with actions, which are, in turn, associated with rules or conditions. Hence, every step with any kind change (present, continuous, or past) is considered an *event*. For example, Start and Stop are events of the workflow.

A workflow can be triggered either automatically or manually. Also, as part of the workflows, you have actions, conditions, and steps, which are the building blocks of the workflow. *Actions* are performed tasks that occur at every event or during an event; for example, an action could be as simple as sending an e-mail. A number of predefined actions are available out of the box from SPD 2010. Each action can be related to a condition. A *condition* is a rule or set of rules, for example, "send an e-mail only when it is approved." In this case, approval becomes the condition. And finally, a condition can have multiple *steps* involved. Considering the same e-mail example, after approval from business office A, the steps might be sending the e-mail to business offices B, C, and D.

Since reusable workflows are new in this version, we will now demonstrate to you how they can be created and reused:

1. First, launch SPD 2010, and click Open Site. In the Open Site dialogue box, type the web application or site URL in the "Site name" text box, and click Open.

2. After the site opens in the designer and all the site objects are loaded, click Workflows on the Site Objects menu.

3. From the ribbon menu under New, click Reusable Workflow.

4. In the Create Reusable Workflow dialogue box, enter a valid name, and provide a description relevant to the workflow, as shown in Figure 4-4.

5. From the available content types, you can either pick a specific content type or choose All. Choosing All will simply make the workflow available to any content type under the site, and choosing a specific one would obviously limit to that content type. For this exercise, pick the Document in the Content Type drop-down, and click Ok.

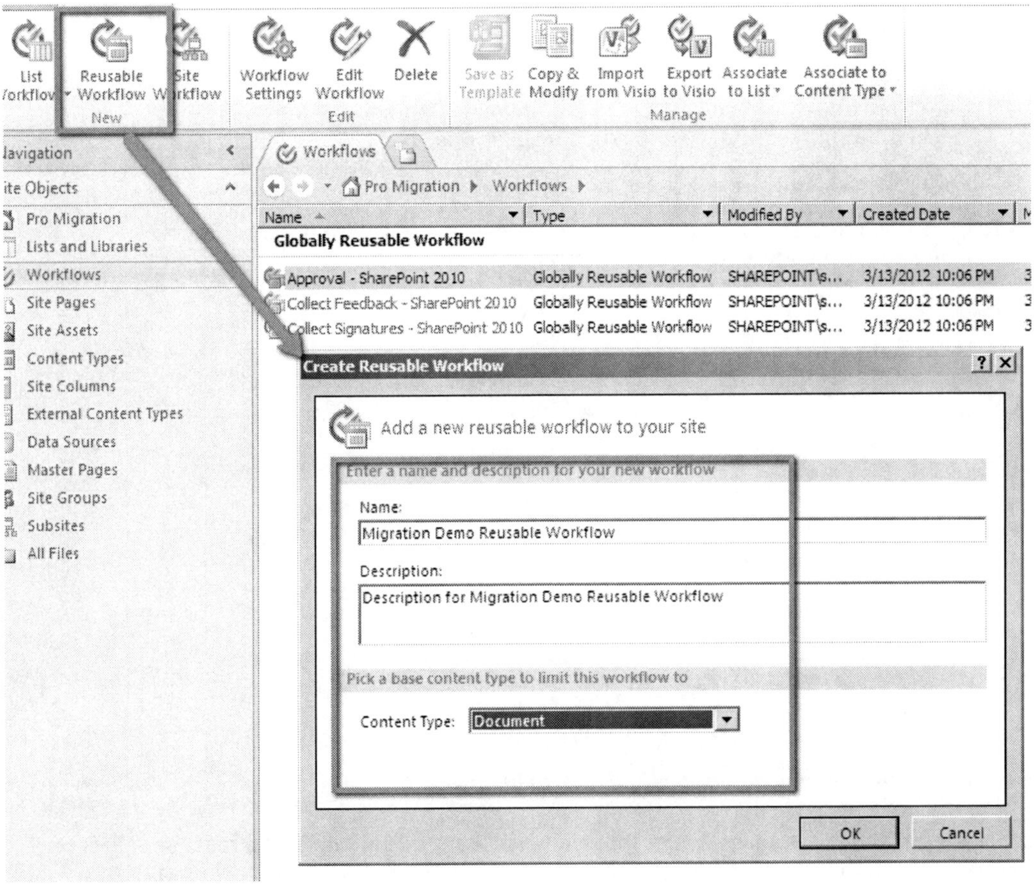

Figure 4-4. Creating a reusable workflow

6. The Workflow editor will open, with Step 1 ready to be defined.

7. As soon as you click Step 1, all the buttons on the ribbon will be enabled, especially Conditions, Actions, and Steps. There are many out-of-the-box conditions and actions that you can choose under each step. You can either start typing in the step if you already know the actions or select one of the actions from the ribbon.

8. Click Condition, and from the common conditions, select "if any value equals value."

9. In the Step 1, condition click the "value" link, and under "define workflow lookup," select Current Item under the "Data source" and Title under "field from source." Click the OK button.

10. Click the "value" link, and choose Display Builder for this parameter.

11. In the String Builder field, type the text Demo Text, and click the OK button.

12. Under the Actions menu, choose Set Field in Current Item, click the "field" link, and choose Title.

13. Click the " value" link, and select Current Item in "Data source" and Name in "Field from source" under the lookup for single line of text. Click OK.

14. From "core actions," select Log to History List.

15. Click the "message" link, and type the text Message Logged from Demo. Your completed workflow editor should look Figure 4-5.

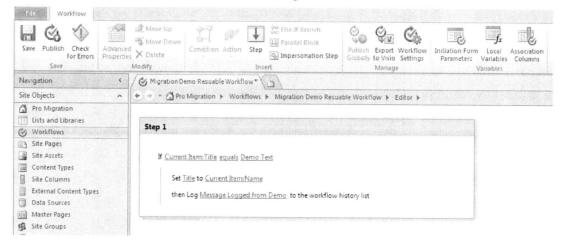

Figure 4-5. Designing workflow conditions and actions in SPD 2010

Notice, on the ribbon's Manage group, the Publish Globally button (only on a root site collection, and not on a subsite). Once you publish globally, a reusable workflow is accesible by the current site and all its subsites. If you would like it to be available globablly, simply click Publish Globally. Click OK when prompted with the message about whether you are sure. This workflow will be then published and added to the Globally Reusable Worflow options, as shown in Figure 4-6.

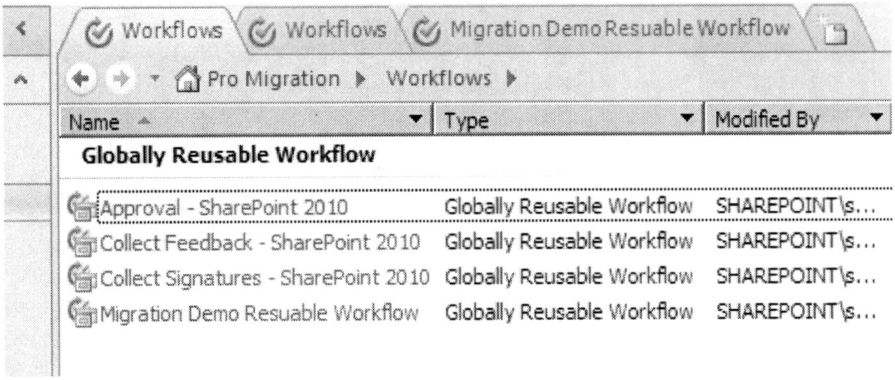

Figure 4-6. Globally Reusable Workflow options

Launch the SharePoint site in a browser, and access any library of the document type, because the globally created workflow is associated for document content type. In this example, let's use Shared Documents library; access the document library, click the Library tab under Library Tools, and then click Workflow Settings. Under the workflows to be configured, choose the Document type. Then click "Add a workflow," and from the Add a Workflow screen, choose the previously created Migration Demo Reusable workflow. Type a unique name, leave the task and history lists as they are, and under Start Options, click "Start this workflow when a new item is created," as shown in Figure 4-7. Click the OK button.

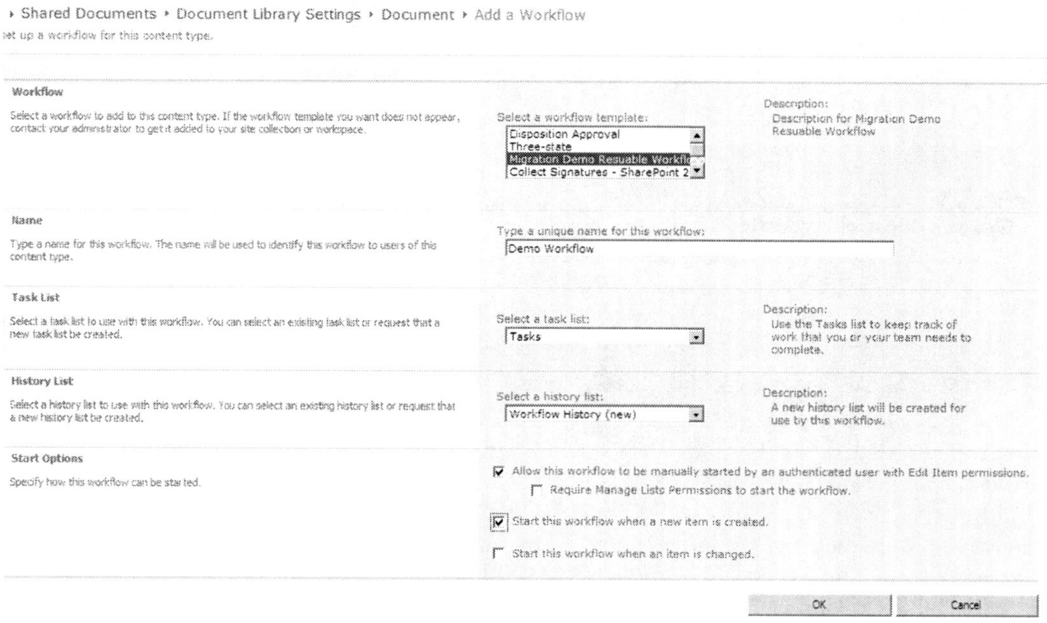

Figure 4-7. *Using the globally reusable workflow created in SPD 2010*

Now, upload a new document to the document library, and edit the item. Set the Title value to Demo Text (since that is the condition), and run the workflow manually. You will receive the status to be completed on the workflow. Return to the document item, edit or view the item to see that the Title is now set to the value of the Name column. Set the workflow's actions so that it kicks off automatically. You can also reuse this workflow with any other document library.

SharePoint 2010 Enterprise and Standard editions have another great feature—editing forms. Unlike in the previous version of MOSS 2007, the edit, new, and display forms are now available as Infopath forms (.xsn) and can be edited using Office Infopath 2010. However, this feature is not available in SharePoint Foundation 2010 edition and these edit forms are available as .aspx files that can be edited using SharePoint Designer itself. We will now discuss how Infopath can be used to edit the workflow forms.

Office Infopath 2010

Like all other areas of improvement, Office InfoPath 2010 has been enhanced a lot over its earlier version, InfoPath 2007. Using InfoPath 2010, we will now customize the workflow form. First, install InfoPath 2010 (x86/x64) if you have not already done so. Return to SharePoint Designer 2010, and click Migration Demo Reusable Workflow. Under the list of available forms, notice the Migration Demo Reusable Workflow.xsn. Clicking the .xsn file should launch the InfoPath 2010 Editor. From the ribbon, click the Insert tab, and click Picture. Select any relevant image from your hard disk, and click the Insert button, which inserts the image onto the InfoPath screen. Click the Start button, and from the Control Tools Properties tab, change the label. Change the label of the Cancel button as well. Once you are satisfied with the changes, click the save icon or save link from the backstage window. This step is important before publishing the InfoPath form. Once you save the form locally, you can return to the backstage window and click Quick Publish. You are then offered a success or failure message box. Click Ok. Your completed InfoPath form should look similar to the one shown in Figure 4-8.

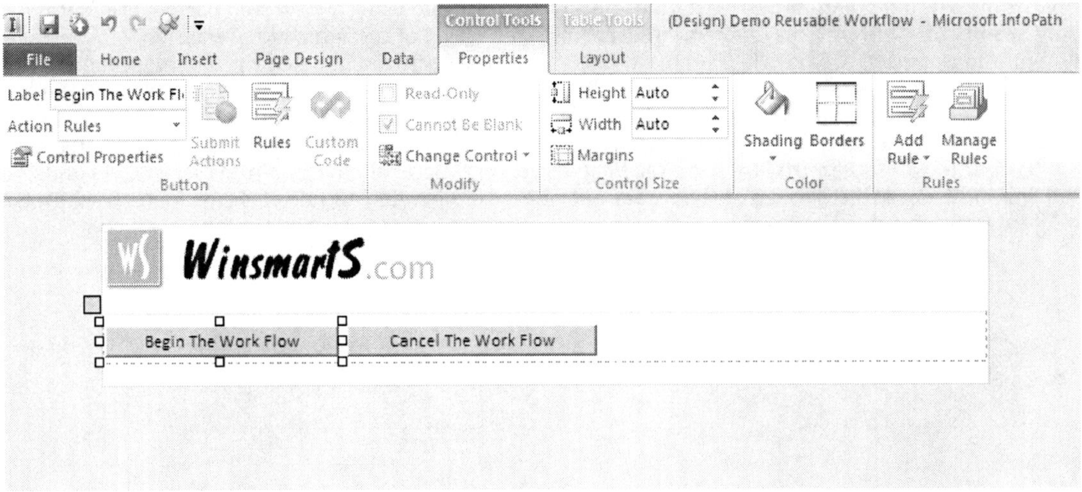

Figure 4-8. Editing workflow forms in Infopath 2010

Return to the SharePoint site and to the document library where you previously set up the workflow. From the content menu of the document item, choose workflows. By clicking the available workflow (in this case Demo Workflow), you are presented with the updated screen, as shown in Figure 4-9.

Figure 4-9. Edited and published workflow form in the browser

---

■ **Note** Form customizations can be performed on any list or document forms, not just on the workflow forms as we just did.

Integrating Visio Diagrams and Visio Services with Workflows

Visio services are newly introduced as one of the service applications in SharePoint 2010. This service application facilitates loading Visio diagrams on a SharePoint site using a Visio web part that renders using Silverlight. Visio services before used to require some level of customization, security configurations, and so on. We will limit our discussion of Visio services in this chapter, but we highly recommend you to read Chapter 2 in *Pro SharePoint 2010 Business Intelligence Solutions* by Sahil Malik, Srini Sistla, and Steve Wright (Apress, 2010) for a deep dive into Visio and Visio Services.

OK, let's assume that you are well versed in using Visio diagrams and that you are a business user who has created a simple workflow from the Visio template "Microsoft SharePoint Workflow (US units)". That workflow would have a start and terminators, one condition, and couple of action items, as shown in Figure 4-10.

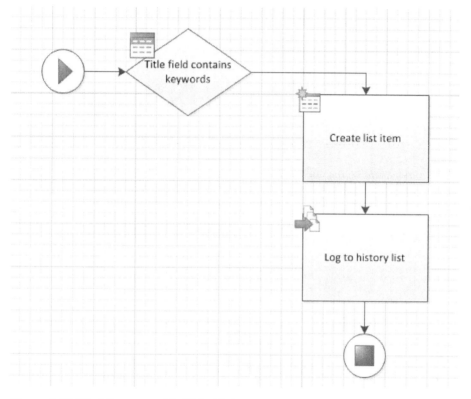

Figure 4-10. Workflow created in Visio 2010

First, save the Visio file locally as a `.vsd` file. Next, from the Process tab, click the Export button under SharePoint Workflow group. Save the file as a Visio Workflow Interchange (`.vwi`) file. When importing Visio workflows, saving the file in `.vwi` format is important. You now provide this file to your designer or business user developer, and the developer will import it using SharePoint Designer. Launch SPD 2010, and click Workflows on the Site Object menu. From the ribbon, click the Import from Visio button under the Manage group, and locate the recently saved `.vwi` file. Click the Next button. You can give the workflow a name, and select the type of workflow to import as. Click Finish, as shown in Figure 4-11.

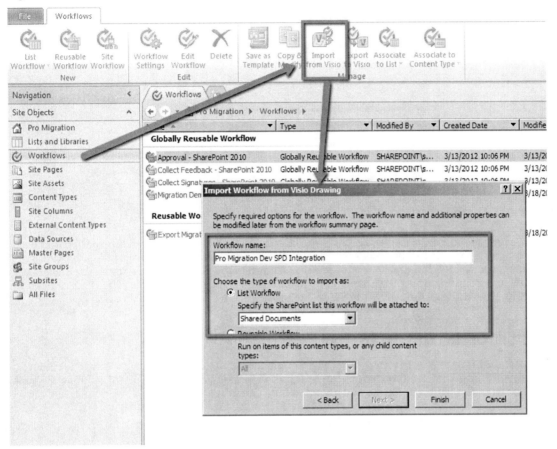

Figure 4-11. *Importing Visio workflows in SPD 2010*

The Visio workflow diagram will be interpreted to the actual workflow conditions and actions, where you can define the conditions, actions, and log messages, as shown in Figure 4-12. Once you are finished, you can check for errors and then publish the same using Publish button as shown in Figure 4-12.

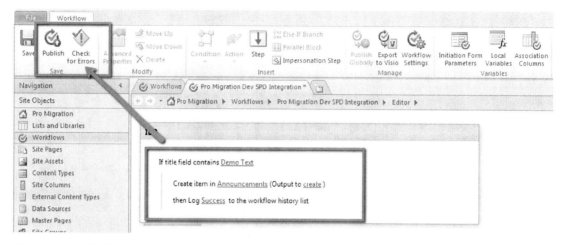

Figure 4-12. Checking for errors and publishing imported workflows

The reverse mechanism is also possible. Workflows designed in SPD 2010 can be exported into Visio formats as well. From the ribbon, click the Export to Visio button under the Manage group, provide a valid name for the .vwi file, and save it to local disk. Return to the Visio client, and under the Process tab, click the Import button under the SharePoint workflow group, and choose the file you just exported from SPD 2010. Visio will load the .vwi file in the design mode for you to make any further changes.

Exporting Customizations As .wsp Files

You have already seen how to export workflows to Visio format in the earlier section. With SharePoint Designer 2010, workflow customizations can be exported from one site and imported on another as well. They can be exported in .wsp format and imported into Visual Studio 2010 as well. Workflows that are defined as reusable can be exported using the Save as Template option shown in Figure 4-13.

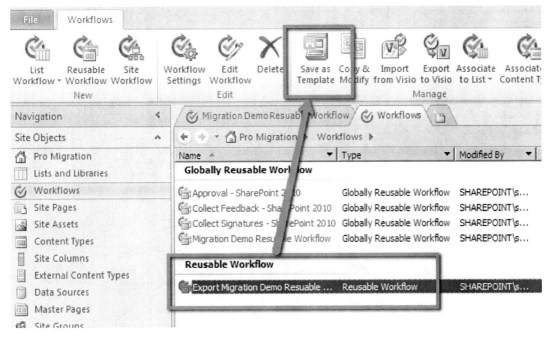

Figure 4-13. Saving and exporting workflows as templates (.wsp files)

■ **Note** Workflows defined as "global" cannot be exported. In such instances, use the Copy & Modify feature and subsequently save the workflow as a template.

Saved templates can be accessed under the Site Assets library of the current site collection. A message is prompted as soon as export is successful. From the Site Assets library, you can simply export the file to your local disk. This exported reusable workflow is saved as a `.wsp` file, which can then be imported back into Visual Studio 2010 using the Import Reusable Workflow template, as shown in Figure 4-14. Once the workflow is imported and customizations are added via code, you can redeploy the project to the SharePoint site and associate the workflow. You can alternatively run the workflow settings wizard and set it to automatically associate as well.

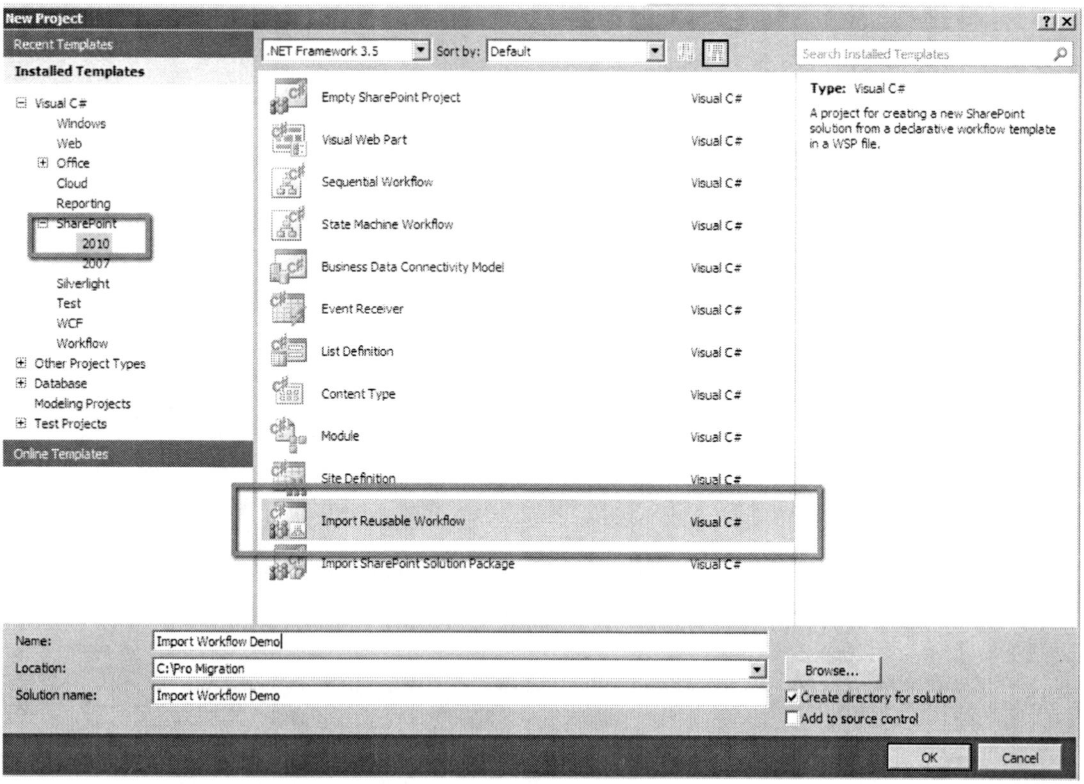

Figure 4-14. Importing reusable workflows in Visual Studio 2010

Exporting customizations can be done at the site level as well. In MOSS 2007, you have the option to export the site as Site Template file (.stp); in SharePoint 2010, you can now export the site in the .wsp format. In fact, SharePoint 2010 does away with STP in favor of WSP. Exporting, or selecting Save as Template, can be done either using SPD 2010 or from the Site Actions menu under the site. This site template is saved to the user's Solution Gallery, as shown in Figure 4-15, and can be downloaded easily. You can import or upload this package file to another site to the Solution Gallery and simply activate the package to use the template while creating another site, as shown in Figure 4-16.

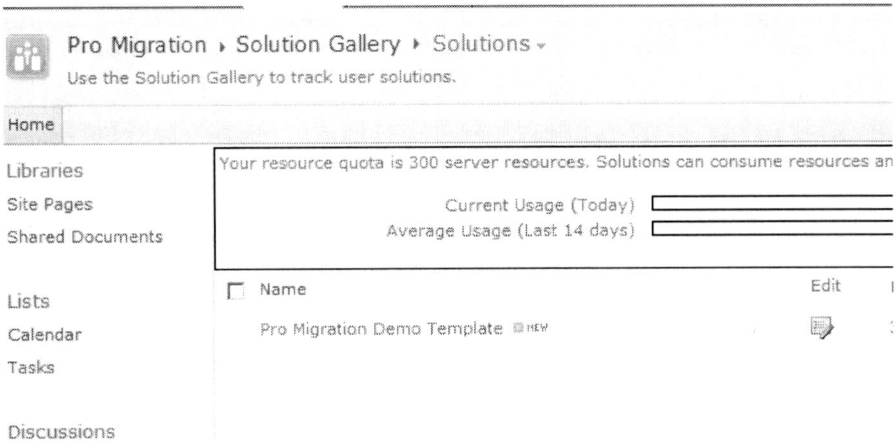

Figure 4-15. *Saved site templates to the Solution Gallery as .wsp files*

The exported package file (shown in Figure 4-16) consists of all the lists and libraries and any customizations that you have made on the site and shall be provisioned back as-is on the imported site.

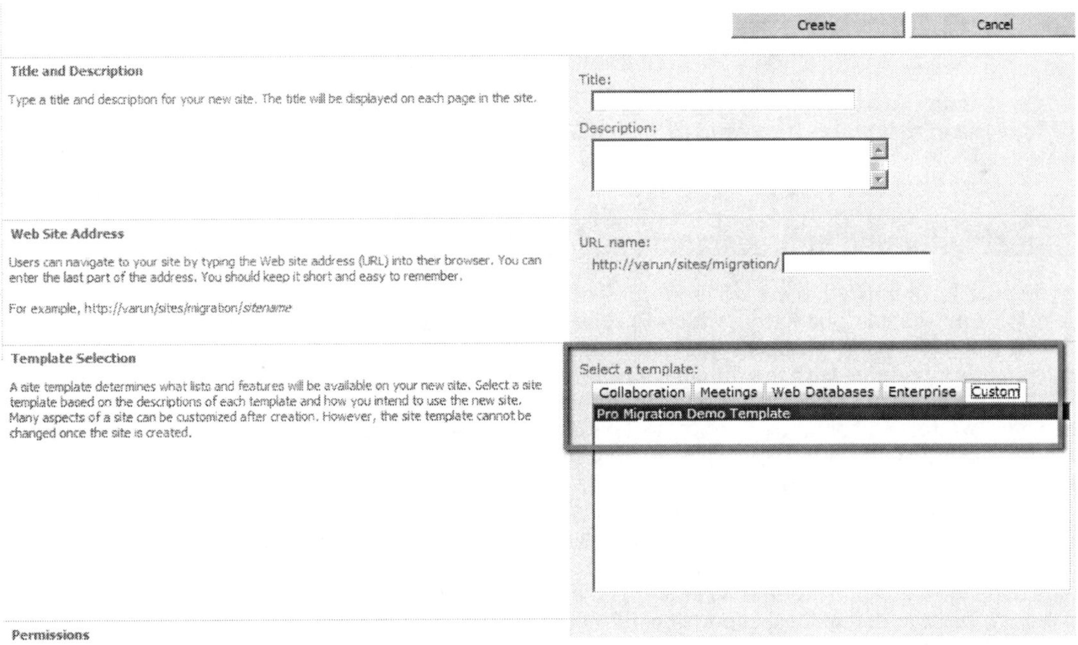

Figure 4-16. *Using the saved site template to create a site*

Another important aspect of SharePoint 2010 is integrating business requirements with SharePoint. While enterprise content management (ECM) in MOSS 2007 is the key factor for success, in SharePoint 2010, ECM became even better with enhancements and new functionalities.

Exploring the New ECM Features

First of all, enterprise content management (ECM) is a huge concept by itself and explaining ECM features in SPS 2010 is either a separate chapter or a miniature book. So we will try to cover the most important and relevant concepts in this section. For general reference, you can read the article `http://msdn.microsoft.com/en-us/library/ee559353.aspx`, and for more detailed information, read Chapter 8 in *Microsoft SharePoint 2010 Building Solutions for SharePoint 2010* by Sahil Malik (Apress, 2010).

For starters, let's define "ECM" as managing the data that is on a large scale or defining or structuring data in a procedural or planned mechanism. This logic can be applied for any level, for tasks as simple as sending e-mail to creating a complex model of managing organization metadata. Either way, it's about how your content is managed and the ways to manage it. And when we say "data" or "content," that can be any documents, videos, record items, or similar files and can be compared to many other things.

However, there were some questions or conerns with ECM features in MOSS 2007 such as:

- How good is it at handling and managing content?

- How much better are the implementation options?

- And how does it best work overall as an tool for the end user?

Considering these questions, SharePoint 2010 has made tremendous enhancements overall in the ECM space and that makes it superior to MOSS 2007. Let's discuss on how certain areas have been improvised.

Content Authoring Improvements and Analytics

As you must have noticed, there is a huge uplift of the user experience in SharePoint 2010. First, there is the newly introduced ribbon, from which you can perform actions within the same page without moving out of it. Then too, page-editing capabilities with an HTML editor and cross-browser compatibility is pretty tightly integrated with the ribbon control. The page editing experience changed as well. You now have very few postbacks, and they also are performed fewer times, and only when needed. Then, you have new controls and types of libraries, such as embedded video, web asset editors, and asset libraries, that are capable of delivering good visuals and skins with streaming content, searching and sorting the assets, increased storage capacities, and so on.

Usage analysis in MOSS 2007 is now part of Web Analytics, which is, by itself, a service application in SPS 2010. Reports can be delivered on the sites that can be ad hoc or scheduled, depending on the various settings including any metric level changes. These reports can be obtained at the site, site collection, and web application level and run on different categories, such as traffic, search, and inventory. You can define these reports on different models, including trends or ranking basis. Finally, a few out-of-the-box web parts can deliver popular content on a site.

Managed Metadata Service

Managed metadata services never existed before, and you will notice that this term is used more than once in this and other chapters of this book. Simply put, that's because of their significant role in SPS 2010, and they are among the reasons why SPS 2010 is very popular, especially with respect to ECM. First, consider these questions: In how many ways can data can be defined? Is there any hierarchy for the data? And can it be managed centrally? And can this data be used on any items in SharePoint as attributes? If the answer to all these questions is "yes," you're working with managed metadata. And the service that enables the managed metadata is the Managed Metadata Service application in SPS 2010. When you begin defining the data, there is always a way to structure it and define a hierarchical level tag to it. For instance, if the United States, Germany, and Canada are countries, they fall respectively as parents to cities—Washington D.C., Berlin, and Ottawa. Here, you can tag the United States Germany, and Canada as Country, and Washington D.C., Berlin, and Ottawa as City, and you can create a hierarchy between them when you define the data. This logical definition technically is called *terms,* and a group of these terms become a *term set;* both terms and term sets are grouped as *term stores.* Similarly, all the cities in United States can be grouped, as can all states. Such hierarchy and grouping can occur and grow to any number of levels in an organization and can be applied to any type of information or data. In SharePoint sites, these terms can be either globally or locally defined, and as they are named, they are scoped the same way. All this naming and grouping is referred to as *metadata taxonomy.* You can define these terms and term sets from the interface known as Term Store Management Tool, as shown in Figure 4-17. For more information on managed metadata services, see http://technet.microsoft.com/en-us/library/ee424402.aspx.

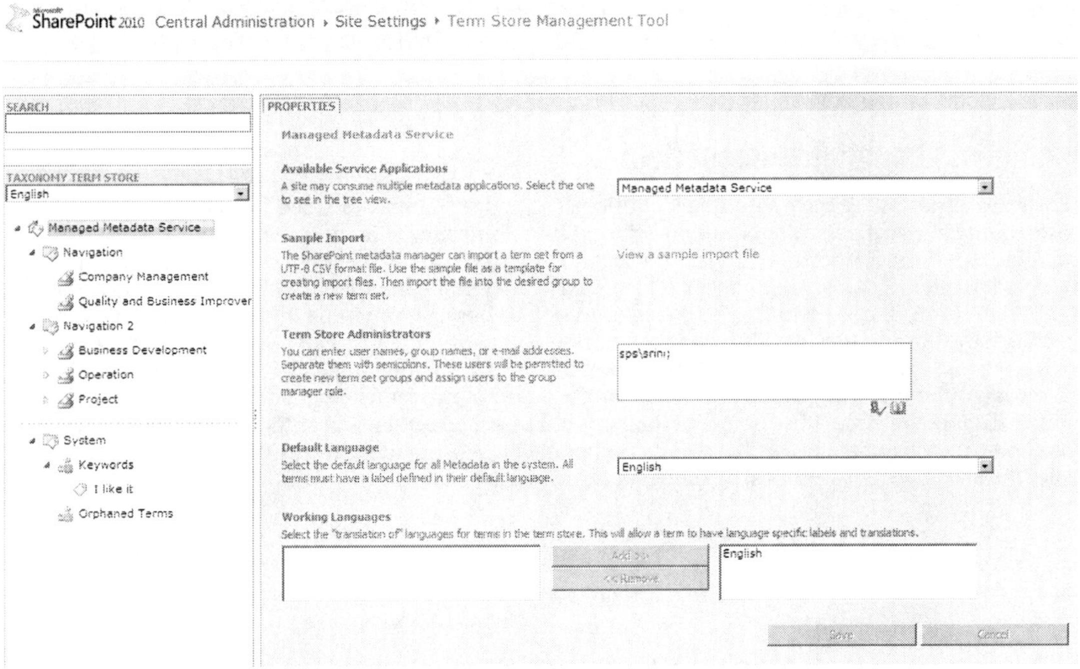

Figure 4-17. Term Store Management Tool

Enterprise Content Types

Content types are an integral part of managing your data. They are very powerful yet sometimes become rusty if you don't know what you are dealing with. Creating content types is not a big deal but understanding what they are is very important. Further, where and when to create and use content types becomes another important factor. Putting all this aside, content types in MOSS 2007 are very much limited to the site collection level. If you need to create a similar content type in a different site collection, you will end up creating a new one there. In SharePoint 2010, you can now create a content type at the enterprise level (or rather, technically, you create it in a content type *hub* and then push it to whatever site collection you need either in the same or in a different farm). This is all achieved via managed metadata services, which allow syndication across sites, site collections, web applications, and farms. At the root of any site collection level (define it as a hub), you will have to activate the new Content Type Syndication Hub feature, and at the other (listener) site collection or site, you need to activate the TaxonomyFieldAdded feature. Then, you can decide on what content type you would like to publish from the hub to the receiver site collections, and the receivers automatically reflect the changes.

■ **Note** Content types at the listener or subsite level are read only and cannot be changed. They can coexist with the general or local content types, and local content types can inherit from enterprise content types.

Use the feature ID 73EF14B1-13A9-416b-A9B5-ECECA2B0604C for TaxonomyFieldAdded during activation instead of the feature name. You can use either STSADM or a PowerShell command to activate.

Document IDs and Document Sets

It is always important to have a unique identifier (ID) for documents uploaded to SharePoint—the reason being that, if a document is uploaded to a SharePoint site, its identity, accessibility, and scalability are rather important, not just the location of the library where it is residing. Similarly, it is important to identify a document when it is moved from one site to other or from one library to other. In MOSS 2007, each item is identified by the column ID and library containing the document. This is very specific to the library level. Another document or item in another library can have the same ID value (which is an integer), and the only differentiation is the library name. In SPS 2010, document provide a unique identifier for an uploaded document, and it does not matter where the document is uploaded or located. The IDs become more or less permanent links, and documents bear the ID even when moved from one library or site to other. To use this functionality, activate the feature Document ID Service under the site collection features, as shown in Figure 4-18.

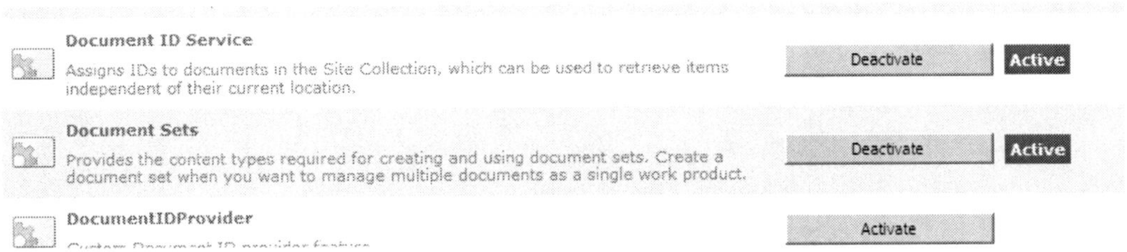

Figure 4-18. Document ID Service and Document Sets site collection features

Once the Document ID Service feature is activated, a Document ID column is added to the document library. As and when a document is uploaded, it is assigned a unique ID, as shown in Figure 4-19. This document can now be accessed via the unique ID, such as `http://{sharepointsite}/_layouts/DocIdRedir.aspx?ID=XWQXDJRV7M27-1-1`.

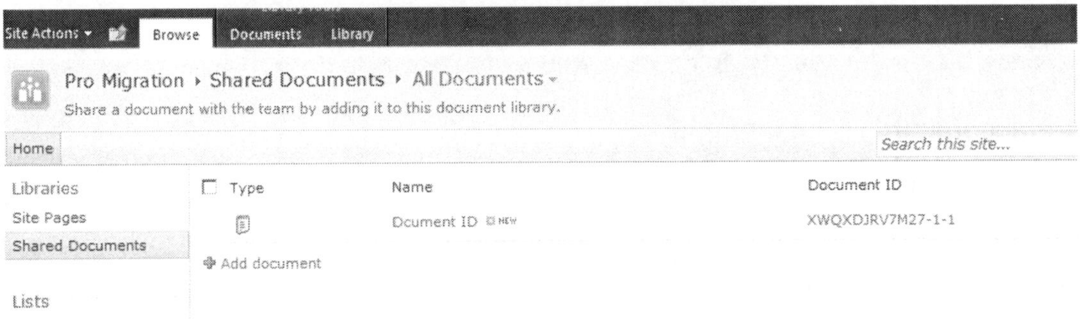

Figure 4-19. Document ID column under Libraries

What if you want to logically group some set of documents? Well, you can live with the concept of folders, as in MOSS 2007, but then, that's the end of the grouping. The *document sets* in SPS 2010 are far beyond just making documents a group. First of all, you are making them a *set* of documents. Second, you are giving them a home welcome page, describing the set, and so on. Third, a document set is implemented as a content type, which means is you get all the powers of the content type, such as versioning, workflows, and policies, as soon as you add the specific content type to the library. To create document sets, activate the site collection feature Document Sets. Once you activate the feature and add the "document set" content type to the document library, you will be able to create a new document set as shown in Figure 4-20. The other factor to notice about the document set is that it has a unique document ID, as we discussed earlier.

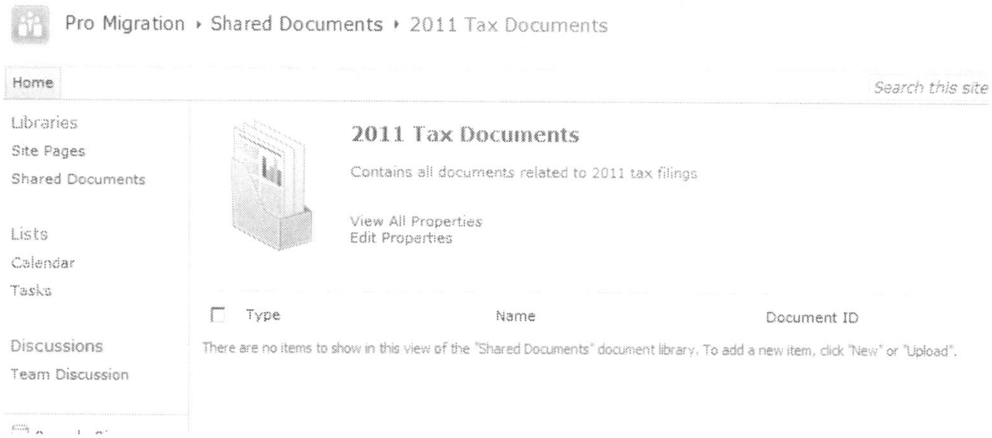

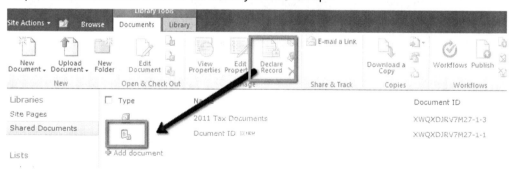

Figure 4-20. Document sets

In-Place Records Management

In MOSS 2007, records management exists but is limited to only the Record Center Site template. If you need to mark a document as a record, you create a site using Record Center Site template and add certain policies. Then, you are able to mark the documents as a record. While the same exist in SharePoint 2010 as well, in-place records management facilitates allow you to mark documents as records on any site, even one not provisioned using the Record Center Site template. To use in-place record management, you will have to activate the In Place Records Management site collection feature. You can define the record declaration settings, rules, restrictions, and auditing settings at the site collection level and, in turn, configure document libraries to inherit these settings by default. The other way is to change the settings at the document library level to allow manual changes. With either of these settings in place, you will be able to set a document as a record. In the document library, select the item or document you would like to mark as a record, and from the ribbon, under Document tab's Manage group, click the Declare Record button. Once you mark the document, you will notice a record lock item on the document, as shown in the Figure 4-21. For an overview of records management, see http://technet.microsoft.com/en-us/library/cc261982.aspx.

Figure 4-21. Declaring and item or document as a record

With all these enhancements, you may notice that there has been a huge investment in not just the ECM features but the platform itself. Switching gears a bit, .NET developers (unlike the SharePoint developers) always resist adapting to SharePoint technologies and developing solutions on the SharePoint platform. When MOSS 2007 was launched, there was a lot to learn and understand, but very few resources were available. And Visual Studio did not have enough tools to fire start developers. Though there are extensions to Visual Studio, it was not always convenient, and you need to have at least two tools over the top of Visual Studio 2008.

.NET Developers

Visual Studio Extensions for Windows SharePoint Services (VSeWSS), WSPBuilder, and STSDEV are some of the extensions for Visual Studio 2008 that developers had to have while developing custom development solutions for MOSS 2007. While VSeWSS provides many SharePoint templates for use, it was a separate installation over Visual Studio, as were WSPBuilder and STSDEV.

Microsoft enhanced Visual Studio 2010 to such an extent that almost all the developer requirements are addressed. The former VSeWSS templates are now an integral part of Visual Studio 2010, and hence, there is no requirement for additional tools' installation. Similarly, developing a `.wsp` file is a piece of cake this time around. Essentially, Visual Studio 2010 brings out-of-the-box SharePoint 2010 development integrated into the IDE. In the next section, you'll see what Visual Studio 2010 can power you with.

SharePoint 2010 Development Tools

SharePoint Server 2010 can now be installed on a client operating system, such as Windows 7 or Vista (64 bit only). This means that developers do not need to have a virtualized environment for developing applications on SharePoint. However, we highly recommend using one because of its obvious advantages. To set up a developer environment, you will have to first go through some of the steps that are discussed in the article at `http://msdn.microsoft.com/en-us/library/ee554869(office.14).aspx`. Then, you can install Visual Studio 2010, as well as the Microsoft SharePoint 2010 Software Development Kit (SDK) `www.microsoft.com/download/en/details.aspx?displaylang=en&id=12323`. Once you have installed your preferred choices, you can launch Visual Studio 2010. However, here are two very important points to consider. First, always run Visual Studio as an administrator. And second, SharePoint supports only .NET Framework 3.5, so build your applications with the target framework as 3.5 only. Usually, there is no need to install any other tools in addition to what Visual Studio provides natively, from SharePoint development standpoint. However, many periodic updates and add-ins are released regularly by Microsoft and so its recommended to have them installed.

Visual Studio 2010

With Visual Studio, you can develop applications based on either MOSS 2007 or SharePoint 2010 in the same sandbox. However, you cannot have both MOSS 2007 and SharePoint 2010 installed in the same box. Again, as a recap, before getting into developing with Visual Studio 2010, these are some of the pain points for MOSS 207 with Visual Studio 2008:

- Relying heavily on Visual Studio extensions and tools for Office in case of WSS 3.0 and MOSS 2007

- Extensively using third-party or community tools, such as those developed and available via CodePlex

- Creating the project structure based on the community tools and understanding the folder structures

- Creating and editing manifest files manually

- Creating and editing CAML files manually

- Building solution package files using community tools or manually

Of course, many more limitations exist. With the arrival of Visual Studio 2010, not only these have been addressed, but many other changes have been introduced. But first, when you launch Visual Studio 2010, you'll notice the default templates shown in Figure 4-22.

■ **Note** One additional installation we recommend is Visual Studio 2010 SharePoint Power Tools (http://visualstudiogallery.msdn.microsoft.com/8e602a8c-6714-4549-9e95-f3700344b0d9). These tools contain the Sandboxed Visual Web part, which you will learn more about in the next section.

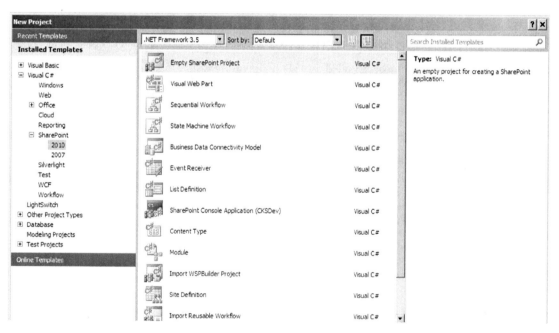

Figure 4-22. Visual Studio 2010 SharePoint templates

To understand the capabilities of Visual Studio 2010, we will walk you through a sample project here and then explain in detail some of the very good features.

Right click on Visual Studio 2010 icon or from program files and select

1. "Run as Administrator," and launch Visual Studio 2010. From the available Installed Templates, select 2010 under the SharePoint category.

2. Select .NET Framework as 3.5. Choose the Empty SharePoint Project type; provide a valid Name, Location, and Solution Name, and click on OK.

3. In the SharePoint Customization Wizard window, select "Deploy as a farm solution", and click the Finish button (we will discuss sandboxed solutions later in this chapter). A project will be created for you, and it will be prepopulated with references to SharePoint Server APIs, an empty feature, and a package.

4. Right-click the project, and click Add. Notice that you have Mapped Folders now available (as marked in Figure 4-22). These mapped folders, when chosen with either images or layouts, are actually mapped to the {SharePoint root} images and layouts folders, respectively. When you choose SharePoint Mapped Folder, you will be prompted with a window that shows all the folders under the {SharePoint root} that you can map to.

5. Next, notice the Deploy, Quick Deploy, Package, and Retract options available when you right-click the project; these are marked in Figure 4-23. These and the mapped folders in step 4 are very important changes, because in Visual Studio 2008, developers used to rely on community tools to get to these mapped folders and manually add them to the project structure.

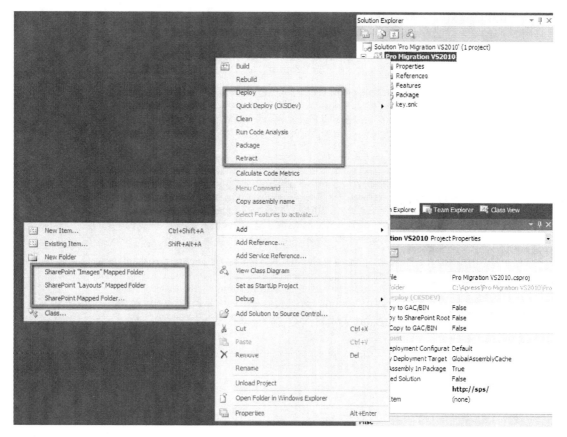

Figure 4-23. Adding SharePoint mapped folders in Visual Studio 2010

■ **Note** Visual Studio 2010 must reside on the same server as SPS 2010 to deploy from Visual Studio 2010; there's no remote deployment mechanism.

6. Under the Server Explorer, select SharePoint Connections. You can add and connect to the SharePoint web application and view all the artifacts that belong to the site. You can launch the site quickly from here as well.

7. Next, right-click the Feature folder, and click Add Feature. A new feature is added to the project with a default name that you can change. However, you now have a feature designer. This will avoid the need to manually edit the feature XML files, although you still can if the need arises. You can provide Name, Description, Feature Scope, and Feature Activation Dependency features as well. If you need to add any resources from the sites, you will have

to first add a module, add assets to it, and then add those assets to the feature files, as shown Figure 4-24.

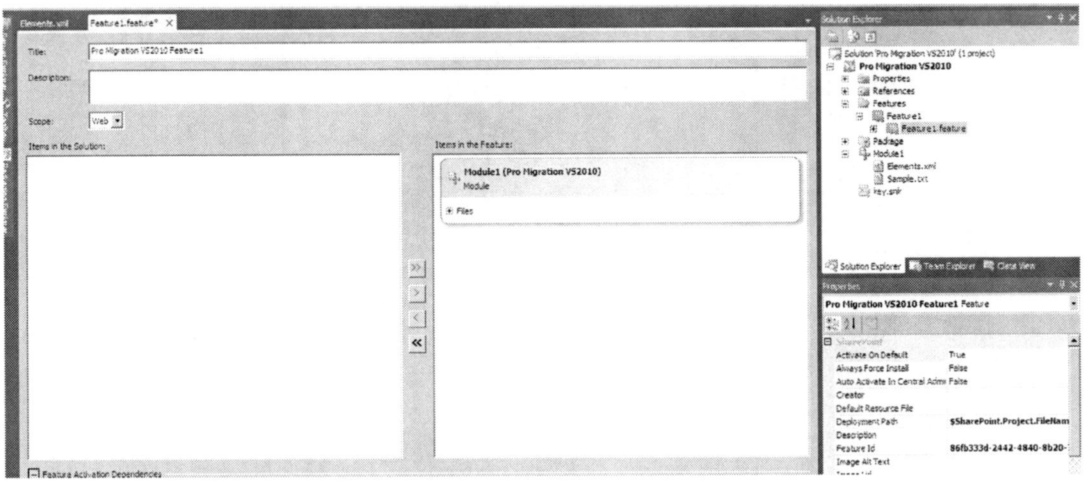

Figure 4-24. Designing features in Visual Studio 2010

There are many other new SharePoint project item templates introduced in Visual Studio 2010 that we will go through in the next section. All in all, the tools are now pretty much standardized or natively available via Visual Studio 2010.

Take a look at Figure 4-25, and you will notice that many new SharePoint project item (SPI) templates are introduced in this version. Some examples of SPI are web part, workflow, site definition, and event receiver. To add an SPI to a project, simply right-click the project, and click *Select*. Then click New Item. You will be prompted with a window in which you can select one of the SPIs, as shown in Figure 4-25. Note that the number of SPI templates available will be greater when you install SharePoint Power Tools.

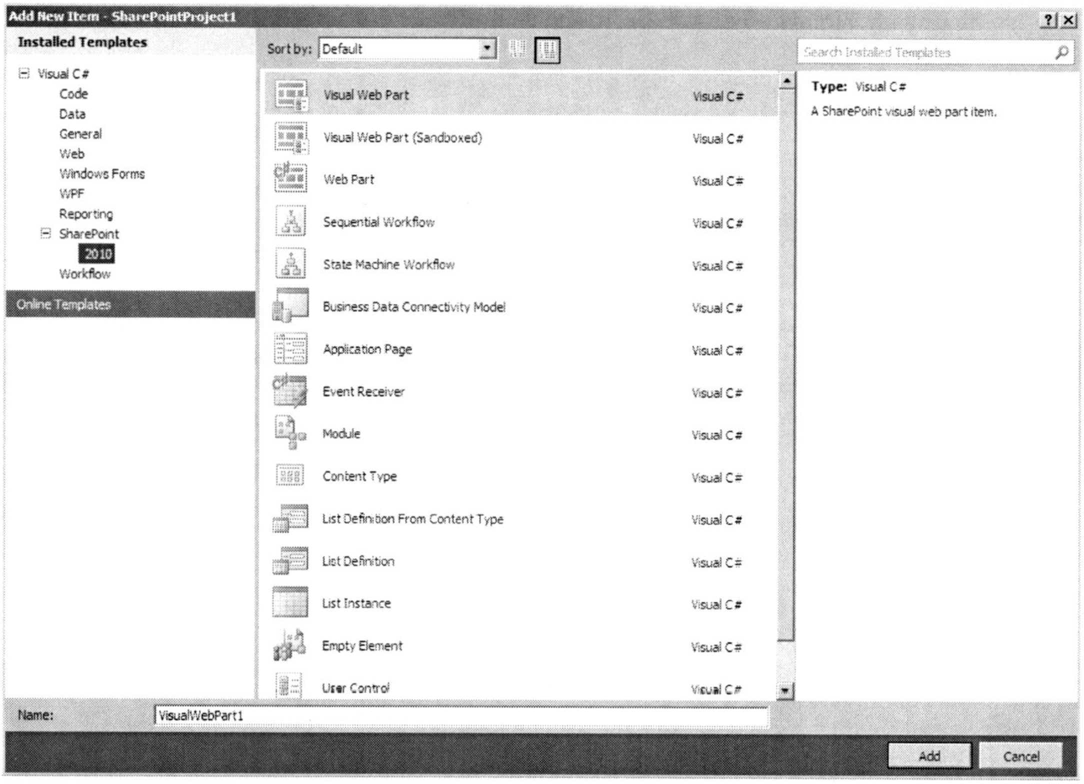

Figure 4-25. *SharePoint project item templates*

With all the above features falling into place, development becomes very easy, and this is the time when ASP.NET developers need to think about switching to SharePoint development. We'll begin by creating a simple solution with one of the SPIs that needs no introduction—building an ASP.NET user control (.ascx), and then, we'll deploy it to SharePoint environment. For SharePoint developers, in MOSS 2007 if you recollect, you must have used the famous smart part to load the user controls. You may have written a custom user control loader as well. Or put them in a layout page? With Visual Studio 2010's SharePoint tool, you now have a visual web part that basically replaces all these custom or community web parts. With it, you can visually build your web part using the Visual Web Part template. The big advantage here is you have a sandbox version as well, about which you shall learn in the next section.

1. Right-click the project that you created earlier, and click Add and then New Item.

2. From the available SPI templates, select Visual Web Part, and under the name, type valid text such as Basic Math Operation. A new user control (.ascx) will be created, along with the code behind file (.cs), web part file (.webpart), and an elements (.xml) file. You can browse through the contents of these files to understand how they are built:

      a. `{control name}.ascx.cs` contains the code behind content for the user control.

      b. `{control name}.ascx` is the actual user control, where you can visually design the control.

      c. `{control name}.cs` is the control loader. This is similar to the smart part we mentioned earlier.

      d. `Elements.xml` is the definition file for the location and logical group where the web part resides after deployment.

      e. `{control name}.webpart` is the XML file that has the definition of the web part metadata, its properties, assembly information and so on.

3. Double-click the user control file to open it, and switch to design mode. From the toolbox, add a Literal control, a text box, and a button. You can follow some basic coding standards here, but for this demonstration, we'll simply leave the default names as they are. However, change the name of the button to Multiply, and double-click the button on the design mode. This creates a click event in the code behind file.

4. Switch to the code behind file, and add the code in Listing 4-1 under the button-click event. The code simply squares the value entered in the text box and displays the result as output in the literal control text.

Listing 4-1. Code Used for the Visual Web Part

```
if (!string.IsNullOrEmpty(TextBox1.Text))
    Literal1.Text = (int.Parse(TextBox1.Text) * int.Parse(TextBox1.Text)).ToString();
else
    Literal1.Text = "Please enter a valid number and click on Multiply button";
```

Let's discuss another important enhancement in this version—the debugging experience. With Visual Studio 2010, you can now simply press F5 for debugging and run the project directly against the SharePoint environment, instead of manually deploying it, before viewing the results. In fact, when you press F5, Visual Studio 2010 basically

- Builds the .WSP file

- Deactivates and activates any features that are part of the package

- Retracts and deletes any old versions of the package

- Checks for conflicts

- Adds and deploys the new version of the package

- Activates any features that are part of the package

- Attaches the debugger to the WWW Worker Process (W3WP) as well

What did Visual Studio replace? All your scripting about STSADM commands and debug attach process is now simply integral part of the F5 experience! We will now walk you through the steps on how simple the debugging experience would be with Visual Studio 2010.

5.   Before you run, make sure, under the project properties, to set the site URL to the target site that you intend to run the web part on. As soon as you press F5 for the first time, you are prompted that the web.config file will be modified to add debug changes, as shown in Figure 4-26. Press the OK button to proceed.

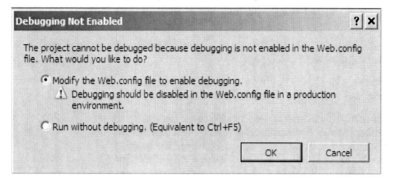

Figure 4-26. *Enabling debugging using F5 debugging*

6.   The SharePoint site launches automatically in the browser and opens the home page. You can edit the page, add the web part created earlier, and insert it on to the page. Once the web part is added, you can exit the edit mode of the page and notice the web part rendered on the page, as shown in Figure 4-27.

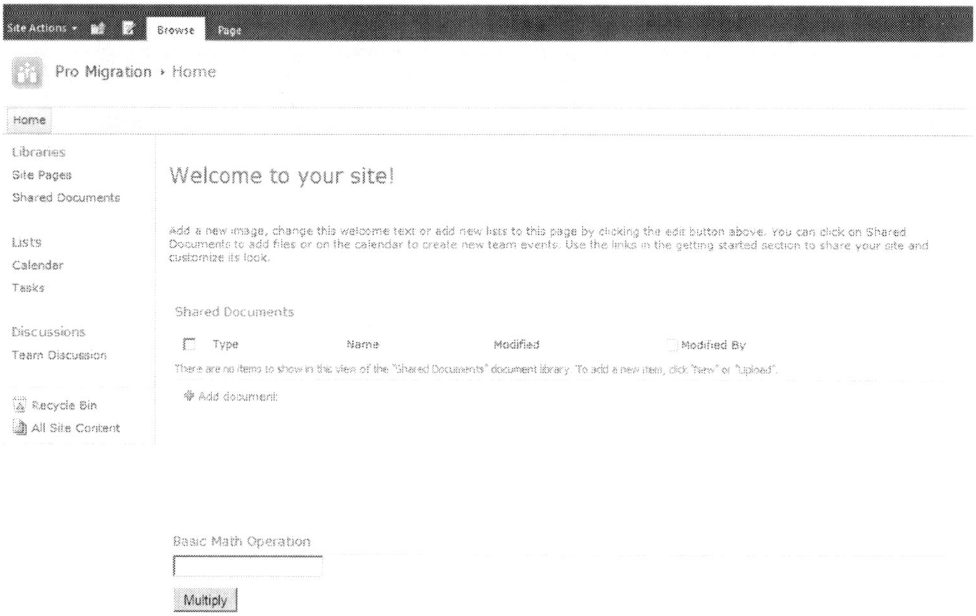

Figure 4-27. *Deployed visual web part on a SharePoint site*

7. F5 debugging integrates and associates very well with the SharePoint environment. It has the right level of trust with the site as well. However, we recommend deploying the package before running in debug mode and then doing a F5 debug.

8. When you are ready for debugging, add a break point, and simply press F5 to work seamlessly with the SharePoint site.

When you deploy this solution, either by using Visual Studio or PowerShell methodology, visual web parts are deployed to the control templates folder and precisely under {SharePoint Root}\CONTROLTEMPLATES\. And as discussed earlier, you can also have a sandbox version of the same visual web part, but sandboxed solutions are not deployed to the database, not to physical. We will walk you through the sandboxed solution architecture in the next section.

Sandbox Solutions

There has been always a need for a better development and deployment pattern. While developers want more control on servers and to learn more about the performance of the code and access logs in case of any errors, IT administrators seek the opposite. They restrict developers as much as possible to maintain code of conduct and secure farms and were always scared of the badly induced code that developers might develop and deploy on their servers. Until SharePoint 2010, there has been no proper bridge between these two groups, and finding a common solution that was a win-win situation for both was difficult. Sandboxed solutions in SharePoint 2010 bring a viable solution to this problem.

Sandboxed solutions are among the new feature introduced in SharePoint 2010; they provide developers and IT administrators a safe way to deploy, monitor, validate, and authorize code using solution packages on SharePoint farms. A *sandboxed solution* is primarily a solution package, similar to that of a Farm Solution except that the code developed using sandboxed solutions runs under partial trust and has limited access to the SharePoint Object API.

■ **Note** Farm solutions are full-trust solutions that are often used in MOSS 2007 and SharePoint 2010; they need to be deployed by farm administrators and have full access to SharePoint Object API.

Unlike farm solutions, sandboxed solutions can be deployed, or technically uploaded, by a site collection administrator to a SharePoint site. Code under these solutions runs under a separate worker process known as SPUCWorkerProcess.exe, making them isolated from the regular code base that runs on the W3WP worker process. The artifacts under these solutions are deployed to a database and not to the file system. This mechanism is highly beneficial, because these solutions' code doesn't bring down your site, and they fail independently.

Farm administrators can assign resource points to control the memory utilized by the code under a sandboxed solution. That way, if the logic is consuming to many memory assets, these solutions can be blocked from running for a specific period of time (say, 24 hours). Farm administrators can relax and worry less about bad code or redeployments. They can also monitor solutions that are uploaded by site collection administrators by using Solution Validator code.

■ **Note** A solution validator deployed at the farm level as a farm solution is used to validate solutions that are uploaded by site collection administrators. Download solution validator code at `http://spsolutionvalidator.codeplex.com`.

As discussed earlier, Visual Studio 2010 has all the development advantages, including creating sandboxed solutions. With Visual Studio 2010, you can choose to create a SB Solution Project (default) while creating a new project, as shown in Figure 4-28. The output of the Visual Studio project is a `.wsp` file, which you can upload to the solutions store under the site collection. You can also directly use the deploy option in Visual Studio (however, that may not be a suitable for staging and production deployments). You simply activate the solution, which is equivalent to deploying the `.wsp` to run the assets under the solution. When you do not need it, simply deactivate it again.

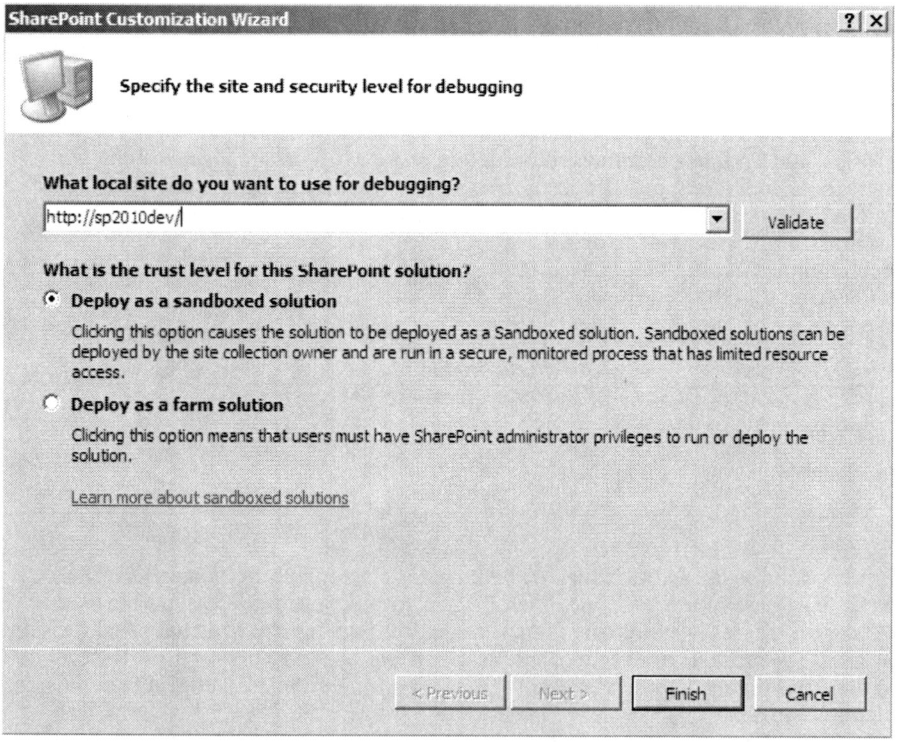

Figure 4-28. Creating proejct as sandboxed solution

While sandbox solutions are a great help, the do have limitations—you cannot achieve everything with sandboxed solutions. Since a sandboxed solution is partially trusted, you cannot attempt to access the full Object API or deploy files to the hive using sandboxed solutions. Here is list of some of the key things that you *can* create in a sandbox:

- Web parts

- Site pages (not application pages with code behind)

- List definitions

- Event and feature receivers

- InfoPath form services

- Custom actions

- Content type and site columns

- JavaScript, AJAX, Silverlight, or jQuery deployed to 14 hive or SharePoint root folder (`C:\Program Files\Common Files\Microsoft Shared\Web Server Extensions\14\`)...

While creating site collections, farm administrators can set preconfigured resource quotas as templates. Resource calculation is based on metric calculation. For instance, for each abnormal process termination, the count is incremented, and when a specific count (which you can configure) is reached, will push the counter to a resource point increase. As soon as the resource storage upper limit is reaches, the solution will be restricted. In other instances, farm administrators can completely block sandboxed solutions using Solution Restrictions, as shown in Figure 4-29.

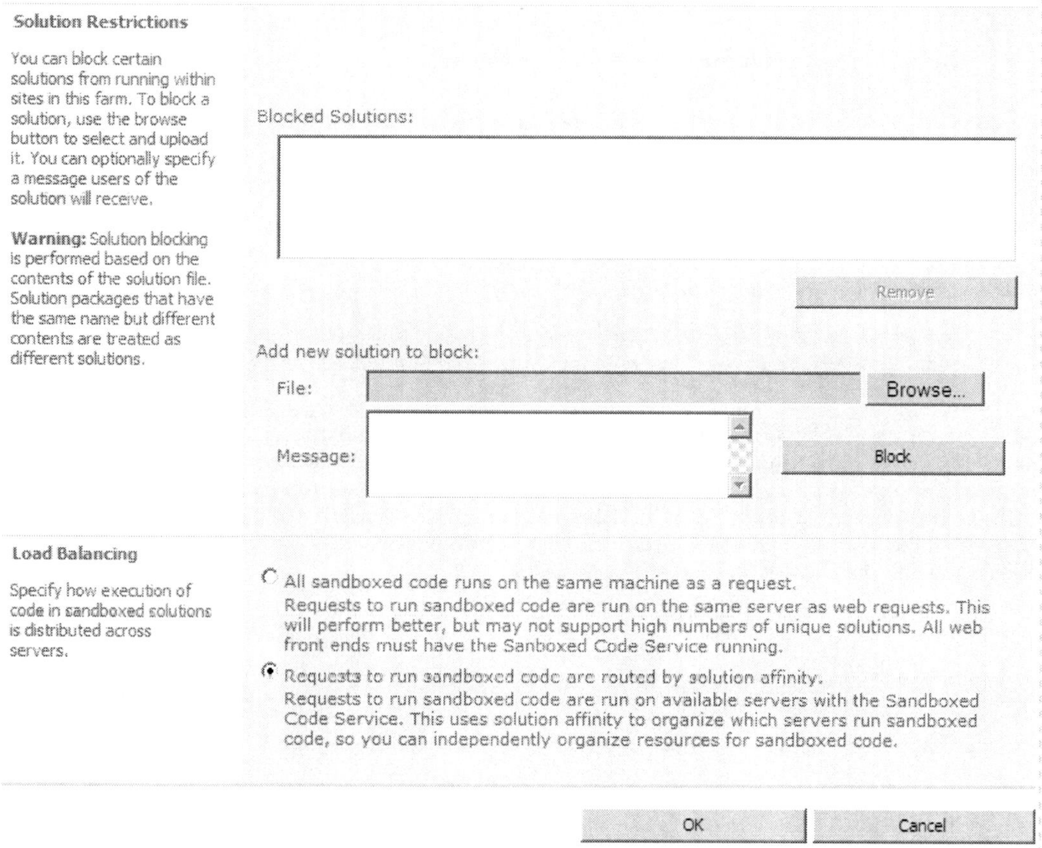

Solution Restrictions

You can block certain solutions from running within sites in this farm. To block a solution, use the browse button to select and upload it. You can optionally specify a message users of the solution will receive.

Warning: Solution blocking is performed based on the contents of the solution file. Solution packages that have the same name but different contents are treated as different solutions.

Blocked Solutions:

Remove

Add new solution to block:

File:

Browse...

Message:

Block

Load Balancing

Specify how execution of code in sandboxed solutions is distributed across servers.

○ All sandboxed code runs on the same machine as a request.
Requests to run sandboxed code are run on the same server as web requests. This will perform better, but may not support high numbers of unique solutions. All web front ends must have the Sandboxed Code Service running.

◉ Requests to run sandboxed code are routed by solution affinity.
Requests to run sandboxed code are run on available servers with the Sandboxed Code Service. This uses solution affinity to organize which servers run sandboxed code, so you can independently organize resources for sandboxed code.

OK

Cancel

Figure 4-29. Sandboxed Solution Restrictions window

As you know, the premise of a sandboxed solution does not exist in MOSS 2007. We recommend use sandboxed solutions as a matter of course. Since sandboxed solutions only allow access to part of your Object API, some of the core functionalities will not work, including these:

- SPSecurity classes

- Web-application–scoped and farm-scoped features

- Layouts folder in the solution

- Sending e-mails using SPUtility.SendEmail

- Custom action groups

- The HideCustomAction element

- Content type binding

- Timer jobs

We are sure your existing MOSS 2007 solutions (farm solutions) have most of these functionalities. If you want to use those and take advantage of sandboxed solutions, what can you do? The solution for such limitations is again quite simple. You will have to write full-trust proxy code to finish the last mile and cross the boundaries. To help you with that, here the URL to an article explaining how to create full-trust proxies for sandboxed solutions in SharePoint 2010: `http://blah.winsmarts.com/2009-12-SharePoint_2010_Sandboxed_Solutions__Full_Trust__Proxies.aspx`.

Refactoring

Though there are ways to get to the functionalities that are restricted by the sandboxed solution model, consider this as a golden opportunity for cleaning and rearranging your code. There is no better time to refactor your existing code. You are not limited to upgrading your solutions to farm solutions; you can break your existing solutions and logically separate them into farm solutions and sandboxed solutions. The rule of thumb is simple: What you cannot achieve using sandboxed solutions should be moved into a farm solution. This way, most of the code is protected, safe, and trustworthy for your IT administrators. And as for developers, they have more control on development aspects. Then too, there is much new functionality in SharePoint 2010. To achieve these functions in MOSS 2007, you might have written custom code-based solutions. Now is a good time to deprecate such solutions and begin using out-of-the-box ones. Also, your existing code does not run on SharePoint 2010 just like that. You will have to remove version 12 DLLs, add version 14 DLLs, and compile. Though this step sounds very simple, we recommend visiting some of the best practice and coding guidelines, cleaning up your code, and removing all the deprecated methods from version 12.

Customizing the Ribbon via CustomActions

If there is something in SharePoint 2010 that needs no introduction, and you will not miss it—the famous and awesome ribbon that you will notice over all the site and application pages. Though the ribbon is part of Office 2007, it was not part of MOSS 2007, and this user interface was needed. It makes all the operations and commands easily accessible to the end user. In MOSS 2007, operations are scattered all over a page, but the ribbon brings them together. The ribbon control comes with a lot of flexibility in customizing it as well. While you can design your master pages for the placement of the ribbon control anywhere logically in the layout, you can as well edit and add actions to the ribbon very easily.

Behind the ribbon architecture is a single file that is part of the site definition and is found under `14hive\TEMPLATE\GLOBAL\XML\CMDUI.XML`. The file contains the definitions for all the components and their actions. So, as you must have noticed, the ribbon base is nothing but an XML file. SharePoint provides an easy mechanism and extends the functionality to modify or add custom actions to ribbon. Listing 4-2 shows an example of adding a custom button on the ribbon. To run the sample, you first have to create an empty SharePoint 2010 project in Visual Studio 2010 and create a feature. Then, create an `Elements.xml` file, and add the code in Listing 4-2 to the file.

Listing 4-2. Ribbon Customizations

```
<Elements xmlns="http://schemas.microsoft.com/sharepoint/">
  <CustomAction
  Id="SkynetCustomRibbonButton"
  RegistrationId="101"
  RegistrationType="List"
  Location="CommandUI.Ribbon"
```

```
       Sequence="5"
       Title="My Custom Ribbon Button">
       <CommandUIExtension>
           <CommandUIDefinitions>
              <CommandUIDefinition Location="Ribbon.Documents.Manage.Controls._children">
                <Button
                  Id="Ribbon.Documents.New.CustomButton"
                  Alt="My Custom Ribbon Button"
                  Sequence="5"
                  Command="NewRibbonButtonCommand"
                  Image32by32="/_layouts/images/PPEOPLE.GIF"
                  Image16by16="/_layouts/images/FILMSTRP.GIF"
                  LabelText="Custom Ribbon Button"
                  TemplateAlias="o1" />
              </CommandUIDefinition>
           </CommandUIDefinitions>
           <CommandUIHandlers>
              <CommandUIHandler
                 Command="NewRibbonButtonCommand"
                 CommandAction="javascript:alert('This is a new button!');" />
           </CommandUIHandlers>
       </CommandUIExtension>
    </CustomAction>
</Elements>
```

Build the project, and deploy the `.wsp` file to your SharePoint web application. Activate the feature deployed, and you'll see the ribbon customization, as shown in Figure 4-30.

Figure 4-30. *Custom ribbon actions*

What Is New in the SharePoint 2010 API?

As always, when out-of-the-box features do not meet your requirements, you can rely on either C# or VB.NET (by referring to the SharePoint API) to craft and design solutions however you want. In the earlier edition, the only option you had was the server-side API, which you used by referring the corresponding DLLs or accessing the available web services. In SharePoint Server 2010, you have a third choice in the form of the Client Object Model. In this section, we will discuss what has been introduced to the Server API as well as define the Client Object Model and its usage and advantages.

Server–Side API

The Server Side API has undergone many changes. Many methods are deprecated (see http://archive.msdn.microsoft.com/sps2010deprecated) in this version, and at the same time, some very interesting additions are really beneficial and easy for developers to use. Three important features that are introduced are the APIs for Language Integrated Query (LINQ), Representational State Transfer (REST), and Business Connectivity Services (BCS).

LINQ

For starters, if you have not used Language Integrated Query (LINQ) to SQL or .NET Objects earlier, you do not need to learn all those now. But if you know the power of LINQ and want to use it with SharePoint, your wish is granted now in the form of LINQ to SharePoint. In fact, compared to the efforts that you must have put in to learn LINQ earlier, you will see that LINQ to SharePoint is very easy, and you hardly need to learn much more. Thanks go to Microsoft for delivering a very nice and simple way to query SharePoint objects.

LINQ provides a way to query *freestyle simple SQL statements* from a data source. Essentially, we are talking about a LINQ provider to any data source, which you can implement using the System.Linq.IQueryable and System.Linq.IQueryProvider interfaces. Again, the primary objective of these providers is to simply translate LINQ queries to the language of the data sources. We are not here to explain basics of LINQ, so let's concentrate on how you can leverage it with SharePoint. But if you are interested in learning its general aspects, please see http://msdn.microsoft.com/en-us/library/bb397919.aspx.

A LINQ to SharePoint provider is defined under the Microsoft.SharePoint.Linq namespace and the data context under Microsoft.SharePoint.Linq.DataContext. Listing 4-3 shows a simple example of retrieving data from a SharePoint list using LINQ. When we refer to "SQL-like" statements, we mean the way you query a database and how that query looks inline. See Listing 4-3 to understand more clearly.

Listing 4-3. Data Context

```
DataContext data = new DataContext(SPContext.GetContext(this.Context).Web.Url);

using (EntitiesDataContext moEntitiesDataContext = new
EntitiesDataContext(SPContext.GetContext(this.Context).Web.Url))
{
    var fn = from fNames in moEntitiesDataContext.FirstNames
            select new { fNames.FirstName };
}
```

Let's explore the preceding code a little bit. The data context classes are built as a result of the new execution tool known as SPMetal available in this edition. SPMetal generates a class that acts like an interface to connect to the SharePoint Foundation 2010 content database, and enable operations such as add, delete, and update. SPMetal can be found under the *14hive\bin* location and can be used as follows:

```
SPMetal /web:http://yourwebapp /code:newdatacontext.cs
```

LINQ actually translate the queries as CAML queries so, you can say "bye-bye" to CAML; you won't need it anymore. Here is a simple, overall outline of LINQ to SharePoint:

- No CAML is required.

- LINQ can be called against both the server and the Client Object Model.

- Tools (like SPMetal) are available to create a business layer (entity classes), and IntelliSense helps query construction

- Query across multiple lists with relationships.

- Allow efficient queries.

- Merge results from multiple lists and multiple data sources.

- Join results from multiple data sources.

What do you have in MOSS 2007 to remotely access server objects? Web services. Well, can web services deliver everything we want? You will end up with filtered server API, but say you can achieve what you need. The issue with web services is that requests are directly proportional to the service overhead. You need proper estimate for performance. Second, can you perform asynchronous operations over the server API? You might end up using third-party tools to accomplish it, but notice that you are not dealing with out-of-the-box stuff.

So, clearly MOSS 2007 features may not address everything and surely need some level of improvement. SharePoint 2010 addressed these issues with the Client Object Model. You can use it when you want to write applications based on the .NET Framework without installing or running the code on actual SharePoint servers—even if the client might be a simple Windows, console application, or Office application.

▪ **Note** "COM" in this chapter does *not* refer to the Component Object Model.

Client–Side API

The Client Object Model (COM) is a new enhancement in SharePoint 2010 and is available with both the Server and Foundation editions. The COM API is the managed code and is rich as service-side API, but of course, with exceptions and limitations that you may not be able to perform in similar lines of the Server API. You can query and access most of the objects, such as site, web, and list, and it does support transactions, such as add, select, and update, on SharePoint data. One of its very good features is that it executes a batch command model rather than executing the commands in isolation, and thus provides huge performance gains.

The Client Object Model can be used with European Computer Manufacture Association Script (ECMAScript), .NET managed, or Silverlight code. To use the COM, you need to first get a reference to the appropriate DLLs. As in the case of the server-side API, where you refer to `Microsoft.SharePoint.dll` from 14hive, for each model within the Client Object Model, you will have to refer the corresponding DLLs as shown Table 4-1. And if you notice the size of each assembly, you can expect that you cannot simply achieve everything that the Server API can achieve. So, as a warning, *do not simply begin developing in the Client Object Model. Understand its limitations first!*

Table 4-1. *Client Object Model Assembly Locations*

Client Object Model	Location
Managed Code	`14hive\ISAPI\Microsoft.SharePoint.Client.dll` `14hive\ISAPI\Microsoft.SharePoint.Client.Runtime.dll`

Silverlight	`14hive\Layouts\ClientBin\Microsoft.SharePoint.Client.Silverlight.dll`
	
	`14hive\Layouts\ClientBin\Microsoft.SharePoint.Client.Silverlight.Runtime.dll`

ECMAScript/ JavaScript	`14hive\Layouts\sp.js`

Coming to development, understanding and learning the Client Object Model is easy, because its classes are built along similar lines to the server side API; the naming conventions are simple to understand, which makes the initial learning curve a little bit shallow (see Table 4-2). You also have full control over the request and response pipeline. However, with the Client Object Model, you cannot access objects beyond the site level, and similarly, you have filtered or less control when using it with sandboxed solutions. However, given the nature of the COM, you will end up with fewer administration tasks.

Table 4-2. *Class Comparison Between Server-Side and Client-Side APIs*

Server-Side API	Client-Side API
SPContext	ClientContext
SPSite	Site
SPWeb	Web
SPList	List
SPListItem	ListItem
SPField	Field

To help you better understand how the COM works, let's see how the architecture is built. Figure 4-31 depicts both scenarios that we discussed earlier: client applications using web services and the COM. In the case of client applications using the COM by sending XML requests, the client services that communicate with the Server Object Model return a response that is JSON compliant. This model works irrespective of whether you use ECMAScript, Silverlight, or managed code. However, remember that the request has to be in XML format.

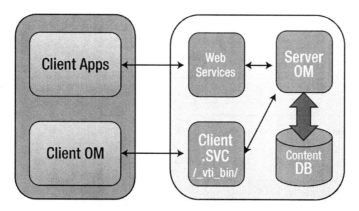

Figure 4-31. Client Object Model architecture

With the basic understanding of the fundamentals of Client Object Model that you have now, you can begin to write simple code using the server API and convert it to the COM, as shown in Listing 4-4.

Listing 4-4. Creating Server Web Context

```
SPWeb web = SPContext.Current.Web;
web.Title = web.Title + " - Hello Srini";
web.AllowUnsafeUpdates = true;
web.Update();
```

The preceding code converted to COM would look like Listing 4-5.

Listing 4-5. Creating Client Context

```
Clientcontext clientContext = new Clientcontext("mysiteurl");
Web web = clientContext.Web;
clientContext.Load(web);
clientContext.ExecuteQuery();
web.Title = web.Title + " - Hello Srini";
web.Update();
clientContext.ExecuteQuery();
```

As discussed earlier, the COM can be used in three flavors. The first one is managed code, which can be used with thick clients, such as Windows, WPF, console, and web thin client applications. Listing 4-6 is from a windows application; it reacts to a button click that retrieves all the list names and loads them to a list control; just keep in mind the appropriate references as mentioned in Table 4-1.

Listing 4-6. Using the Client Object Model in Windows Applciations

```
private void button1_Click(object sender, RoutedEventArgs e)
        {
            listBox1.Items.Clear();
            using (Microsoft.SharePoint.Client.ClientContext ctx = new
ClientContext(textBox1.Text))
            {
```

```
Microsoft.SharePoint.Client.ListCollection listCollection = ctx.Web.Lists;
var query = from list in ctx.Web.Lists
            select list;
var lists = ctx.LoadQuery(query);
ctx.ExecuteQuery();
foreach (var list in lists)
{
    listBox1.Items.Add(list.Title);
}
      }
   }
```

The second approach with the COM is by using Silverlight. Unlike managed code, Silverlight needs a host, and in your case, that could be the SharePoint infrastructure. First of all, why Silverlight? Well, obviously, because of the rich interface and asynchronous support that Silverlight offers. Though Silverlight is not a related topic in this book, let's see how to write a bit of simple code using Silverlight and the COM. Similar to the previous example, you can create a simple button and list box to the Silverlight panel, and with a button click, you can write logic and use the COM as shown in Listing 4-7. However, one important factor to keep in mind here is that, when you build a Silverlight project, the output generated is a .xap file. We recommend adding this file to the clientbin folder, in the 14hive\layouts folder.

Listing 4-7. Using the Client Object Model in Silverlight

```
private void button1_Click(object sender, RoutedEventArgs e)
    {
        ctx = new ClientContext(ApplicationContext.Current.Url);
        web = ctx.Web;
        ctx.Load(web);
        ctx.Load(web.Lists);
        ctx.ExecuteQueryAsync(new ClientRequestSucceededEventHandler(OnSuccess), new
ClientRequestFailedEventHandler(OnFailed));
    }
    private void OnSuccess(Object sender, ClientRequestSucceededEventArgs args)
    {
        Dispatcher.BeginInvoke(FillListBox);
    }
    private void OnFailed(Object sender, ClientRequestFailedEventArgs args)
    {
        listBox1.Items.Clear();
        listBox1.Items.Add("Error!");
    }
```

The last model with the COM uses ECMAScript. Similar to the previous model, this one does not need a host, and of course, it is SharePoint. In this case, you will have to have the reference to sp.js (refer to Table 4-1 for its location). If you are using an out-of-the-box SharePoint master page, the sp.js file is already referenced in it. However, if you are building a custom master page, ensure that you have reference to the appropriate location of the file. Like using Silverlight, when using ECMAScript you have the advantage of performing asynchronous operations. Since the script is a reference to a JavaScript file, this can technically work on any page under your site as long as you refer to it. In ECMAScript, you have different definitions for accessing classes and objects from SharePoint COM; these are Get and Set methods. One of the added advantage of this model is that you have debug version available. Let's look at a simple example to help you understand COM and ECMAScript more clearly. Listing 4-8 shows simple code that retrieves title of the current site.

Listing 4-8. Client OM using ECMA script

```
function GetSiteTitle() {
        var context = new SP.ClientContext.get_current();
        web = context.get_web();
        context.load(web);
        context.executeQueryAsync(Function.createDelegate(this, this.onSuccess),
Function.createDelegate(this, this.onFailure));
        }
function onSuccess(sender, args) {
        alert("Site title: " + web.get_title());
        }
function onFailure(sender, args) {
        alert("Request failed " + args.get_message() + "\n" + args.get_stackTrace());
        }
```

As you have seen, the Client Object Model is a huge improvement in this version. It might look very convenient, but at the same time, its power might add a fear factor. You obviously have concerns about the data security and how your servers are protected. First of all, can the code in the listings be executed as is? If so, where is the security? Well, you can rest assured that your SharePoint servers and data are secured and cannot be accessed easily from a remote client. To achieve these results, you will have to go through the authentication model first.

The COM supports three models of security; using them, you can actually access your SharePoint servers, and on subsequent access, you can access data:

- *Default*: Default authentication mode

- *Forms Authentication*: Uses ASP.NET authentication

- *Anonymous*: For anonymous authentication

Listing 4-9 specifies how to authenticate to a site protected using forms-based authentication (FBA) before you actually access site data.

Listing 4-9. Creating Client Context Authentication Mode

```
clientContext.AuthenticationMode = ClientAuthenticationMode.FormsAuthentication;
FormsAuthenticationLoginInfo fbaInfo = new FormsAuthenticationLoginInfo("userid", "password");
clientContext.FormsAuthenticationLoginInfo = fbaInfo;
```

Summary

In this chapter, we looked at the following (see Figure 4-32):

- New concepts from the savvy business and .NET developers' standpoints

- New features and tools, including SharePoint Designer 2010, Visio 2010, and InfoPath 2010

- New ECM Features such as enterprise content types, document IDs, document sets, in-place records management, and managed metadata services

- How Visual Studio was improved to support .NET developers

- Sandboxed solutions and various aspects related their use

- Changes in the server API and the new Client API

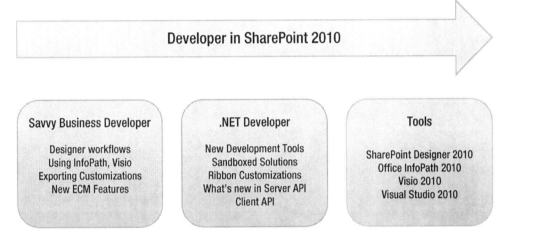

Figure 4-32. Developer roadmap in SharePoint 2010

This is the final chapter in this book. The appendix section primarily seeks to provide you information on some of the API changes, master page references, differences between STSADM and PowerShell, and good references from MSDN that can help you in the migration process from MOSS 2007 to SharePoint 2010.

Appendix

Though this section is an appendix, it has very valuable information and details that will be helpful for you while performing your migration from MOSS 2007 to SharePoint 2010. Again, we are limiting information to only what is important and relevant, rather than providing you with what's already available from TechNet or MSDN. However, we have included external links that you can refer to for more specific and detailed information.

STSADM vs. PowerShell

As discussed through out this book, PowerShell is going to lead the way moving forward from SharePoint 2010, and because of its many advantages, we suggest that you understand, learn, practice, and implement PowerShell as much as possible. Though STSADM commands still work, we strongly suggest using of PowerShell, and to help you do so, Table A-1 offers a comparison between STSADM and PowerShell.

Table A-1. STSADM Operations and Their PowerShell Cmdlet Counterparts

STSADM Operation	Windows PowerShell Cmdlet
Activatefeature	Enable-SPFeature
Activateformtemplate	Enable-SPInfoPathFormTemplate
Addalternatedomain	New-SPAlternateUrl
Addcontentdb	Mount-SPContentDatabase
	New-SPContentDatabase
Adddataconnectionfile	Install-SPDataConnectionFile
Add-ecsfiletrustedlocation	New-SPExcelFileLocation
Add-ecssafedataprovider	New-SPExcelDataProvider

153

STSADM Operation	Windows PowerShell Cmdlet
Add-ecstrusteddataconnectionlibrary	New-SPExcelDataConnectionLibrary
Add-ecsuserdefinedfunction	New-SPExcelUserDefinedFunction
Addexemptuseragent	Add-SPInfoPathUserAgent
Addpath	New-SPManagedPath
Addpermissionpolicy	None
Addsolution	Add-SPSolution
Addtemplate	Install-SPWebTemplate
Adduser	New-SPUser
Addwppack	Install-SPWebPartPack
Addzoneurl	New-SPAlternateUrl
Allowuserformwebserviceproxy	Set-SPInfoPathWebServiceProxy Use the AllowForUserForms and Identity parameters.
Allowwebserviceproxy	Set-SPInfoPathWebServiceProxy Use the AllowWebServiceProxy and Identity parameters.
Authentication	Set-SPWebApplication Use the AuthenticationMethod or AuthenticationProvider parameters.
Backup	Backup-SPConfigurationDatabase Backup-SPFarm Backup-SPSite
Backuphistory	Get-SPBackupHistory
Binddrservice	None
Blockedfilelist	None

Canceldeployment	None
Changepermissionpolicy	None
Copyappbincontent	None
Createadminvs	New-SPCentralAdministration
Creategroup	None
Createsite	New-SPSite
Createsiteinnewdb	New-SPSite Use the ContentDatabase parameter. New-SPContentDatabase
Createweb	New-SPWeb
Databaserepair	None
Deactivatefeature	Disable-SPFeature
Deactivateformtemplate	Disable-SPInfoPathFormTemplate
Deleteadminvs	None
Deletealternatedomain	Remove-SPAlternateUrl
Deleteconfigdb	Remove-SPConfigurationDatabase
Deletecontentdb	Dismount-SPContentDatabase
Deletegroup	None
Deletepath	Remove-SPManagedPath
Deletepermissionpolicy	None
Deletesite	Remove-SPSite
Deletesolution	Remove-SPSolution
Deletetemplate	Uninstall-SPWebTemplate

STSADM Operation	Windows PowerShell Cmdlet
Deleteuser	Remove-SPUser
Deleteweb	Remove-SPWeb
Deletewppack	Uninstall-SPWebPartPack
Deletezoneurl	Remove-SPAlternateUrl
Deploysolution	Install-SPSolution
Deploywppack	Install-SPWebPartPack
Disablessc	None
Displaysolution	Get-SPSolution
Editcontentdeploymentpath	Set-SPContentDeploymentPath
Email	None
Enablessc	None
Enumalternatedomains	Get-SPAlternateURL
Enumcontentdbs	Get-SPContentDatabase
Enumdataconnectionfiledependants	Get-SPDataConnectionFileDependent
Enumdataconnectionfiles	Get-SPDataConnectionFile
Enumdeployments	None
Enumexemptuseragents	Get-SPInfoPathUserAgent
Enumformtemplates	Get-SPInfoPathFormTemplate
Enumgroups	None
Enumroles	None
Enumservices	Get-SPServiceInstance

Enumsites	Get-SPSiteAdministration (To run this cmdlet, you must be a member of the Farm Administrators group.) Get-SPSite (To run this cmdlet, you must be a local administrator on the computer where SharePoint 2010 Products is installed.)
Enumsolutions	Get-SPSolution
Enumsubwebs	Get-SPWeb
Enumtemplates	Get-SPWebTemplate
Enumusers	Get-SPUser
Enumwppacks	Get-SPWebPartPack
Enumzoneurls	Get-SPAlternateURL
Execadmsvcjobs	Start-SPAdminJob
Export	Export-SPWeb
Extendvs	New-SPWebApplication
Extendvsinwebfarm	New-SPWebApplicationExtension
Forcedeletelist	None
Getadminport	Get-SPWebApplication Use the following syntax: Get-SPWebApplication -IncludeCentralAdministration | ? {$_.IsAdministrationWebApplication -eq $true}
Getdataconnectionfileproperty property	Get-SPDataConnectionFile Use the following syntax: Get-SPDataConnectionFile | where {$_.Name -eq "dataConFileName"} | format-list

STSADM Operation	Windows PowerShell Cmdlet
Getformtemplateproperty property	Get-SPInfoPathFormTemplate Use the following syntax: Get-SPInfoPathFormTemplate | where {$_.DisplayName -e "formTemplateName"} | format-list
Getosearchsetting	None
Getproperty	Get-SPFarmConfig Get-SPTimerJob Disable-SPTimerJob Enable-SPTimerJob Set-SPTimerJob Start-SPTimerJob
Getsitelock	Get-SPSiteAdministration
Getsiteuseraccountdirectorypath	None
Geturlzone	Get-SPAlternateURL
Import	Import-SPWeb
Installfeature	Install-SPFeature
Listlogginglevels	Get-SPLogLevel
Listqueryprocessoroptions	None
Listregisteredsecuritytrimmers	Get-SPEnterpriseSearchSecurityTrimmer
Localupgradestatus	None

Managepermissionpolicylevel	None
Mergecontentdbs	Move-SPSite
Migrateuser	Move-SPUser
Osearch	For the Osearch parameters farmcontactemail, farmperformancelevel, farmserviceaccount, and farmservicepassword, use the Get-SPEnterpriseSearchService and Set-SPEnterpriseSearchService cmdlets. For the Osearch parameters start and stop, use the Start-SPEnterpriseSearchServiceInstance and Stop-SPEnterpriseSearchServiceInstance cmdlets, respectively. For the Osearch parameter defaultindexlocation, use the Get-SPEnterpriseSearchServiceInstance and Set-SPEnterpriseSearchServiceInstance cmdlets.
Osearchdiacriticsensitive	Use the Get-SPEnterpriseSearchServiceApplication cmdlet to retrieve the specific search service application, and then use DiacriticSensitive parameter from the Set-SPEnterpriseSearchServiceApplication cmdlet.
Provisionservice	Start-SPServiceInstance
Quiescefarm	None
Quiescefarmstatus	None
Quiesceformtemplate	Stop-SPInfoPathFormTemplate
Reconvertallformtemplates	Update-SPInfoPathFormTemplate
Refreshdms	None
Refreshsitedms	None
Registersecuritytrimmer	New-SPEnterpriseSearchSecurityTrimmer
Registerwsswriter	None
Removedataconnectionfile	Uninstall-SPDataConnectionFile
Remove-ecsfiletrustedlocation	Remove-SPExcelFileLocation

STSADM Operation	Windows PowerShell Cmdlet
Remove-ecssafedataprovider	Remove-SPExcelDataProvider
Remove-ecstrusteddataconnectionlibrary	Remove-SPExcelDataConnectionLibrary
Remove-ecsuserdefinedfunction	Remove-SPExcelFileLocation
Removedrservice	None
Removeexemptuseragent	Remove-SPInfoPathUserAgent
Removeformtemplate	Uninstall-SPInfoPathFormTemplate
Removesolutiondeploymentlock	None
Renameserver	Rename-SPServer
Renamesite	Set-SPSite Use the Url parameter.
Renameweb	Set-SPWeb Use the RelativeUrl parameter.
Restore	Restore-SPFarm Restore-SPSite
Retractsolution	Uninstall-SPSolution
Retractwppack	None
Runcontentdeploymentjob	Start-SPContentDeploymentJob
Scanforfeatures	Install-SPFeature Use the Scanforfeatures parameter.
Setadminport	Set-SPCentralAdministration
Setapppassword	None
Setconfigdb	Connect-SPConfigurationDatabase

Setcontentdeploymentjobschedule	Set-SPContentDeploymentJob
Setdataconnectionfileproperty	Set-SPDataConnectionFile
Set-ecsexternaldata	Set-SPExcelFileLocation
Set-ecsloadbalancing	Set-SPExcelServiceApplication Use the LoadBalancingScheme parameter.
Set-ecsmemoryutilization	Set-SPExcelServiceApplication Use the MemoryCacheThreshold and PrivateBytesMax parameters.
Set-ecssecurity	Set-SPExcelServiceApplication Use the CrossDomainAccessAllowed, EncryptedUserConnectionRequired, and FileAccessMethod parameters.
Set-ecssessionmanagement	Set-SPExcelServiceApplication Use the SessionsPerUserMax and SiteCollectionAnonymousSessionsMax parameters.
Set-ecsworkbookcache	Set-SPExcelServiceApplication Use the Workbookcache and WorkbookCacheSizeMax parameters.
Setformtemplateproperty	Set-SPInfoPathFormTemplate
Setlogginglevel	Set-SPLogLevel
Setosearchsetting	None

STSADM Operation	Windows PowerShell Cmdlet
Setproperty	Set-SPFarmConfig
	Get-SPTimerJob
	Disable-SPTimerJob
	Enable-SPTimerJob
	Set-SPTimerJob
	Start-SPTimerJob
Setqueryprocessoroptions	None
Setsitelock	Set-SPSiteAdministration
	Use the LockState parameter.
Setsiteuseraccountdirectorypath	Get-SPSiteSubscription
	New-SPSiteSubscription
	Remove-SPSiteSubscription
Setworkflowconfig	Set-SPWorkflowConfig
Siteowner	Set-SPSiteAdministration
Syncsolution	Install-SPSolution
	Use the Synchronize parameter.
Unextendvs	Remove-SPWebApplication

Uninstallfeature	Uninstall-SPFeature
Unquiescefarm	None
Unquiesceformtemplate	Start-SPInfoPathFormTemplate
Unregistersecuritytrimmer	Remove-SPEnterpriseSearchSecurityTrimmer
Unregisterwsswriter	None
Updateaccountpassword	Set-SPManagedAccount
Updatealerttemplates	None
Updatefarmcredentials	None
Upgrade	None
Upgradeformtemplate	Install-SPInfoPathFormTemplate
Upgradesolution	Update-SPSolution
Upgradetargetwebapplication	None
Uploadformtemplate	Install-SPInfoPathFormTemplate
Userrole	Get-SPUser Move-SPUser New-SPUser Remove-SPUser Set-SPUser
Verifyformtemplate	Test-SPInfoPathFormTemplate

Content Placeholders

This section is for designers who create, design, and implement master pages. In Table A-2, we are providing information about content placeholders—new ones and those that already exist (in MOSS 2007) and are part of the master pages.

Table A-2. Master Page Content Place Holders

Placeholder	Description	New
`<asp:ContentPlaceHolder id="PlaceHolderQuickLaunchTop" runat="server">`	The top of the Quick Launch menu.	Yes
`<asp:ContentPlaceHolder id="PlaceHolderQuickLaunchBottom" runat="server">`	The bottom of the Quick Launch menu.	Yes
`<asp:ContentPlaceHolder id="PlaceHolderPageTitle" runat="server"/>`	The title of the site.	No
`<asp:ContentPlaceHolder id="PlaceHolderAdditionalPageHead" runat="server"/>`	A placeholder in the head section of the page used to add extra components such as ECMAScript (JavaScript, JScript) and Cascading Style Sheets (CSS) to the page.	No
`<asp:ContentPlaceHolder id="PlaceHolderBodyAreaClass" runat="server"/>`	The class of the body area.	No
`<asp:ContentPlaceHolder ID="SPNavigation" runat="server">`	A control used for additional page editing controls.	No
`<asp:ContentPlaceHolder id="PlaceHolderSiteName" runat="server">`	The name of the site where the current page resides.	No
`<asp:ContentPlaceHolder id="PlaceHolderPageTitleInTitleArea" runat="server" />`	The title of the page, which appears in the title area on the page.	No
`<asp:ContentPlaceHolder id="PlaceHolderPageDescription" runat="server"/>`	The description of the current page.	No
`<asp:ContentPlaceHolder id="PlaceHolderSearchArea" runat="server">`	The section of the page for the search controls.	No
`<asp:ContentPlaceHolder id="PlaceHolderGlobalNavigation" runat="server">`	The breadcrumb control on the page.	No

`<asp:ContentPlaceHolder id="PlaceHolderTitleBreadcrumb" runat="server">`	The breadcrumb text for the breadcrumb control.	No
`<asp:ContentPlaceHolder id="PlaceHolderGlobalNavigationSiteMap" runat="server">`	The list of subsites and sibling sites in the global navigation on the page.	No
`<asp:ContentPlaceHolder id="PlaceHolderTopNavBar" runat="server">`	The container used to hold the top navigation bar.	No
`<asp:ContentPlaceHolder id="PlaceHolderHorizontalNav" runat="server">`	The navigation menu that is inside the top navigation bar.	No
`<asp:ContentPlaceHolder id="PlaceHolderLeftNavBarDataSource" runat="server" />`	The placement of the data source used to populate the left navigation bar.	No
`<asp:ContentPlaceHolder id="PlaceHolderCalendarNavigator" runat="server" />`	The date picker used when a calendar is visible on the page.	No
`<asp:ContentPlaceHolder id="PlaceHolderLeftNavBarTop" runat="server"/>`	The top section of the left navigation bar.	No
`<asp:ContentPlaceHolder id="PlaceHolderLeftNavBar" runat="server">`	The Quick Launch bar.	No
`<asp:ContentPlaceHolder id="PlaceHolderLeftActions" runat="server">`	The additional objects above the Quick Launch bar.	No
`<asp:ContentPlaceHolder id="PlaceHolderMain" runat="server">`	The main content of the page.	No
`<asp:ContentPlaceHolder id="PlaceHolderFormDigest" runat="server">`	The container where the page form digest control is stored.	No
`<asp:ContentPlaceHolder id="PlaceHolderUtilityContent"`	The additional content at the bottom of the page, outside of the form tag.	No

Placeholder	Description	New
`runat="server"/>`		
`<asp:ContentPlaceHolder id="PlaceHolderTitleAreaClass" runat="server"/>`	The class for the title area. This is now in the head tag. Any customizations that add a web part zone in a content tag to this placeholder will cause an error on the page.	No
`<asp:ContentPlaceHolder id="PlaceHolderPageImage" runat="server"/>`	Does not appear as part of the UI but must be present for backward compatibility.	No
`<asp:ContentPlaceHolder id="PlaceHolderTitleLeftBorder" runat="server">`	Does not appear as part of the UI but must be present for backward compatibility.	No
`<asp:ContentPlaceHolder id="PlaceHolderMiniConsole" runat="server"/>`	Does not appear as part of the UI but must be present for backward compatibility.	No
`<asp:ContentPlaceHolder id="PlaceHolderTitleRightMargin" runat="server"/>`	Does not appear as part of the UI but must be present for backward compatibility.	No
`<asp:ContentPlaceHolder id="PlaceHolderTitleAreaSeparator" runat="server"/>`	Does not appear as part of the UI but must be present for backward compatibility.	No
`<asp:ContentPlaceHolder id="PlaceHolderNavSpacer" runat="server">`	Does not appear as part of the UI but must be present for backward compatibility.	No
`<asp:ContentPlaceHolder id="PlaceHolderLeftNavBarBorder" runat="server">`	Does not appear as part of the UI but must be present for backward compatibility.	No
`<asp:ContentPlaceHolder id="PlaceHolderBodyLeftBorder" runat="server">`	Does not appear as part of the UI but must be present for backward compatibility.	No
`<asp:ContentPlaceHolder id="PlaceHolderBodyRightMargin" runat="server">`	Does not appear as part of the UI but must be present for backward compatibility.	No

Team Site Elements and CSS Classes

Table A-3 is intended to help designers with some of the changes related to the team sites and relevant CSS classes that you will have to understand and override based on the need in your master pages.

Table A-3. Core V4 CSS Elements and corresponding classes

Element	CSS Classes	Notes
<body>	v4master	Applies CSS styles in corev4.css to the page.
Ribbon container	s4-pr	Makes the Ribbon container the full width of the page row.
	s4-ribbonrowhidetitle	Used to show or hide the ribbon title area when the ribbon is opened or closed.
	ms-cui-ribbon	Defines the main ribbon CSS class.
	ms-cui-ribbonTopBars	Defines the elements above the ribbon body, from the top of the page up to and including the ribbon tab titles.
Site Actions menu	ms-siteactionsmenu	Sets styles for the Site Actions menu as a whole.
	ms-siteactionsmenuinner	Sets styles for the inner Site Actions menu.
	ms-menu-a	Sets the margin-right property on the top menu.
Breadcrumb menu	s4-breadcrumb-menu	Sets styles for the Breadcrumb menu as a whole.
	s4-breadcrumb-anchor	Sets styles on hover over the Breadcrumb menu.
Breadcrumb menu header	s4-breadcrumb-top	Sets styles on the Breadcrumb menu top area when the drop-down tree is open.
	s4-breadcrumb-header	Sets styles on the breadcrumb folder icon when the breadcrumb

		tree drop-down menu is selected.
Breadcrumb menu items	`s4-breadcrumb`	Sets breadcrumb item styles.
	`s4-breadcrumbRootNode`	Sets styles on the breadcrumb team site root tree element.
	`s4-breadcrumbCurrentNode`	Sets styles on the breadcrumb home tree element.
Edit tab	`ms-qatbutton`	Sets styles on the Edit tab.
Browse tab	`ms-cui-tts`	Sets styles for the container for the tab title.
	`ms-cui-tt`	Sets styles for the tab title.
	`ms-browseTab`	Sets styles specific to the Browse tab.
	`ms-cui-tt-s`	Sets styles for a selected tab title.
	`ms-cui-tt-a`	Sets styles for the Ribbon tab title anchor (the link element that makes the table title clickable).
	`ms-cui-tt-span`	Sets styles for tab title span.
Page tab	`ms-cui-tt`	Sets styles for the tab title.
	`ms-cui-tt-a`	Sets styles for the Ribbon tab title anchor (the link element that makes the table title clickable).
	`ms-cui-tt-span`	Sets styles for tab title span.
User menu	`s4-trc-container-menu`	Sets styles for the top-right corner container menu.
	`ms-SPLink`	Sets styles applied to a menu item.
	`ms-welcomeMenu`	Sets the `margin-right` property on a drop-down menu item.

Element	CSS Classes	Notes
	ms-menu-a	Sets the margin-right property on the top menu.
Title row	s4-pr	Makes the title row the full width of the page row.
	s4-title	Sets styles on page title elements.
	s4-lp	Sets styles for elements on the left part of the page.
	s4-titlelogo	Sets margin and alignment on the title logo image.
	s4-titletext	Sets styles on all text to the right of the page logo graphic.
Search area	s4-search	Sets padding values on the search control in the secondary menu.
	s4-rp	Sets styles for elements on the right part of the page.
Quick Launch menu items	menu-item	Sets styles for the Home button located under the site logo.
	menu-item-text	Sets styles on the text of the Home button.
Recycle Bin link	s4-rcycl	Sets styles specific to the Recycle Bin link element.
	ms-splinkbutton-text	Sets styles on the link element.
All Site Content link	s4-specialNavIcon	Sets styles specific to the All Site Content link element.
	ms-splinkbutton-text	Sets styles on the link element.
Shared Documents link	ms-WPHeaderTd	Sets styles on the header section in the web part.
	ms-standardheader	Sets standard header styles.

	ms-WPTitle	Sets styles on the web part title.
Web Part menu	ms-WPHeaderTdMenu	Sets styles on the Web Part menu.
	ms-WPHeaderMenuImg	Sets styles on the Web Part menu image.
Selection check box	ms-WPHeaderTdSelection	Sets styles on the Web Part selection check box.
	ms-WPHeaderTdSelSpan	Sets span styles on the Web Part selection check box.
Item selection check box	ms-vh-icon	Sets styles on the item selection check box icon.
	ms-vh2	Sets the height property.
Type, Name, Modified, and Modified By options	ms-vh-div	Sets the padding-top property.
	s4-ctx	Sets padding, position, and display properties on the drop-down menu.
	ms-vh2	Sets the height property.
Shared Documents text	ms-vb	Sets styles on the Shared Documents control group text area (bottom of group).
Add document link	ms-addnew	Sets styles specified to the Add document link.
Photo image	ms-rte-layoutszone-outer	Rich text editor class that sets the float property on controls of the team site home web part.
	ms-rte-layoutszone-inner	Rich text editor class that sets styles on content areas of the team site home web part.
	ms-rteThemeForeColor-5-5	Rich text editor class that sets the theme foreground color (to dark blue) on the Getting Started wiki

Element	CSS Classes	Notes
		area.
Getting Started area	ms-rte-layoutszone-outer	Rich text editor class that sets the float property on controls of the team site home web part.
	ms-rte-layoutszone-inner	Rich text editor class that sets styles on content areas of the team site home web part.
	ms-rteThemeForeColor-5-5	Rich text editor class that sets the theme foreground color (to dark blue) on the Getting Started wiki area.
Share this site Change site theme Set site icon Customize Quick Launch links	ms-rteTable-0, ms-rteTableEvenRow-0 ms-rteTableEvenCol-0 ms-rteTableOddCol-0 ms-rteTableOddRow-0	Rich text editor classes that set styles on the controls under the Getting Started wiki area.

MOSS 2007 Deprecated Methods

Table A-4 lists some of the deprecated methods from TechNet resource; for the full list, see http://blog.srinisistla.com/Lists/Posts/Post.aspx?ID=219.

Table A-4. Deprecated Methods in SharePoint 2010

Namespace: Microsoft.SharePoint.WebPartPages **Type:** GetRequiresData **Details:** Use IConnectionData.GetRequiresData() instead.
Namespace: Microsoft.SharePoint.WebPartPages **Type:** GetData **Details:** Use IConnectionData.GetData() instead.
Namespace: Microsoft.SharePoint.WebPartPages

Type: GetRequiresData   **Details:** Use IConnectionData.GetRequiresData() instead.
Namespace: Microsoft.SharePoint.WebPartPages   **Type:** EnsureInterfaces   **Details:** Use the ConnectionProvider or ConnectionConsumer attribute to create ConnectionPoint instead.
Namespace: Microsoft.SharePoint.WebPartPages   **Type:** GetInitEventArgs   **Details:** Use ConnectionProvider or ConnectionConsumer to create ConnectionPoint instead.
Namespace: Microsoft.SharePoint.WebPartPages   **Type:** CanRunAt   **Details:** Use ConnectionProvider or ConnectionConsumer to create ConnectionPoint instead.
Namespace: Microsoft.SharePoint.WebPartPages   **Type:** PartCommunicationMain   **Details:** Use ConnectionProvider or ConnectionConsumer to create ConnectionPoint instead.
Namespace: Microsoft.SharePoint.WebPartPages   **Type:** GetRequiresData   **Details:** Use IConnectionData.GetRequiresData() instead.
Namespace: Microsoft.SharePoint.WebPartPages   **Type:** GetRequiresData   **Details:** Use IConnectionData.GetRequiresData() instead.
Namespace: Microsoft.SharePoint.WebPartPages.Communication   **Type:** IParametersInProvider   **Details:** Use System.Web.UI.WebControls.WebParts.IWebPartParameters instead.
Namespace: Microsoft.SharePoint.WebPartPages.Communication   **Type:** IParametersOutProvider   **Details:** Use System.Web.UI.WebControls.WebParts.IWebPartParameters instead.
Namespace: Microsoft.SharePoint.WebPartPages.Communication   **Type:** IParametersOutConsumer

Details: Use System.Web.UI.WebControls.WebParts.IWebPartParameters instead.

Namespace: Microsoft.SharePoint.WebPartPages
Type: GetRequiresData
Details: Use IConnectionData.GetRequiresData() instead.

Namespace: Microsoft.SharePoint.WebPartPages
Type: GetData
Details: Use IConnectionData.GetData() instead.

Namespace: Microsoft.SharePoint.WebPartPages
Type: GetPostBackEventReference
Details: The recommended alternative is ClientScript.GetPostBackEventReference. For more information, see http://go.microsoft.com/fwlink/?linkid=14202.

Namespace: Microsoft.SharePoint.WebPartPages
Type: GetPostBackEventReference
Details: The recommended alternative is ClientScript.GetPostBackEventReference. For more information, see http://go.microsoft.com/fwlink/?linkid=14202.

Namespace: Microsoft.SharePoint.WebPartPages
Type: GetPostBackClientEvent
Details: The recommended alternative is ClientScript.GetPostBackEventReference. For more information, see http://go.microsoft.com/fwlink/?linkid=14202.

Namespace: Microsoft.SharePoint.WebPartPages
Type: GetPostBackClientHyperlink
Details: The recommended alternative is ClientScript.GetPostBackClientHyperlink. For more information, see http://go.microsoft.com/fwlink/?linkid=14202.

Namespace: Microsoft.SharePoint.WebPartPages
Type: IsClientScriptBlockRegistered
Details: The recommended alternative is ClientScript.IsClientScriptBlockRegistered(string key) http://go.microsoft.com/fwlink/?linkid=14202.

Namespace: Microsoft.SharePoint.WebPartPages
Type: IsStartupScriptRegistered
Details: The recommended alternative is ClientScript.IsStartupScriptRegistered(string key). For

more information, see http://go.microsoft.com/fwlink/?linkid=14202.

Namespace: Microsoft.SharePoint.WebPartPages

Type: RegisterHiddenField

Details: The recommended alternative is ClientScript.RegisterHiddenField(string hiddenFieldName, string hiddenFieldInitialValue). For more information, see http://go.microsoft.com/fwlink/?linkid=14202.

Namespace: Microsoft.SharePoint.WebPartPages

Type: RegisterClientScriptBlock

Details: The recommended alternative is ClientScript.RegisterClientScriptBlock(Type type, string key, string script). For more information, see http://go.microsoft.com/fwlink/?linkid=14202.

Namespace: Microsoft.SharePoint.WebPartPages

Type: RegisterStartupScript

Details: The recommended alternative is ClientScript.RegisterStartupScript(Type type, string key, string script). For more information, see http://go.microsoft.com/fwlink/?linkid=14202.

Namespace: Microsoft.SharePoint.WebControls

Type: RegisterOnSubmitStatement

Details: The recommended alternative is ClientScript.RegisterOnSubmitStatement(Type type, string key, string script). For more information, see http://go.microsoft.com/fwlink/?linkid=14202.

Namespace: Microsoft.SharePoint.Administration

Type: SPGlobalAdmin

Details: Most of the functionality in this class is available in SPFarm or SPWebService.

Namespace: Microsoft.SharePoint.Administration

Type: OpenVirtualServer

Details: OpenVirtualServer is obsolete. Use SPWebApplication.Lookup() instead.

Namespace: Microsoft.SharePoint.Administration

Type: ExtendVirtualServer

Details: SPGlobalAdmin.ExtendVirtualServer is obsolete. To create a new web application,

use the SPWebApplicationBuilder class.

Namespace: Microsoft.SharePoint.Administration

Type: ExtendVirtualServerInWebFarm

Details: To extend a web application to a new IIS web site, add a new entry to `SPWebApplication.IisSettings`. Duplicating IIS web sites on other machines in the farm is now handled automatically.
Namespace: `Microsoft.SharePoint.Administration` **Type:** `UnextendVirtualServer` **Details:** To remove SharePoint from an IIS web site, remove the `IISSettings` object from the web application that the site is serving, and call `SPWebApplication.Unprovision()`.
Namespace: `Microsoft.SharePoint.Administration` **Type:** `CreateAdminVirtualServer` **Details:** The Administration web application is now created at the same time as the server farm. To provision the Central Administration site on a server, enable its web service instance.
Namespace: `Microsoft.SharePoint.Administration` **Type:** `SetAdminPort` **Details:** To change the port of the administration site, update the `SPIisSettings` associated with `SPAdministrationWebApplication.Local` and call `SPWebApplication.Provision()`.
Namespace: `Microsoft.SharePoint.Administration` **Type:** `SetAdminPortAppPool` **Details:** Use `SPAdministrationWebApplication.Local` to change this setting.
Namespace: `Microsoft.SharePoint.Administration` **Type:** `DeleteAdminVirtualServer` **Details:** `DeleteAdminVirtualServer` is obsolete. Call `SPWebServiceInstance.LocalAdministration.Unprovision()` instead.
Namespace: `Microsoft.SharePoint.Administration` **Type:** `CreateConfigDatabase` **Details:** Use `SPFarm.Create` instead.
Namespace: `Microsoft.SharePoint.Administration` **Type:** `UpgradeApplication` **Details:** `UpgradeApplication()` is a deprecated method.
Namespace: `Microsoft.SharePoint.Administration` **Type:** `UpgradeConfigDB`

Details: `UpgradeConfigDB()` is a deprecated method.
Namespace: `Microsoft.SharePoint.Administration` **Type:** `UpdateConfigDatabaseConnection` **Details:** Use `SPFarm.Join()` instead.
Namespace: `Microsoft.SharePoint.Administration` **Type:** `DeleteConfigDB` **Details:** Use `SPFarm.UnJoin()` instead.
Namespace: `Microsoft.SharePoint.Administration` **Type:** `RegisterASPNETClient` **Details:** This method is no longer necessary.
Namespace: `Microsoft.SharePoint.Administration` **Type:** `StartDBService` **Details:** Call `SPWindowsServiceInstance.Provision()` instead.
Namespace: `Microsoft.SharePoint.Administration` **Type:** `StartTimerService` **Details:** Call `SPWindowsServiceInstance.Provision()` instead.
Namespace: `Microsoft.SharePoint.Administration` **Type:** `Log` **Details:** This method is obsolete.
Namespace: `Microsoft.SharePoint.Administration` **Type:** `ListCustomGlobalWebTemplates` **Details:** Web templates are now accessed via `SPWebService`.
Namespace: `Microsoft.SharePoint.Administration` **Type:** `AddCustomGlobalWebTemplate` **Details:** Web templates are now accessed via `SPWebService`.
Namespace: `Microsoft.SharePoint.Administration` **Type:** `DeleteCustomGlobalWebTemplate` **Details:** Web templates are now accessed via `SPWebService`.

Namespace: `Microsoft.SharePoint.Administration` **Type:** `AddWPPack` **Details:** Use the SPSolution objects instead.
Namespace: `Microsoft.SharePoint.Administration` **Type:** `RemoveWPPack` **Details:** Use the SPSolution objects instead.
Namespace: `Microsoft.SharePoint.Administration` **Type:** `RefreshConfigCache` **Details:** `SPGlobalAdmin.RefreshConfigCache()` is obsolete. The configuration cache is now refreshed automatically by the timer service.
Namespace: `Microsoft.SharePoint.Administration` **Type:** `IsCurrentUserGlobalAdmin` **Details:** This method is no longer necessary.
Namespace: `Microsoft.SharePoint.Administration` **Type:** `Close` **Details:** This method is no longer necessary.
Namespace: `Microsoft.SharePoint.Administration` **Type:** `Dispose` **Details:** This method is no longer necessary.
Namespace: `Microsoft.SharePoint.Administration` **Type:** `SPGlobalConfig` **Details:** Most of the functionality in this class is available in `SPFarm` or `SPWebService`.
Namespace: `Microsoft.SharePoint.Administration` **Type:** `SPVirtualServer` **Details:** Use `SPWebApplication` or `SPIisSettings` instead.
Namespace: `Microsoft.SharePoint.Administration` **Type:** `UpgradeVirtualServer` **Details:** `UpgradeVirtualServer()` is a deprecated method.

Namespace: `Microsoft.SharePoint.Administration`

Type: `SPVirtualServerConfig`

Details: Use `SPWebApplication` or `SPIisSettings` instead.

Namespace: `Microsoft.SharePoint.SoapServer`

Type: `GetPostBackEventReference`

Details: The recommended alternative is `ClientScript.GetPostBackEventReference`. For more information, see `http://go.microsoft.com/fwlink/?linkid=14202`.

Namespace: `Microsoft.SharePoint.SoapServer`

Type: `RegisterStartupScript`

Details: The recommended alternative is `ClientScript.RegisterStartupScript(Type type, string key, string script)`. For more information, see `http://go.microsoft.com/fwlink/?linkid=14202`.

Namespace: `Microsoft.SharePoint.SoapServer`

Type: `RegisterOnSubmitStatement`

Details: The recommended alternative is `ClientScript.RegisterOnSubmitStatement(Type type, string key, string script)`. For more information, see `http://go.microsoft.com/fwlink/?linkid=14202`.

Namespace: `Microsoft.SharePoint.SoapServer`

Type: `GetWebPartPageDocument`

Details: Use `GetWebPartPage` instead.

Namespace: `Microsoft.SharePoint.SoapServer`

Type: `GetWebPart`

Details: Use `GetWebPart2` instead.

Namespace: `Microsoft.SharePoint.SoapServer`

Type: `GetWebPartProperties`

Details: Use `GetWebPartProperties2` instead.

Namespace: `Microsoft.SharePoint.SoapServer`

Type: `SaveWebPart`

Details: Use `SaveWebPart2` instead.

Namespace: `Microsoft.SharePoint`

Type: `SPRights`

Details: Use SPBasePermissions instead.
Namespace: Microsoft.SharePoint **Type:** GetWebPartCollection **Details:** Use SPFile.GetLimitedWebPartManager instead.
Namespace: Microsoft.SharePoint **Type:** SPRoleCollection **Details:** Use the SPRoleDefinitionCollection class instead.
Namespace: Microsoft.SharePoint **Type:** GetWebPartCollection **Details:** Use SPWeb.GetLimitedWebPartManager instead.
Namespace: Microsoft.SharePoint **Type:** SPWebPartCollection **Details:** Use SPLimitedWebPartManager instead.
Namespace: Microsoft.SharePoint.Utilities **Type:** EnsureSessionCredentials **Details:** Use SPUtility.EnsureAuthentication instead.
Namespace: Microsoft.SharePoint.Utilities **Type:** ValidateDatabaseConnectionString **Details:** This method is no longer needed.
Namespace: Microsoft.SharePoint.Utilities **Type:** GuessLoginNameFromEmail **Details:** Use SPUtility.ResolvePrincipal instead.
Namespace: Microsoft.SharePoint.Utilities **Type:** GetLoginNameFromEmail **Details:** Use SPUtility.ResolvePrincipal instead.
Namespace: Microsoft.SharePoint.WebControls **Type:** OWSForm **Details:** This class has been deprecated.

Namespace: `Microsoft.SharePoint.WebControls`   **Type:** `OWSControl`   **Details:** This class has been deprecated.
Namespace: `Microsoft.SharePoint.WebControls`   **Type:** `OWSSubmitButton`   **Details:** This class has been deprecated.
Namespace: `Microsoft.SharePoint.WebControls`   **Type:** `OWSDateField`   **Details:** This class has been deprecated.
Namespace: `Microsoft.SharePoint.WebControls`   **Type:** `OWSNumberField`   **Details:** This class has been deprecated.
Namespace: `Microsoft.SharePoint.Meetings`   **Type:** `GetRequiresData`   **Details:** Use `IConnectionData.GetRequiresData()` instead.
Namespace: `Microsoft.SharePoint.Meetings`   **Type:** `GetData`   **Details:** Use `IConnectionData.GetData()` instead.
Namespace: `Microsoft.SharePoint.Meetings`   **Type:** `PartCommunicationMain`   **Details:** Use `ConnectionProvider` or `ConnectionConsumer` to create `ConnectionPoint` instead.
Namespace: `Microsoft.SharePoint.ApplicationRuntime`   **Type:** `ProcessRequest`   **Details:** This method has been deprecated.
Namespace: `Microsoft.SharePoint.ApplicationRuntime`   **Type:** `SPProcessRequest`   **Details:** This method has been deprecated.

Namespace: `Microsoft.SharePoint.ApplicationRuntime` **Type:** `DisposeResources` **Details:** This method has been deprecated.
Namespace: `Microsoft.SharePoint.WebPartPages.Communication` **Type:** `InitEventArgs` **Details:** Use `ConnectionProvider` or `ConnectionConsumer` to create `ConnectionPoint` instead.
Namespace: `Microsoft.SharePoint.WebPartPages.Communication` **Type:** `ConnectionRunAt` **Details:** Use `ConnectionProvider` or `ConnectionConsumer` to create `ConnectionPoint` instead.
Namespace: `Microsoft.SharePoint.WebPartPages.Communication` **Type:** `InterfaceTypes` **Details:** Use `ConnectionProvider` or `ConnectionConsumer` to create `ConnectionPoint` instead.
Namespace: `Microsoft.SharePoint.WebPartPages.Communication` **Type:** `ListReadyEventArgs` **Details:** Use `System.Web.UI.WebControls.WebParts.IWebPartTable` instead.
Namespace: `Microsoft.SharePoint.WebPartPages.Communication` **Type:** `ParametersOutProviderInitEventHandler` **Details:** Use `System.Web.UI.WebControls.WebParts.IWebPartParameters` instead.
Namespace: `Microsoft.SharePoint.WebPartPages.Communication` **Type:** `ParametersOutReadyEventHandler` **Details:** Use `System.Web.UI.WebControls.WebParts.IWebPartParameters` instead.
Namespace: `Microsoft.SharePoint.Publishing.WebControls` **Type:** `GetRequiresData` **Details:** Use `IConnectionData.GetRequiresData()` instead.
Namespace: `Microsoft.SharePoint.Publishing.WebControls` **Type:** `GetData` **Details:** Use `IConnectionData.GetData()` instead.

Namespace: `Microsoft.SharePoint.Publishing.WebControls`

Type: `EnsureInterfaces`

Details: Use `ConnectionProvider` or `ConnectionConsumer` to create `ConnectionPoint` instead.

Namespace: `Microsoft.SharePoint.Publishing.WebControls`

Type: `GetInitEventArgs`

Details: Use `ConnectionProvider` or `ConnectionConsumer` to create `ConnectionPoint` instead.

Namespace: `Microsoft.SharePoint.Publishing.WebControls`

Type: `InitializeNonDefault`

Details: This method has been deprecated. Use `InitializeExistingComponent` instead. For more information, see `http://go.microsoft.com/fwlink/?linkid=14202`.

Namespace: `Microsoft.SharePoint.Publishing.WebControls`

Type: `OnSetComponentDefaults`

Details: This method has been deprecated. Use `InitializeNewComponent` instead. For more information, see `http://go.microsoft.com/fwlink/?linkid=14202`.

Namespace: `Microsoft.SharePoint.Publishing.WebControls`

Type: `GetRequiresData`

Details: Use `IConnectionData.GetRequiresData()` instead.

Namespace: `Microsoft.SharePoint.Publishing.WebControls`

Type: `GetData`

Details: Use `IConnectionData.GetData()` instead.

Namespace: `Microsoft.SharePoint.Publishing.WebControls`

Type: `EnsureInterfaces`

Details: Use `ConnectionProvider` or `ConnectionConsumer` to create `ConnectionPoint` instead.

Namespace: `Microsoft.SharePoint.Publishing.WebControls`

Type: `GetInitEventArgs`

Details: Use `ConnectionProvider` or `ConnectionConsumer` to create `ConnectionPoint` instead.

Namespace: `Microsoft.SharePoint.Publishing.WebControls`

Type: `CanRunAt`

Details: Use ConnectionProvider or ConnectionConsumer to create ConnectionPoint instead.
Namespace: Microsoft.SharePoint.Publishing.WebControls **Type:** PartCommunicationConnect **Details:** Use ConnectionProvider or ConnectionConsumer to create ConnectionPoint instead.
Namespace: Microsoft.SharePoint.Publishing.WebControls **Type:** PartCommunicationInit **Details:** Use ConnectionProvider or ConnectionConsumer to create ConnectionPoint instead.
Namespace: Microsoft.SharePoint.Publishing.WebControls **Type:** PartCommunicationMain **Details:** Use ConnectionProvider or ConnectionConsumer to create ConnectionPoint instead.
Namespace: Microsoft.SharePoint.Publishing.WebControls **Type:** GetRequiresData **Details:** Use IConnectionData.GetRequiresData() instead.
Namespace: Microsoft.SharePoint.Publishing.WebControls **Type:** GetData **Details:** Use IConnectionData.GetData() instead.
Namespace: Microsoft.SharePoint.Publishing.WebControls **Type:** EnsureInterfaces **Details:** Use ConnectionProvider or ConnectionConsumer to create ConnectionPoint instead.
Namespace: Microsoft.SharePoint.Publishing.WebControls **Type:** GetInitEventArgs **Details:** Use ConnectionProvider or ConnectionConsumer to create ConnectionPoint instead.
Namespace: Microsoft.SharePoint.Publishing.WebControls **Type:** CanRunAt **Details:** Use ConnectionProvider or ConnectionConsumer to create ConnectionPoint instead.
Namespace: Microsoft.SharePoint.Publishing.WebControls **Type:** PartCommunicationConnect **Details:** Use ConnectionProvider or ConnectionConsumer to create ConnectionPoint instead.

Namespace: Microsoft.SharePoint.Publishing.WebControls **Type:** PartCommunicationInit **Details:** Use ConnectionProvider or ConnectionConsumer to create ConnectionPoint instead.
Namespace: Microsoft.SharePoint.Publishing.WebControls **Type:** PartCommunicationMain **Details:** Use ConnectionProvider or ConnectionConsumer to create ConnectionPoint instead.
Namespace: Microsoft.SharePoint.Publishing.WebControls **Type:** GetRequiresData **Details:** Use IConnectionData.GetRequiresData() instead.
Namespace: Microsoft.SharePoint.Publishing.WebControls **Type:** GetData **Details:** Use IConnectionData.GetData() instead.
Namespace: Microsoft.SharePoint.Publishing.WebControls **Type:** EnsureInterfaces **Details:** Use ConnectionProvider or ConnectionConsumer to create ConnectionPoint instead.
Namespace: Microsoft.SharePoint.Publishing.WebControls **Type:** GetInitEventArgs **Details:** Use ConnectionProvider or ConnectionConsumer to create ConnectionPoint instead.
Namespace: Microsoft.SharePoint.Publishing.WebControls **Type:** CanRunAt **Details:** Use ConnectionProvider or ConnectionConsumer to create ConnectionPoint instead.
Namespace: Microsoft.SharePoint.Publishing.WebControls **Type:** PartCommunicationConnect **Details:** Use ConnectionProvider or ConnectionConsumer to create ConnectionPoint instead.
Namespace: Microsoft.SharePoint.Publishing.WebControls **Type:** PartCommunicationInit **Details:** Use ConnectionProvider or ConnectionConsumer to create ConnectionPoint instead.

Namespace: `Microsoft.SharePoint.Publishing.WebControls` **Type:** `PartCommunicationMain` **Details:** Use `ConnectionProvider` or `ConnectionConsumer` to create `ConnectionPoint` instead.
Namespace: `Microsoft.SharePoint.Publishing.WebControls` **Type:** `GetRequiresData` **Details:** Use `IConnectionData.GetRequiresData()` instead.
Namespace: `Microsoft.SharePoint.Publishing.WebControls` **Type:** `GetData` **Details:** Use `IConnectionData.GetData()` instead.
Namespace: `Microsoft.SharePoint.Publishing.WebControls` **Type:** `EnsureInterfaces` **Details:** Use `ConnectionProvider` or `ConnectionConsumer` to create `ConnectionPoint` instead.
Namespace: `Microsoft.SharePoint.Publishing.WebControls` **Type:** `GetInitEventArgs` **Details:** Use `ConnectionProvider` or `ConnectionConsumer` to create `ConnectionPoint` instead.
Namespace: `Microsoft.SharePoint.Publishing.WebControls` **Type:** `CanRunAt` **Details:** Use `ConnectionProvider` or `ConnectionConsumer` to create `ConnectionPoint` instead.
Namespace: `Microsoft.SharePoint.Publishing.WebControls` **Type:** `PartCommunicationConnect` **Details:** Use `ConnectionProvider` or `ConnectionConsumer` to create `ConnectionPoint` instead.
Namespace: `Microsoft.SharePoint.Publishing.WebControls` **Type:** `PartCommunicationInit` **Details:** Use `ConnectionProvider` or `ConnectionConsumer` to create `ConnectionPoint` instead.
Namespace: Microsoft.SharePoint.Publishing.WebControls **Type:** PartCommunicationMain **Details:** Use `ConnectionProvider` or `ConnectionConsumer` to create `ConnectionPoint` instead.

Namespace: `Microsoft.SharePoint.Publishing.Internal.CodeBehind` **Type:** `GetPostBackEventReference` **Details:** The recommended alternative is `ClientScript.GetPostBackEventReference`. For more information, see http://go.microsoft.com/fwlink/?linkid=14202.
Namespace: `Microsoft.SharePoint.Publishing.Internal.CodeBehind` **Type:** `GetPostBackEventReference` **Details:** The recommended alternative is `ClientScript.GetPostBackEventReference`. For more information, see http://go.microsoft.com/fwlink/?linkid=14202.
Namespace: `Microsoft.SharePoint.Publishing.Internal.CodeBehind` **Type:** `GetPostBackClientEvent` **Details:** The recommended alternative is `ClientScript.GetPostBackEventReference`. For more information, see http://go.microsoft.com/fwlink/?linkid=14202.
Namespace: `Microsoft.SharePoint.Publishing.Internal.CodeBehind` **Type:** `GetPostBackClientHyperlink` **Details:** The recommended alternative is `ClientScript.GetPostBackClientHyperlink`. For more information, see http://go.microsoft.com/fwlink/?linkid=14202.
Namespace: `Microsoft.SharePoint.Publishing.Internal.CodeBehind` **Type:** `IsClientScriptBlockRegistered` **Details:** The recommended alternative is `ClientScript.IsClientScriptBlockRegistered(string key)`. For more information, see http://go.microsoft.com/fwlink/?linkid=14202.
Namespace: `Microsoft.SharePoint.Publishing.Internal.CodeBehind` **Type:** `IsStartupScriptRegistered` **Details:** The recommended alternative is `ClientScript.IsStartupScriptRegistered(string key)`. For more information, see http://go.microsoft.com/fwlink/?linkid=14202.
Namespace: `Microsoft.SharePoint.Publishing.Internal.CodeBehind` **Type:** `GetPostBackEventReference` **Details:** The recommended alternative is `ClientScript.GetPostBackEventReference`. For more information, see http://go.microsoft.com/fwlink/?linkid=14202.
Namespace: `Microsoft.SharePoint.Publishing.Internal.CodeBehind` **Type:** `GetPostBackEventReference` **Details:** The recommended alternative is `ClientScript.GetPostBackEventReference`. For more

information, see http://go.microsoft.com/fwlink/?linkid=14202.

Namespace: Microsoft.SharePoint.Publishing.Internal.CodeBehind

Type: GetPostBackClientEvent

Details: The recommended alternative is ClientScript.GetPostBackEventReference. For more information, see http://go.microsoft.com/fwlink/?linkid=14202.

Namespace: Microsoft.SharePoint.Publishing.Internal.CodeBehind

Type: GetPostBackClientHyperlink

Details: The recommended alternative is ClientScript.GetPostBackClientHyperlink. For more information, see http://go.microsoft.com/fwlink/?linkid=14202.

Namespace: Microsoft.SharePoint.Publishing.Internal.CodeBehind

Type: IsClientScriptBlockRegistered

Details: The recommended alternative is ClientScript.IsClientScriptBlockRegistered(string key). For more information, see http://go.microsoft.com/fwlink/?linkid=14202.

Namespace: Microsoft.SharePoint.Publishing.Internal.CodeBehind

Type: IsStartupScriptRegistered

Details: The recommended alternative is ClientScript.IsStartupScriptRegistered(string key). For more information, see http://go.microsoft.com/fwlink/?linkid=14202.

Namespace: Microsoft.SharePoint.Publishing.Internal.CodeBehind

Type: RegisterArrayDeclaration

Details: The recommended alternative is ClientScript.RegisterArrayDeclaration(string arrayName, string arrayValue). For more information, see http://go.microsoft.com/fwlink/?linkid=14202.

Namespace: Microsoft.SharePoint.Publishing.Internal.CodeBehind

Type: GetPostBackClientEvent

Details: The recommended alternative is ClientScript.GetPostBackEventReference. For more information, see http://go.microsoft.com/fwlink/?linkid=14202.

Namespace: Microsoft.SharePoint.Publishing.Internal.CodeBehind

Type: IsStartupScriptRegistered

Details: The recommended alternative is ClientScript.IsStartupScriptRegistered(string key). For more information, see http://go.microsoft.com/fwlink/?linkid=14202.

Namespace: Microsoft.SharePoint.Publishing.Internal.CodeBehind

Type: RegisterArrayDeclaration

Details: The recommended alternative is `ClientScript.RegisterArrayDeclaration(string arrayName, string arrayValue)`. For more information, see `http://go.microsoft.com/fwlink/?linkid=14202`.

Namespace: `Microsoft.SharePoint.Publishing.Internal.CodeBehind`

Type: `RegisterHiddenField`

Details: The recommended alternative is `ClientScript.RegisterHiddenField(string hiddenFieldName, string hiddenFieldInitialValue)`. For more information, see `http://go.microsoft.com/fwlink/?linkid=14202`.

Namespace: `Microsoft.SharePoint.Publishing.Internal.CodeBehind`

Type: `RegisterClientScriptBlock`

Details: The recommended alternative is `ClientScript.RegisterClientScriptBlock(Type type, string key, string script)`. For more information, see `http://go.microsoft.com/fwlink/?linkid=14202`.

Namespace: `Microsoft.SharePoint.Publishing.Internal.CodeBehind`

Type: `RegisterStartupScript`

Details: The recommended alternative is `ClientScript.RegisterStartupScript(Type type, string key, string script)`. For more information, see `http://go.microsoft.com/fwlink/?linkid=14202`.

Namespace: `Microsoft.SharePoint.Publishing.Internal.CodeBehind`

Type: `RegisterOnSubmitStatement`

Details: The recommended alternative is `ClientScript.RegisterOnSubmitStatement(Type type, string key, string script)`. For more information, see `http://go.microsoft.com/fwlink/?linkid=14202`.

Namespace: `Microsoft.SharePoint.Publishing.Internal.CodeBehind`

Type: `GetPostBackEventReference`

Details: The recommended alternative is `ClientScript.GetPostBackEventReference`. For more information, see `http://go.microsoft.com/fwlink/?linkid=14202`.

Namespace: `Microsoft.SharePoint.Publishing.Internal.CodeBehind`

Type: `GetPostBackEventReference`

Details: The recommended alternative is `ClientScript.GetPostBackEventReference`. For more information, see `http://go.microsoft.com/fwlink/?linkid=14202`.

Namespace: `Microsoft.SharePoint.Publishing.Internal.CodeBehind`

Type: `GetPostBackClientEvent`

Details: The recommended alternative is `ClientScript.GetPostBackEventReference`. For more information, see `http://go.microsoft.com/fwlink/?linkid=14202`.

Namespace: Microsoft.SharePoint.Publishing.Internal.CodeBehind

Type: GetPostBackClientHyperlink

Details: The recommended alternative is ClientScript.GetPostBackClientHyperlink. For more information, see http://go.microsoft.com/fwlink/?linkid=14202.

Namespace: Microsoft.SharePoint.Publishing.Internal.CodeBehind

Type: IsClientScriptBlockRegistered

Details: The recommended alternative is ClientScript.IsClientScriptBlockRegistered(string key). For more information, see http://go.microsoft.com/fwlink/?linkid=14202.

Namespace: Microsoft.SharePoint.Publishing.Internal.CodeBehind

Type: IsStartupScriptRegistered

Details: The recommended alternative is ClientScript.IsStartupScriptRegistered(string key). For more information, see http://go.microsoft.com/fwlink/?linkid=14202.

Namespace: Microsoft.SharePoint.Publishing.Internal.CodeBehind

Type: RegisterArrayDeclaration

Details: The recommended alternative is ClientScript.RegisterArrayDeclaration(string arrayName, string arrayValue). For more information, see http://go.microsoft.com/fwlink/?linkid=14202.

Namespace: Microsoft.SharePoint.Publishing.Internal.CodeBehind

Type: RegisterHiddenField

Details: The recommended alternative is ClientScript.RegisterHiddenField(string hiddenFieldName, string hiddenFieldInitialValue). For more information, see http://go.microsoft.com/fwlink/?linkid=14202.

Namespace: Microsoft.SharePoint.Publishing.Internal.CodeBehind

Type: RegisterClientScriptBlock

Details: The recommended alternative is ClientScript.RegisterClientScriptBlock(Type type, string key, string script). For more information, see http://go.microsoft.com/fwlink/?linkid=14202.

Namespace: Microsoft.SharePoint.Publishing.Internal.CodeBehind

Type: RegisterStartupScript

Details: The recommended alternative is ClientScript.RegisterStartupScript(Type type, string key, string script). For more information, see http://go.microsoft.com/fwlink/?linkid=14202.

Namespace: Microsoft.SharePoint.Publishing.Internal.CodeBehind

Type: RegisterOnSubmitStatement

Details: The recommended alternative is ClientScript.RegisterOnSubmitStatement(Type type, string

---

key, string script). For more information, see http://go.microsoft.com/fwlink/?linkid=14202.

Namespace: Microsoft.SharePoint.Publishing.Internal.CodeBehind

Type: GetPostBackEventReference

Details: The recommended alternative is ClientScript.GetPostBackEventReference. For more information, see http://go.microsoft.com/fwlink/?linkid=14202.

Namespace: Microsoft.SharePoint.Publishing.Internal.CodeBehind

Type: GetPostBackEventReference

Details: The recommended alternative is ClientScript.GetPostBackEventReference. For more information, see http://go.microsoft.com/fwlink/?linkid=14202.

Namespace: Microsoft.SharePoint.Publishing.Internal.CodeBehind

Type: GetPostBackClientEvent

Details: The recommended alternative is ClientScript.GetPostBackEventReference. For more information, see http://go.microsoft.com/fwlink/?linkid=14202.

Namespace: Microsoft.SharePoint.Publishing.Internal.CodeBehind

Type: GetPostBackClientHyperlink

Details: The recommended alternative is ClientScript.GetPostBackClientHyperlink. For more information, see http://go.microsoft.com/fwlink/?linkid=14202.

Namespace: Microsoft.SharePoint.Publishing.Internal.CodeBehind

Type: IsClientScriptBlockRegistered

Details: The recommended alternative is ClientScript.IsClientScriptBlockRegistered(string key). For more information, see http://go.microsoft.com/fwlink/?linkid=14202.

Namespace: Microsoft.SharePoint.Publishing.Internal.CodeBehind

Type: IsStartupScriptRegistered

Details: The recommended alternative is ClientScript.IsStartupScriptRegistered(string key). For more information, see http://go.microsoft.com/fwlink/?linkid=14202.

Namespace: Microsoft.SharePoint.Publishing.Internal.CodeBehind

Type: RegisterArrayDeclaration

Details: The recommended alternative is ClientScript.RegisterArrayDeclaration(string arrayName, string arrayValue). For more information, see http://go.microsoft.com/fwlink/?linkid=14202.

Namespace: Microsoft.SharePoint.Publishing.Internal.CodeBehind

Type: RegisterHiddenField

Details: The recommended alternative is `ClientScript.RegisterHiddenField(string hiddenFieldName, string hiddenFieldInitialValue)`. For more information, see `http://go.microsoft.com/fwlink/?linkid=14202`.

Namespace: `Microsoft.SharePoint.Publishing.Internal.CodeBehind`
Type: `RegisterClientScriptBlock`
Details: The recommended alternative is `ClientScript.RegisterClientScriptBlock(Type type, string key, string script)`. For more information, see `http://go.microsoft.com/fwlink/?linkid=14202`.

Namespace: `Microsoft.SharePoint.Publishing.Internal.CodeBehind`
Type: `RegisterStartupScript`
Details: The recommended alternative is `ClientScript.RegisterStartupScript(Type type, string key, string script)`. For more information, see `http://go.microsoft.com/fwlink/?linkid=14202`.

Namespace: `Microsoft.SharePoint.Publishing.Internal.CodeBehind`
Type: `RegisterOnSubmitStatement`
Details: The recommended alternative is `ClientScript.RegisterOnSubmitStatement(Type type, string key, string script)`. For more information, see `http://go.microsoft.com/fwlink/?linkid=14202`.

Namespace: `Microsoft.SharePoint.Publishing.Internal.CodeBehind`
Type: `GetPostBackEventReference`
Details: The recommended alternative is `ClientScript.GetPostBackEventReference`. For more information, see `http://go.microsoft.com/fwlink/?linkid=14202`.

Namespace: `Microsoft.SharePoint.Publishing.Internal.CodeBehind`
Type: `GetPostBackEventReference`
Details: The recommended alternative is `ClientScript.GetPostBackEventReference`. For more information, see `http://go.microsoft.com/fwlink/?linkid=14202`.

Namespace: `Microsoft.SharePoint.Publishing.Internal.CodeBehind`
Type: `GetPostBackClientEvent`
Details: The recommended alternative is `ClientScript.GetPostBackEventReference`. For more information, see `http://go.microsoft.com/fwlink/?linkid=14202`.

Namespace: `Microsoft.SharePoint.Publishing.Internal.CodeBehind`
Type: `GetPostBackClientHyperlink`
Details: The recommended alternative is `ClientScript.GetPostBackClientHyperlink`. For more information, see `http://go.microsoft.com/fwlink/?linkid=14202`.

Namespace: Microsoft.SharePoint.Publishing.Internal.CodeBehind

Type: IsClientScriptBlockRegistered

Details: The recommended alternative is ClientScript.IsClientScriptBlockRegistered(string key). For more information, see http://go.microsoft.com/fwlink/?linkid=14202.

Namespace: Microsoft.SharePoint.Publishing.Internal.CodeBehind

Type: IsStartupScriptRegistered

Details: The recommended alternative is ClientScript.IsStartupScriptRegistered(string key). For more information, see http://go.microsoft.com/fwlink/?linkid=14202.

Namespace: Microsoft.SharePoint.Publishing.Internal.CodeBehind

Type: RegisterArrayDeclaration

Details: The recommended alternative is ClientScript.RegisterArrayDeclaration(string arrayName, string arrayValue). For more information, see http://go.microsoft.com/fwlink/?linkid=14202.

Namespace: Microsoft.SharePoint.Publishing.Internal.CodeBehind

Type: RegisterHiddenField

Details: The recommended alternative is ClientScript.RegisterHiddenField(string hiddenFieldName, string hiddenFieldInitialValue). For more information, see
http://go.microsoft.com/fwlink/?linkid=14202.

Namespace: Microsoft.SharePoint.Publishing.Internal.CodeBehind

Type: RegisterClientScriptBlock

Details: The recommended alternative is ClientScript.RegisterClientScriptBlock(Type type, string key, string script). For more information, see http://go.microsoft.com/fwlink/?linkid=14202.

Namespace: Microsoft.SharePoint.Publishing.Internal.CodeBehind

Type: RegisterStartupScript

Details: The recommended alternative is ClientScript.RegisterStartupScript(Type type, string key, string script). For more information, see http://go.microsoft.com/fwlink/?linkid=14202.

Namespace: Microsoft.SharePoint.Publishing.Internal.CodeBehind

Type: RegisterOnSubmitStatement

Details: The recommended alternative is ClientScript.RegisterOnSubmitStatement(Type type, string key, string script). For more information, see http://go.microsoft.com/fwlink/?linkid=14202.

Namespace: Microsoft.SharePoint.Publishing.Design.WebControls

Type: GetPersistInnerHtml

Details: The recommended alternative is GetPersistenceContent(). For more information, see http://go.microsoft.com/fwlink/?linkid=14202.

Namespace: Microsoft.SharePoint.Publishing.Design.WebControls
Type: IsPropertyBound
Details: The recommended alternative is DataBindings.Contains(string). The DataBindings collection allows more control of the data bindings associated with the control. For more information, see http://go.microsoft.com/fwlink/?linkid=14202.

Namespace: Microsoft.SharePoint.Publishing.Design.WebControls
Type: RaiseResizeEvent
Details: Use of this method is not recommended because resizing is handled by the OnComponentChanged() method. For more information, see http://go.microsoft.com/fwlink/?linkid=14202.

Namespace: Microsoft.SharePoint.Publishing.Design.WebControls
Type: InitializeNonDefault
Details: This method has been deprecated. Use InitializeExistingComponent instead. For more information, see http://go.microsoft.com/fwlink/?linkid=14202.

Namespace: Microsoft.SharePoint.Publishing.Design.WebControls
Type: OnSetComponentDefaults
Details: This method has been deprecated. Use InitializeNewComponent instead. For more information, see http://go.microsoft.com/fwlink/?linkid=14202.

Namespace: Microsoft.SharePoint.Publishing
Type: GetPostBackEventReference
Details: The recommended alternative is ClientScript.GetPostBackEventReference. For more information, see http://go.microsoft.com/fwlink/?linkid=14202.

Namespace: Microsoft.SharePoint.Publishing
Type: GetPostBackEventReference
Details: The recommended alternative is ClientScript.GetPostBackEventReference. For more information, see http://go.microsoft.com/fwlink/?linkid=14202.

Namespace: Microsoft.SharePoint.Publishing
Type: GetPostBackClientEvent
Details: The recommended alternative is ClientScript.GetPostBackEventReference. For more information, see http://go.microsoft.com/fwlink/?linkid=14202.

Namespace: Microsoft.SharePoint.Publishing

Type: GetPostBackClientHyperlink

Details: The recommended alternative is ClientScript.GetPostBackClientHyperlink. For more information, see http://go.microsoft.com/fwlink/?linkid=14202.

Namespace: Microsoft.SharePoint.Publishing

Type: IsClientScriptBlockRegistered

Details: The recommended alternative is ClientScript.IsClientScriptBlockRegistered(string key). For more information, see http://go.microsoft.com/fwlink/?linkid=14202.

Namespace: Microsoft.SharePoint.Publishing

Type: IsStartupScriptRegistered

Details: The recommended alternative is ClientScript.IsStartupScriptRegistered(string key). For more information, see http://go.microsoft.com/fwlink/?linkid=14202.

Namespace: Microsoft.SharePoint.Publishing

Type: RegisterArrayDeclaration

Details: The recommended alternative is ClientScript.RegisterArrayDeclaration(string arrayName, string arrayValue). For more information, see http://go.microsoft.com/fwlink/?linkid=14202.

Namespace: Microsoft.SharePoint.Publishing

Type: RegisterHiddenField

Details: The recommended alternative is ClientScript.RegisterHiddenField(string hiddenFieldName, string hiddenFieldInitialValue). For more information, see http://go.microsoft.com/fwlink/?linkid=14202.

Namespace: Microsoft.SharePoint.Publishing

Type: RegisterClientScriptBlock

Details: The recommended alternative is ClientScript.RegisterClientScriptBlock(Type type, string key, string script). For more information, see http://go.microsoft.com/fwlink/?linkid=14202.

Namespace: Microsoft.SharePoint.Publishing

Type: RegisterStartupScript

Details: The recommended alternative is ClientScript.RegisterStartupScript(Type type, string key, string script). For more information, see http://go.microsoft.com/fwlink/?linkid=14202.

Namespace: Microsoft.SharePoint.Publishing

Type: RegisterOnSubmitStatement

Details: The recommended alternative is `ClientScript.RegisterOnSubmitStatement(Type type, string key, string script)`. For more information, see http://go.microsoft.com/fwlink/?linkid=14202.

Namespace: `Microsoft.SharePoint.Publishing` **Type:** `GetPostBackEventReference` **Details:** The recommended alternative is `ClientScript.GetPostBackEventReference`. For more information, see http://go.microsoft.com/fwlink/?linkid=14202.

Namespace: `Microsoft.SharePoint.Publishing` **Type:** `GetPostBackEventReference` **Details:** The recommended alternative is `ClientScript.GetPostBackEventReference`. For more information, see http://go.microsoft.com/fwlink/?linkid=14202.

Namespace: `Microsoft.SharePoint.Publishing` **Type:** `GetPostBackClientEvent` **Details:** The recommended alternative is `ClientScript.GetPostBackEventReference`. For more information, see http://go.microsoft.com/fwlink/?linkid=14202.

Namespace: `Microsoft.SharePoint.Publishing` **Type:** `GetPostBackClientHyperlink` **Details:** The recommended alternative is `ClientScript.GetPostBackClientHyperlink`. For more information, see http://go.microsoft.com/fwlink/?linkid=14202.

Namespace: `Microsoft.SharePoint.Publishing` **Type:** `IsClientScriptBlockRegistered` **Details:** The recommended alternative is `ClientScript.IsClientScriptBlockRegistered(string key)`. For more information, see http://go.microsoft.com/fwlink/?linkid=14202.

Namespace: `Microsoft.SharePoint.Publishing` **Type:** `IsStartupScriptRegistered` **Details:** The recommended alternative is `ClientScript.IsStartupScriptRegistered(string key)`. For more information, see http://go.microsoft.com/fwlink/?linkid=14202.

Namespace: `Microsoft.SharePoint.Publishing` **Type:** `RegisterArrayDeclaration` **Details:** The recommended alternative is `ClientScript.RegisterArrayDeclaration(string arrayName, string arrayValue)`. For more information, see http://go.microsoft.com/fwlink/?linkid=14202.

Namespace: `Microsoft.SharePoint.Publishing`

Type: RegisterHiddenField
Details: The recommended alternative is ClientScript.RegisterHiddenField(string hiddenFieldName, string hiddenFieldInitialValue). For more information, see http://go.microsoft.com/fwlink/?linkid=14202.

Namespace: Microsoft.SharePoint.Publishing
Type: RegisterClientScriptBlock
Details: The recommended alternative is ClientScript.RegisterClientScriptBlock(Type type, string key, string script). For more information, see http://go.microsoft.com/fwlink/?linkid=14202.

Namespace: Microsoft.SharePoint.Publishing
Type: RegisterStartupScript
Details: The recommended alternative is ClientScript.RegisterStartupScript(Type type, string key, string script). For more information, see http://go.microsoft.com/fwlink/?linkid=14202.

Namespace: Microsoft.SharePoint.Publishing
Type: RegisterOnSubmitStatement
Details: The recommended alternative is ClientScript.RegisterOnSubmitStatement(Type type, string key, string script). For more information, see http://go.microsoft.com/fwlink/?linkid=14202.

Namespace: Microsoft.SharePoint.Publishing
Type: GetPostBackEventReference
Details: The recommended alternative is ClientScript.GetPostBackEventReference. For more information, see http://go.microsoft.com/fwlink/?linkid=14202.

Namespace: Microsoft.SharePoint.Publishing
Type: GetPostBackEventReference
Details: The recommended alternative is ClientScript.GetPostBackEventReference. For more information, see http://go.microsoft.com/fwlink/?linkid=14202.

Namespace: Microsoft.SharePoint.Publishing
Type: GetPostBackClientEvent
Details: The recommended alternative is ClientScript.GetPostBackEventReference. For more information, see http://go.microsoft.com/fwlink/?linkid=14202.

Namespace: Microsoft.SharePoint.Publishing
Type: GetPostBackClientHyperlink
Details: The recommended alternative is ClientScript.GetPostBackClientHyperlink. For more information, see http://go.microsoft.com/fwlink/?linkid=14202.

Namespace: Microsoft.SharePoint.Publishing **Type:** IsClientScriptBlockRegistered **Details:** The recommended alternative is ClientScript.IsClientScriptBlockRegistered(string key). For more information, see http://go.microsoft.com/fwlink/?linkid=14202.
Namespace: Microsoft.SharePoint.Publishing **Type:** IsStartupScriptRegistered **Details:** The recommended alternative is ClientScript.IsStartupScriptRegistered(string key). For more information, see http://go.microsoft.com/fwlink/?linkid=14202.
Namespace: Microsoft.SharePoint.Publishing **Type:** RegisterArrayDeclaration **Details:** The recommended alternative is ClientScript.RegisterArrayDeclaration(string arrayName, string arrayValue). For more information, see http://go.microsoft.com/fwlink/?linkid=14202.
Namespace: Microsoft.SharePoint.Publishing **Type:** RegisterHiddenField **Details:** The recommended alternative is ClientScript.RegisterHiddenField(string hiddenFieldName, string hiddenFieldInitialValue). For more information, see http://go.microsoft.com/fwlink/?linkid=14202.
Namespace: Microsoft.SharePoint.Publishing **Type:** RegisterClientScriptBlock **Details:** The recommended alternative is ClientScript.RegisterClientScriptBlock(Type type, string key, string script). For more information, see http://go.microsoft.com/fwlink/?linkid=14202.
Namespace: Microsoft.SharePoint.Publishing **Type:** RegisterStartupScript **Details:** The recommended alternative is ClientScript.RegisterStartupScript(Type type, string key, string script). For more information, see http://go.microsoft.com/fwlink/?linkid=14202.
Namespace: Microsoft.SharePoint.Search.Internal.WebControls **Type:** GetRequiresData **Details:** Use IConnectionData.GetRequiresData() instead.
Namespace: Microsoft.SharePoint.Search.Internal.WebControls **Type:** GetData **Details:** Use IConnectionData.GetData() instead.

197

Namespace: `Microsoft.SharePoint.Search.Internal.WebControls` **Type:** `EnsureInterfaces` **Details:** Use `ConnectionProvider` or `ConnectionConsumer` to create `ConnectionPoint` instead.
Namespace: `Microsoft.SharePoint.Search.Internal.WebControls` **Type:** `GetInitEventArgs` **Details:** Use `ConnectionProvider` or `ConnectionConsumer` to create `ConnectionPoint` instead.
Namespace: `Microsoft.SharePoint.Search.Internal.WebControls` **Type:** `PartCommunicationConnect` **Details:** Use `ConnectionProvider` or `ConnectionConsumer` to create `ConnectionPoint` instead.
Namespace: `Microsoft.SharePoint.Search.Internal.WebControls` **Type:** `GetRequiresData` **Details:** Use `IConnectionData.GetRequiresData()` instead.
Namespace: `Microsoft.SharePoint.Search.Internal.WebControls` **Type:** `GetData` **Details:** Use `IConnectionData.GetData()` instead.
Namespace: `Microsoft.SharePoint.Security` **Type:** `WebPartPermission` **Details:** Web part permissions are obsolete and no longer required.
Namespace: `Microsoft.SharePoint.Security` **Type:** `WebPartPermissionAttribute` **Details:** Web part permissions are obsolete and no longer required.
Namespace: `Microsoft.Office.RecordsManagement.Internal` **Type:** `Init` **Details:** The `ResourceManager` is statically initialized.
Namespace: `Microsoft.Office.RecordsManagement.Internal` **Type:** `Init` **Details:** The `ResourceManager` is statically initialized.

Namespace: Microsoft.Office.RecordsManagement.Internal

Type: Init

Details: The ResourceManager is statically initialized.

Namespace: Microsoft.Office.InfoPath.Server.ApplicationPages

Type: GetPostBackEventReference

Details: The recommended alternative is ClientScript.GetPostBackEventReference. For more information, see http://go.microsoft.com/fwlink/?linkid=14202.

Namespace: Microsoft.Office.InfoPath.Server.ApplicationPages

Type: GetPostBackEventReference

Details: The recommended alternative is ClientScript.GetPostBackEventReference. For more information, see http://go.microsoft.com/fwlink/?linkid=14202.

Namespace: Microsoft.Office.InfoPath.Server.ApplicationPages

Type: GetPostBackClientEvent

Details: The recommended alternative is ClientScript.GetPostBackEventReference. For more information, see http://go.microsoft.com/fwlink/?linkid=14202.

Namespace: Microsoft.Office.InfoPath.Server.ApplicationPages

Type: GetPostBackClientHyperlink

Details: The recommended alternative is ClientScript.GetPostBackClientHyperlink. For more information, see http://go.microsoft.com/fwlink/?linkid=14202.

Namespace: Microsoft.Office.InfoPath.Server.ApplicationPages

Type: IsClientScriptBlockRegistered

Details: The recommended alternative is ClientScript.IsClientScriptBlockRegistered(string key). For more information, see http://go.microsoft.com/fwlink/?linkid=14202.

Namespace: Microsoft.Office.InfoPath.Server.ApplicationPages

Type: IsStartupScriptRegistered

Details: The recommended alternative is ClientScript.IsStartupScriptRegistered(string key). For more information, see http://go.microsoft.com/fwlink/?linkid=14202.

Namespace: Microsoft.Office.InfoPath.Server.ApplicationPages

Type: RegisterArrayDeclaration

Details: The recommended alternative is ClientScript.RegisterArrayDeclaration(string arrayName, string arrayValue). For more information, see http://go.microsoft.com/fwlink/?linkid=14202.

Namespace: `Microsoft.Office.InfoPath.Server.ApplicationPages`

Type: `RegisterHiddenField`

Details: The recommended alternative is `ClientScript.RegisterHiddenField(string hiddenFieldName, string hiddenFieldInitialValue)`. For more information, see http://go.microsoft.com/fwlink/?linkid=14202.

Namespace: `Microsoft.Office.InfoPath.Server.ApplicationPages`

Type: `RegisterClientScriptBlock`

Details: The recommended alternative is `ClientScript.RegisterClientScriptBlock(Type type, string key, string script)`. For more information, see http://go.microsoft.com/fwlink/?linkid=14202.

Namespace: `Microsoft.Office.InfoPath.Server.ApplicationPages`

Type: `RegisterStartupScript`

Details: The recommended alternative is `ClientScript.RegisterStartupScript(Type type, string key, string script)`. For more information, see http://go.microsoft.com/fwlink/?linkid=14202.

Namespace: `Microsoft.Office.InfoPath.Server.ApplicationPages`

Type: `RegisterOnSubmitStatement`

Details: The recommended alternative is `ClientScript.RegisterOnSubmitStatement(Type type, string key, string script)`. For more information, see http://go.microsoft.com/fwlink/?linkid=14202.

Namespace: `Microsoft.SharePoint.Publishing.WebControls`

Type: `PartCommunicationConnect`

Details: Use `ConnectionProvider` or `ConnectionConsumer` to create `ConnectionPoint` instead.

Namespace: `Microsoft.SharePoint.Publishing.WebControls`

Type: `PartCommunicationInit`

Details: Use `ConnectionProvider` or `ConnectionConsumer` to create `ConnectionPoint` instead.

Namespace: `Microsoft.SharePoint.Publishing.WebControls`

Type: `PartCommunicationMain`

Details: Use `ConnectionProvider` or `ConnectionConsumer` to create `ConnectionPoint` instead.

Namespace: `Microsoft.SharePoint.Publishing.Internal.CodeBehind`

Type: `GetPostBackEventReference`

Details: The recommended alternative is `ClientScript.GetPostBackEventReference`. For more information, see http://go.microsoft.com/fwlink/?linkid=14202.

Namespace: Microsoft.SharePoint.Publishing

Type: IsClientScriptBlockRegistered

Details: The recommended alternative is ClientScript.IsClientScriptBlockRegistered(string key). For more information, see http://go.microsoft.com/fwlink/?linkid=14202.

Namespace: Microsoft.SharePoint.Publishing

Type: IsStartupScriptRegistered

Details: The recommended alternative is ClientScript.IsStartupScriptRegistered(string key). For more information, see http://go.microsoft.com/fwlink/?linkid=14202.

Namespace: Microsoft.SharePoint.Publishing

Type: RegisterArrayDeclaration

Details: The recommended alternative is ClientScript.RegisterArrayDeclaration(string arrayName, string arrayValue). For more information, see http://go.microsoft.com/fwlink/?linkid=14202.

Namespace: Microsoft.SharePoint.Publishing

Type: RegisterHiddenField

Details: The recommended alternative is ClientScript.RegisterHiddenField(string hiddenFieldName, string hiddenFieldInitialValue). For more information, see http://go.microsoft.com/fwlink/?linkid=14202.

Namespace: Microsoft.SharePoint.Publishing

Type: RegisterClientScriptBlock

Details: The recommended alternative is ClientScript.RegisterClientScriptBlock(Type type, string key, string script). For more information, see http://go.microsoft.com/fwlink/?linkid=14202.

Namespace: Microsoft.SharePoint.Publishing

Type: RegisterStartupScript

Details: The recommended alternative is ClientScript.RegisterStartupScript(Type type, string key, string script). For more information, see http://go.microsoft.com/fwlink/?linkid=14202.

Namespace: Microsoft.SharePoint.Publishing

Type: RegisterOnSubmitStatement

Details: The recommended alternative is ClientScript.RegisterOnSubmitStatement(Type type, string key, string script). For more information, see http://go.microsoft.com/fwlink/?linkid=14202.

New SharePoint Server Controls

Some new server controls introduced in SharePoint 2010 are relevant to designers, power users and developers. Table A-5 contains the comprehensive list of new server controls and their description.

Table A-5. *New SharePoint Service Controls*

Server Control	Description
SharePoint:SPShortcutIcon	Sets the favicon in the top left of the browser URL ba
SharePoint:CssRegistration After="corev4.css"	Tells SharePoint what to load after Corev4 css
SharePoint:SPRibbon	Adds the Fluent UI (the ribbon) to the page
SharePoint:PopoutMenu	Adds the breadcrumb that, when clicked, shows the pop-out that displays your current location in the sit a hierarchical tree structure
SharePoint:SPRibbonPeripheralContent	Adds various items that are attached to the ribbon
SharePoint:PageStateActionButton	Loads the page edit and save icon buttons near the t left of the page
SharePoint:LanguageSpecificContent	Displays content specific to the selected language
Sharepoint:DeveloperDashboardLauncher	Launches the developer dashboard (which is hidden default but can be enabled with STSADM or PowerSh
SharePoint:ClusteredDirectionalSeparatorArrow	Loads the arrow near the site icon after the page title
SharePoint:AspMenu UseSimpleRendering="true"	Renders tableless navigation
SharePoint:VisualUpgradePreviewStatus	Displays the visual upgrade status in the status bar
SharePoint:VersionedPlaceHolder UIVersion="3"	Enables the capability to target page elements to version 3 or 4 capabilities
SharePoint:ClusteredSPLinkButton	Allows SharePoint 2010 to make use of CSS sprites
SharePoint:DeveloperDashboard	Loads the actual developer dashboard at the bottom the master page, which is hidden until the launcher i clicked
SharePoint:WarnOnUnsupportedBrowsers	Displays a warning to users who are trying to access t site with an unsupported browser (e.g., Internet

	Explorer 6)
`wssuc:MUISelector`	Sets the Multilingual User Interface (MUI) language selected that shows up in the welcome menu if language packs are installed
`SPSWC:MySiteCssRegistration`	Allows the use of specific CSS

The Administration Toolkit

By Microsoft and third-party vendors, many tools have been introduced to facilitate process, management, and data in SharePoint 2010. Various tools are available for developers and designers, and we have introduced few of the noteworthy and important ones in previous chapters. However, one very important tool we would recommend to administrators is the Administration toolkit. Using it, administrators can perform load testing, configure security, replicate user profiles, ensure interoperability with content management, and run diagnostics on the SharePoint platform. You can obtain the Administration toolkit here: `http://technet.microsoft.com/en-us/library/cc508851.aspx`.

Must-Read Articles and Blogs

As final note, Microsoft has made available a significant amount of information on migration to SharePoint 2010 on both the MSDN and TechNet sites. You'll also find a lot about general architecture, designs, development, and so on. Then too, many community groups and users have contributed a lot the SharePoint community, and we strongly recommend reading all the information available. To help you find what you need, we list here some of the important articles, blogs, and books that might help you in your migration process.

MSDN Blogs

There are many blog posts on MSDN related to migration to SharePoint 2010. These are the MSDN blogs we recommend:

- `http://msdn.microsoft.com/en-us/sharepoint/ee514557.aspx`
- `http://msdn.microsoft.com/en-us/library/gg454789.aspx`
- `http://msdn.microsoft.com/en-us/library/ee539981.aspx`
- `http://msdn.microsoft.com/en-us/library/ee816116.aspx`
- `http://msdn.microsoft.com/en-us/library/ee662217.aspx`
- `http://msdn.microsoft.com/en-us/library/gg430141.aspx`
- `http://blogs.msdn.com/opal/archive/2009/11/16/installation-notice-for-sharepoint-2010-public-beta.aspx`
- `http://sharepoint.microsoft.com/blog/Pages/BlogPost.aspx?pID=431`

- http://sharepoint.microsoft.com/Blogs/GetThePoint/Lists/Posts/Post.aspx?ID
  =389

- http://sharepoint.microsoft.com/Blogs/GetThePoint/Lists/Posts/Post.aspx?ID
  =398

- http://sharepoint.microsoft.com/Blogs/GetThePoint/Lists/Posts/Post.aspx?ID
  =409

TechNet Articles

These are the TechNet articles we recommend:

- http://technet.microsoft.com/en-us/library/hh801868.aspx

- http://technet.microsoft.com/en-us/sharepoint/ee517214.aspx

- http://technet.microsoft.com/en-us/sharepoint/ff465365

- http://technet.microsoft.com/en-us/library/cc303420.aspx

- http://technet.microsoft.com/en-us/library/hh801868.aspx

- http://technet.microsoft.com/en-us/library/ff191199.aspx

- http://technet.microsoft.com/en-us/library/cc262155.aspx

- http://technet.microsoft.com/en-us/library/cc262967.aspx

Other Blogs

There are many community groups and SharePoint experts who contributed a lot. Here are a few other blogs you might want to follow:

- www.sharepointjoel.com/Lists/Posts/Post.aspx?ID=337

- http://weblogs.asp.net/jan/archive/2009/05/06/querying-sharepoint-list-
  items-using-jquery.aspx

- http://blah.winsmarts.com/2009-11-
  SharePoint_2010_Development_Environment_-and-ndash;_Practical_Tips.aspx

- www.win2008workstation.com/win2008/windows-server-2008-workstation-
  converter

- www.aiim.org/community/blogs/expert/SharePoint-2010-Web-Standards-
  Accessibility-and-Usability-Quick-Reference-Guide

Books

For more detailed information we recommend the following books:

- *Microsoft SharePoint 2010: Building Solutions for SharePoint 2010* by Sahil Malik (Apress, 2010)

- *Pro SharePoint 2010 Business Intelligence Solutions* by Sahil Malik, Srini Sistla, and Steve Wright (Apress, 2010)

- *Pro SharePoint 2010 Branding and User Interface Design* by Randy Drisgill, John Ross, and Jacob J. Sanford (Wrox, 2010)

Authors' Blogs

And finally, here are the authors' blogs. Our blogs contain a lot of information about migration and many other topics on SharePoint 2010:

- http://blah.winsmarts.com
- http://blog.srinisistla.com

Index

CPSIA information can be obtained at www.ICGtesting.com
Printed in the USA
LVOW070508280612

287991LV00012B/6/P